THE
LONDON BLITZ

1. Firemen fighting fires off Chancery Lane.

Chapmans Publishers Ltd
141–143 Drury Lane
London WC2B 5TB

BRITISH LIBRARY CATALOGUING IN PUBLICATION DATA
The London Blitz.
1. London (City). Air raids by Germany. Luftwaffe, 1939–
1945
I. Hill, Maureen
940.542121

ISBN 1–85592–700–4
ISBN 1–85592–709–8 pbk

First published by Chapmans 1990

Photoset in Helvetica Narrow by Macmillan Production Limited, London WC2

Originated, printed and bound in Great Britain by Butler and Tanner Limited,
Frome and London

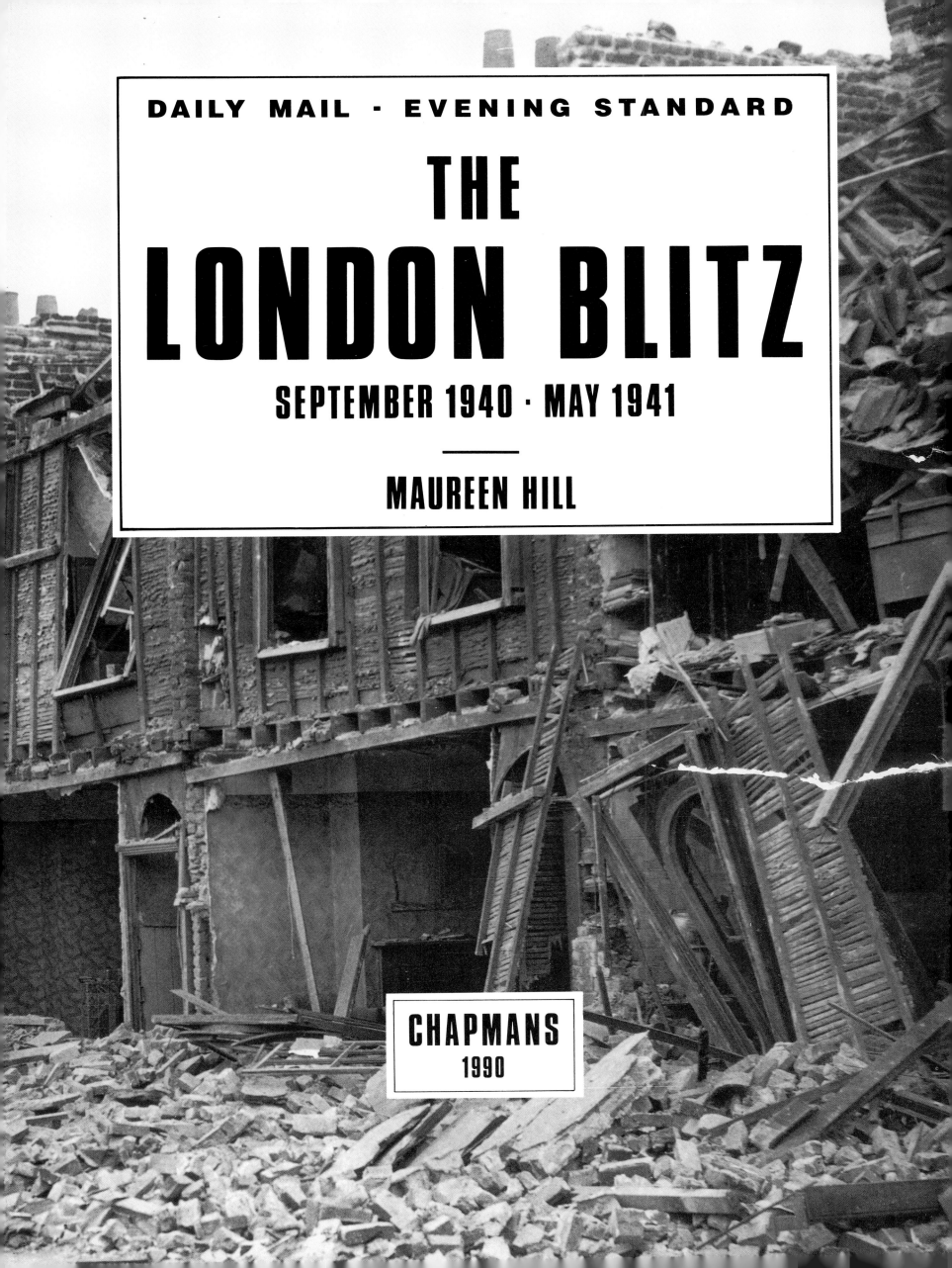

DAILY MAIL · EVENING STANDARD

THE
LONDON BLITZ

SEPTEMBER 1940 · MAY 1941

—

MAUREEN HILL

CHAPMANS
1990

Introduction

The Blitz, as it came to be known, was the most devastating aerial bombardment the world had ever seen. From September 1940 until May 1941, wave upon wave of German aircraft bombed not only London but cities as far apart as Bristol, Glasgow and Belfast. The damage was massive and it was London that suffered the most. Much of the old City and East End simply vanished under a hail of high explosive and incendiaries.

Aerial bombardment was nothing new. Many people still remembered the Zeppelin raids on London during the First World War; and only a few years before, during the Spanish Civil War, air raids had been deployed to awesome effect. In the uneasy years that led up to the declaration of war on 3 September 1939, therefore, many people's perception of the inevitable conflict was that of carnage unleashed from the air upon a civilian population.

By the time the war broke out a system of Air Raid Protection (ARP) was already in place. Wardens were trained, some shelters built, gas masks manufactured and plans laid to deal with the estimated 3000 deaths per day. Evacuation plans were also in position and in the first week of the war some four million people, mainly women and children, moved out of their homes and away to rural areas that would be safer from attack.

The next few months, however, were those of the Phoney War while the Germans concentrated on building an impregnable base in continental Europe. The bombs did not fall as predicted and many evacuees began to trickle back to their homes. Soon, the trickle became a flood. It was not until the summer of 1940, after the retreat from Dunkirk, that Hitler felt capable of an invasion of Britain. The plans for Operation Sealion, as the invasion was codenamed, began with the massing of barges in French Channel ports. So began the Battle of Britain and the first real aerial warfare over the British Isles.

At first the German air force, the *Luftwaffe*, attacked Britain's production lines, airfields, aircraft and air crew in an attempt to destroy the Royal Air Force's capacity to mount defensive action in the event of an invasion. A landing by sea, the only possible route for an invasion of Britain, left the soldiers on board ships and landing-craft very vulnerable to attack from the air. For Operation Sealion to succeed, it was imperative to defeat the RAF.

The RAF, however, proved a more formidable adversary than the *Luftwaffe* had anticipated. Throughout that dramatic summer of 1940, Spitfire and Hurricane pilots flew sortie after sortie while workers on the production lines fought their own battle to supply and maintain the hardware. Finally, in the autumn, the *Luftwaffe's* failure to destroy Britain's air defences provoked a change of tactics. In future, the targets were to be civilian. On 4 September 1940

2. A heap of rubble is all that is left of two newly-built houses in South West London.

Hitler threatened to raze British cities to the ground and reduce London to rubble.

Three days later, London was burning. 'I personally have assumed the leadership of this attack,' Goering announced, 'and today I have heard above me the roaring of the victorious German squadrons.'

This book chronicles the air attacks on London through the archives of the *Daily Mail* and the London *Evening Standard* (the latter then owned by Lord Beaverbrook, Minister of Aircraft Production). Material for the text came from a number of different sources, including the pages of the papers, both printed throughout the Blitz, and the details on the prints in the picture library. But inevitably, and especially in wartime, newspapers can tell only part of the story and I have also used a number of published books. *The Blitz Then and Now* (After the Battle Publications) is a wonderfully detailed and meticulously researched book which proved an invaluable source of information. Another book which provides details of the raids, the aircraft and the air forces is *Blitz on Britain 1939–1945* by Alfred Price. Several books were useful in building a picture of the social effects of the bombing and wartime life in general. Among them are Angus Calder's classic account *The People's War, Living Through the Blitz* by Tom Harrisson *How We Lived Then* by Norman Longmate; Robert

Westall's *Children of the Blitz* and *Bombers and Mash* by Raynes Minn. I would also like to thank friends and relatives who recounted their memories of wartime life and air raids – all of which helped to create a picture of day-to-day life under aerial attack.

Finally, a few technicalities about the book and its contents.

When an attack is referred to as 'major' it means a raid in which more than 100 tons of high explosive (HE) dropped. By comparison with the RAF raids on Germany later in the war when thousands of tons of HE were dropped in a night, 100 tons seems insignificant – but the photographs and stories in the book show the enormous damage that even a small quantity of explosive can inflict.

As most of the bombing occurred at night I have ascribed a night's bombing to the date on which the first attacks were made. For example, the bombs that fell on Oxford Street around 3.00 a.m. on the morning of September 18th 1940 are described in the entry for September 17th as that was when the first party of raiders appeared over London.

Maureen Hill,
June 1990

SEPT

7 Saturday

The first bombs in what was to become known as the Blitz fell during daylight hours on a beautiful, sunny September day. Hundreds of incendiary bombs were dropped around London's docks and the fires they started provided a guide and target for the night-time raiders. All night, until 4.30 a.m. on the morning of Sunday the 8th, the *Luftwaffe* bombed the East End. Throughout the day and night fire-fighters battled to control 19 major, 40 serious and nearly 1000 small fires. Doctors, nurses, ARP wardens, policemen, rescue workers and a host of others fought to save lives, maintain order and offer comfort. 430 civilians died, 1600 were injured and thousands more made homeless on this one night.

3
4

3. *London's Front Line Civilians Carry On: The world has been thrilled by London's ARP workers, who have had little or no rest since Saturday evening. Fire-fighting has become one of the most important duties of the front-line civilian. Daily Mail*, 12th September 1940. Fire-fighters attacking one of the many dockside fires.

4. A silhouette of the East End skyline ablaze.

Evening Standard

Amusements ....
Radio ....

BLACK-OUT 7.55 pm. 6.0 am
MOON Rises 4.2 pm : Sets 1.7 am.

No. 36,198   LONDON, TUESDAY, SEPTEMBER 10, 1940   ONE PENNY

Maternity and Children's Hospitals Hit, Fires Near St. Paul's, in 9-Hour Night Raid

FIGHTS OVER CITY TO-DAY

"Enemy Has Thrown Off All Pretence"

Enemy raiders were again over the London area this afternoon, after night-long terrorist bombings in which —for the second successive night—three hospitals were among the buildings damaged.

To-day's warning lasted from 12.55 p.m. to 1.22. The noise of dogfights could be heard in the City.

A HEAVY ANTI-AIRCRAFT BARRAGE GREETED THE RAIDERS AS THEY CROSSED THE COAST AND APPROACHED LONDON.

They were flying very high and could not be seen through clouds.

The all-night attack—the third in succession of Germany's "terror raids"—lasted from 8.40 p.m. to 5.40 a.m.

It is believed that about 150 German airplanes were engaged over London last night. Some of the bombs they used were so big that a raider would probably carry only two of them.

The opinion was expressed in authoritative quarters in London to-day that the enemy are trying to smash our communications in these night raids; but that the raiders scattered their bombs at random when they failed to locate an objective.

FIRES IN CITY

An Air Ministry and Ministry of Home Security communiqué, issued at 8 a.m. to-day, said:—

"Following the heavy losses inflicted on him by our fighters, and the repulse of his attacks yesterday evening, the enemy has now thrown off all pretence of confining himself to military targets.

"Reports received during the night show that bombs have been scattered at random over London without any distinction of objectives.

"They have fallen in the City and caused fires in the immediate vicinity of St. Paul's Cathedral and the Guildhall.

"They have fallen on a large maternity hospital, which was twice attacked, a number of casualties being caused.

"They have fallen on a Poor Law institution for the aged, on an L.C.C. housing estate, and on a large number of workmen's cottages, especially in the East End of London, which were heavily and repeatedly attacked.

"And they have also been scattered in the residential districts of West and North London.

"There was little enemy activity in the rest of Great Britain during the night, but some bombs were dropped in a town in the North-West of England and in rural districts of the South-West. They caused some damage, but no casualties have been reported.

52 SHOT DOWN

"The number of casualties in London last night is not yet available. The casualties known to have been caused in the enemy's attacks on Sunday night are 286 dead and approximately 1400 seriously injured.

"It is now confirmed that 52 enemy aircraft were destroyed yesterday, 49 by our fighters and three by A.A. guns.

"Three of our pilots previously reported missing are now known to be safe."

Going Away To Safety

To-day, after bombs on a London children's hospital in the night, these babies were being taken away to safety.

Avoid Travel To London
TRANSPORT MINISTRY REQUEST

The Ministry of Transport announces:—

The violent and indiscriminate bombing of London during the past two or three days has naturally caused some temporary dislocation of travelling facilities.

In order to enable the work of restoring the services to proceed with the least possible delay, the public are asked to refrain from unnecessary travelling to and from the London area.

Bus and Tube Services

Underground railway services, states London Transport, are being maintained on all lines, except for a few sections where the services are temporarily interrupted.

Passengers should inquire at their local stations as to the best means of making their journeys.

Railway tickets are being accepted on the road services where necessary.

Bus, tram and trolleybus services are running on all routes except where curtailments, or diversions have been necessary.

Passengers in doubt should make inquiries of the local London Transport officials.

An official of the Transport Workers' Union said to-day that, owing to the difficulties caused by recent raids details of a scheme for operating buses after warnings had not yet been settled with the London Transport Board. A statement would be issued as soon as possible.

Fires Rage in the City

Warehouses in the vicinity of St Paul's Cathedral were ablaze to-day. There was little hope, it was stated, of saving the buildings, all efforts being concentrated on preventing the spread of the flames.

Large forces of firemen and A.F.S. men were working to stop the spread of the fires in the warehouses.

During the night more and more loads of high explosive and incendiary bombs were dropped. Fire after fire was started.

By the time of the all clear the flames and sparks were being blown away from St Paul's Cathedral. St Mary-le-Bow Church, of Bow Bells fame, was, after a long time of anxiety, reported out of danger.

Not even one window was cracked in St. Paul's Cathedral.

The Dean, Dr. W. R. Matthews, and other members of the administrative staff were in the cathedral most of the night.

Raids: The New Technique

A watcher from the roof of factory premises in the City said to-day that the technique of the night's raiders appeared to be plain.

For the first two hours there was not great activity in the air. The scattered machines which flew over the London area seemed to concentrate on starting fires at various points.

As the flames increased—probably providing landmarks for the Germans—the number of raiders increased, as did the intensity of the bombing.

30 Mothers Lay In Bombed Home

OPERATION TABLE DRAMA

Evening Standard Reporter

When high-explosive bombs crashed on a maternity hospital in Central London last night one woman patient had just undergone a blood transfusion operation.

Not a thing was left intact in the ward except the operating table on which she lay and the bottle containing the blood which saved her life.

R.A.F. AGAIN BOMB BERLIN
In Spite of Bad Weather

The R.A.F. again attacked military objectives in Germany, including Berlin, during the night, according to an authoritative statement in London to-day.

The statement added that the attack was carried out in spite of adverse weather conditions which hampered our bombers.

The raid was reported by German radio to-day, says Reuter.

"In particular bombs were dropped in the northern suburbs of Berlin," the announcer said.

"All these attacks," he added "were carried out haphazardly against non-military objectives A number of dwelling houses was hit.

"About midnight last night a few British airplanes flew over the town of Wesermuende, near Bremerhaven, which was strongly defended by A.A. fire," states the official German news agency.

The German agency adds that the R.A.F. penetrated the centre of Berlin, where bombs were dropped.

"In the north of Berlin," it adds, "several incendiary bombs struck houses in a main street and roofs were set on fire."

Airplanes Before Alarm

British United Press says that the alarm was sounded in Berlin at 1 45 a.m. and the all clear was given at 2 28 a.m.

Before the alarm the sound of engines was heard distinctly in the centre of the city, interspersed with heavy anti-aircraft fire. A flare was dropped in the north of Berlin

The agency adds that four waves of British airplanes apparently approached Berlin. During the first and third they could be heard in the metropolitan area and anti-aircraft fire and tracer bullets were plentiful.

The second and fourth waves apparently grazed the outskirts, where flashes from anti-aircraft guns could be seen.

Stettin was raided early to-day, it is learned in Berlin.

Workers Protest

Workers in parts of Germany have protested that they are unable to continue work because of lack of sleep caused by British air raids : production has dropped.

Penalties imposed by the German authorities for leakage of information regarding raid damage are so harsh that eyewitnesses hardly care to discuss these happenings even with friends.

Rhineland arms works moved.—PAGE TWO.

"It was impossible to move her because of her condition," the 32-year-old doctor in charge told me, "but she stayed there quite calm. When we were able to remove her she was none the worse."

The doctor told me how the 30 mothers and 22 children escaped injury, although every pane of glass in the hospital was broken and several wards and offices wrecked.

"As soon as the sirens sounded we transferred the patients from the wards to the corridors," he told me. "We placed all the babies in their cots beneath the beds of the mothers. Most of them were asleep when the bombs fell.

"There was not the slightest panic. I have never seen such fortitude among women."

An SOS was sent to another London hospital for a fleet of ambulances to remove the mothers and babies to the country.

Police Cleared Way

Within half an hour the hospital staff, helped by the A.F.S. had removed every patient while the raid was still in progress, and they were on their way to safe quarters. Police in the area prepared a clear road for them and guided the ambulances past a huge crater in the main road while the raiders flew overhead.

Another hospital in the London area was seriously damaged by a
(Continued on Back Page, Col. Five)

Mr. Churchill Sees Raid Damage

Mr. Winston Churchill, accompanied by Sir Hugh Turnbull, City Police Commissioner, visited the City to-day to inspect last night's raid damage.

He was recognised by crowds of City workers and loudly cheered.

One man raised a shout of "Are we downhearted?" and thousands roared "No." A few yards further on, a shout was raised of "Are we going to win," and immediately the crowd yelled "Yes."

The Prime Minister lunched with the King and Queen at Buckingham Palace.

Divorce Judgment in Refuge Room

A divorce appeal was being heard to-day when the sirens sounded.

The judges went to the refuge room in the basement of the Law Courts and there Lord Justice Mackinnon gave judgment, remarking:

"This is the first occasion on which the Court of Appeal has given judgment in such a place."

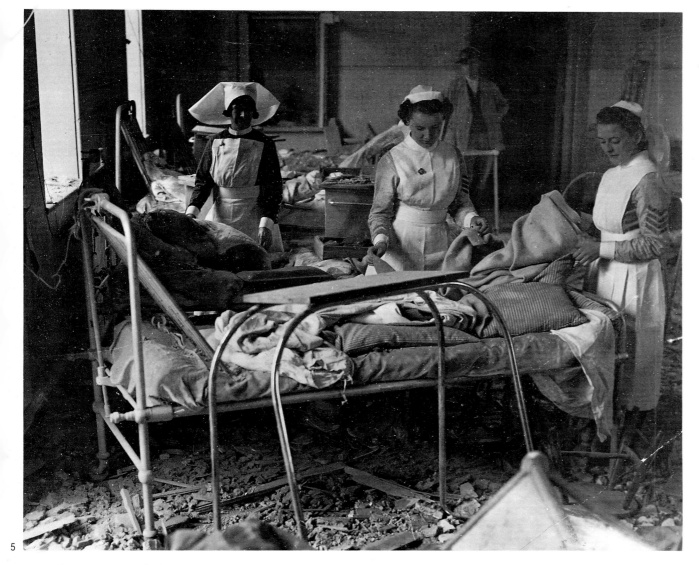

SEPTEMBER

8 Sunday

Winston Churchill, the Prime Minister, toured the East End in the afternoon and found the population in good spirits, despite the severity of the previous night's raid. In the early evening thousands of East Enders trekked towards the West End to seek shelter in the basements of the larger stores or the Tube, although the *Luftwaffe* were soon to include these areas in their targets.

Guided by the still-burning fires from Saturday's raids, the bombers returned at about 8.00 p.m. on the night of Sunday the 8th and the attack continued until 5.00 a.m. the following morning. Again many fires were started and damage was severe, particularly to roads and railways where all main lines to the south were blocked.

9 Monday

The King toured many of the damaged sites in the East End during the day. Minor raids in daylight were followed by another night of heavy attack that left 370 people dead.

10 Tuesday

Bombing was less severe than on the previous nights and there were fewer casualties. Nevertheless the prolonged attack caused fires in the dock area and some damage to railways. The northern outfall sewer which discharged into the River Lea was breached.

5. *And this was the scene inside a bombed South London hospital – one of three hit during the night. In spite of their nerve-racking night, the nurses were there on duty, cleaning up in damaged wards. Daily Mail,* 10th September 1940.

6. St Thomas's Hospital, damaged in an air raid on 8th September.

IMPREGNABLE TARGET. (Copyright in All Countries.)

Body blow for Hitler

THE R.A.F. drop bombs and set the Black Forest ablaze. This sends Hitler into a violent rage. Why?

Because next to oil and iron, wood is Germany's greatest need. The whole of the *ersatz* economy of the country is based on a plentiful supply of timber.

Fibrated wood is in general use as a cloth substitute. A German *hausfrau* advised her husband not to hang his new suit in the wardrobe.

"Why?" he asked.

"Because it might take root," was the reply.

The Nazi civilian wears boots with soles and uppers both made from wood.

Wood, chemically disintegrated and then plastically moulded, is used to replace glass.

Wood in the form of veneers, impregnated with phenolic resin and compressed under High pressure, is used as a substitute for metal.

Wood supplies essential alcohol for German aircraft.

Every barracks, airfield and naval base uses wood for constructional purposes. Every military wagon or lorry consists largely of wood. Almost every ammunition-box is made of wood. The railway depends on wood for sleepers; telegraphy demands wooden poles.

The German aircraft industry made its remarkable pre-war expansion, principally through the substitution of wood for metal. *To-day it is still dependent on wood to keep up its rate of production.*

HITLER'S annexations of the last four years have trebled his timber resources. His invasion of Norway and Denmark had as one of its many purposes the exclusion of the Allies from the Baltic, thus cutting off Britain from the Scandinavian countries, formerly her chief sources of timber.

On the other hand, Hitler has easy access to the soft-wood, plywood and wood pulp exports of Russia.

We ourselves have a trade agreement to buy three million pounds worth of Russian timber, an agreement which was not implemented owing to the Russo-Finnish war.

We should remember that every yard of timber we get from Russia means a yard less for him.

Maurice Edelman

HERO IN EVERY STREET

By Patricia Ward

LET me introduce you to a hero —you've got one like him in your street.

You may not have noticed him much till now, for it wasn't until the first wave of German bombers came droning over London that he stood out against the background of the war. He wears a tin hat and overalls, the helmet and armour in which, night after dangerous night, he is out on the streets looking after everybody's interests except his own.

He is, in fact, an air-raid warden, one of the legion of great-hearted men and women who since the Battle of London began have been going without sleep or rest to bring succour and comfort to their fellow citizens.

MY warden is typical of thousands. He is a married man of fifty, whose name, we'll say, is Jones.

He is a telephonist in a City office, and his working day begins at 7.30 in the morning. Before the war it used to end at half-past four, but now it goes on, with only the briefest break, until five of the following morning.

For Jones is a senior warden in the North-East suburb where he lives. Since the blitzkrieg started over London he has been on duty every night and has averaged exactly two hours' sleep out of the 24.

He's very gay about it. Much gayer than a number of people I've come across of late moaning and groaning about the loss of sleep involved in going to and from a shelter. Jones has a twinkle in his eye and an infectious grin; neither has suffered since he's been working night and day.

He rarely sees his wife and two young children, for almost as soon as he gets home the sirens send him out to his post to collect the six men under him and start their patrol.

That area includes two huge blocks of mansion flats, a 200-yard stretch of main road bordered by houses and shops, and half a dozen communal shelters shared by the tenants of the flats.

"I live in one of those flats," he said, "so I come across my wife and kids in one or other of the shelters when I get time to pop down and see how everybody's getting on. That's about all I see of them these days, but that's better than nothing.

WHEN the sirens go, Jones's first duty is to see that everyone takes cover in the shelters. At first, he told me, people treated him as a sort of mixture of ogre and governess. "But now we're all quite friendly; and the first time they offered me a cup of tea down in the shelter and asked me to stay and talk to them awhile I felt so complimented that I wouldn't have changed places with anyone in the world."

Jones and the six men under him join forces with the whole-time wardens in the district and patrol in groups of two and three for two-hourly stretches. In the intervals, at their post, they brew endless cups of tea to keep themselves awake.

He spoke proudly of his colleagues. "I was all through the last war, as a gunner; but I've never come across a finer bunch of men than these," he told me. "They're keen and quick on the job, and their spirit is fine—something Hitler will never crush."

He told me the story of his "second-in-command," a part-time warden like himself and the owner of a silk manu-

facturing business in the City. This man's wife is also trained in A.R.P. work, and every night this week she has been going from one to another of the shelters in the district, doing what she could to help and cheer the people in them.

"Yesterday morning," said Jones, "the husband went to his office when he came off duty and found it wasn't there—a bomb had dropped on it and wrecked it.

"It means the end of all their hopes, but they were both on duty again in the evening, and from their manner you would never have guessed that anything had happened."

That's the sort of spirit which Jones himself possesses. The sort of spirit which has proved him and his fellow-wardens the heroes and heroines of these days and nights of blitzkrieg.

TWO nights ago, when the All-Clear went in the small hours of the morning, I went up to the top landing of the block of flats where I live to get a view of the fires that were blazing down on the docks.

The top flat belongs to the landlord. Together we hung over the balcony on the landing, gazed at the distant blaze, and sniffed the air.

"Isn't it odd," said the landlord, "that one can smell burning from a fire all those miles away?"

The smell of burning grew stronger, and we grew suddenly apprehensive. We opened the door of the sitting-room, and there, smouldering away on the carpet, lay an incendiary bomb.

The landlord went down into the street and found two wardens. They fetched a stirrup-pump and a bucket, and within six minutes of the discovery had taken the bomb away in the bucket and so drenched the carpet and floor-boards that they ceased to smoulder.

They wasted not a second, nor indulged in any fuss or shouted any orders. They smiled so cheerfully on the assembled tenants that the result, in a house of not particularly brave people, was no one was frightened.

THERE should be more men of this calibre on the streets. At the moment, it is only in some districts that there are enough wardens to ensure that each one gets at least one night off in three. More often there are not enough of them to relieve each other, so they come on duty every night like Jones.

It is not possible to distribute them evenly, for though many are willing to help out in other districts short of wardens, they cannot, under present conditions, be certain of transport.

There is only one way by which these men and women can be guaranteed the rest they need, and that is by more people volunteering to be part-time wardens to help them out.

It is not difficult to discover whether your district is short of wardens or not; you have only got to ask at the A.R.P. headquarters. If there should be a dearth, and the wardens, like Jones, are going without any sleep at all in order to look after you, the power to help them is right there in your own hands.

Winston Churchill broadcast on radio to the nation. He drew attention to the fact that the bombing and the battle between the RAF and the *Luftwaffe* were part of Hitler's plans for an invasion of Britain. His speech rejected the idea that the bombing would demoralise the 'British Nation, or the tough fibre of the Londoners...' Instead Hitler's incendiary and explosive bombs had 'lighted a fire which will burn with a steady and consuming flame until the last vestiges of Nazi tyranny have been burnt out of Europe'.

During daylight hours a number of bombers attacking London got through the defences and caused considerable damage. At night raiding continued right across London from around 8.00 p.m. until 5.30 a.m. on the morning of Thursday the 12th, but a massive anti-aircraft (AA) barrage scored some successes.

7. Another view of the damage to St Thomas's Hospital. Many hospitals were damaged during the Blitz. Much was made of Hitler's claims to be bombing only 'military objectives' in respect of the bombing of hospitals.

8. Regent Street, bombed when the Luftwaffe spread their target areas from the East End and docks to include the West End with its shops, cinemas, theatres and restaurants.

SEPTEMBER
12 Thursday

At 2.25 a.m. a raiding German aircraft dropped a bomb in the vicinity of St Paul's Cathedral. It failed to explode, wormed its way into the ground and lodged near the Cathedral's foundations. The news of this peril was not released to the public until Sunday the 15th, after it had been bodily removed, put on a lorry and driven at high speed to Hackney Marshes where it was exploded.

Unexploded bombs or UXBs were not new, but to have one in such a prominent position drew a great deal of attention both to the threat of UXBs and to the Bomb Disposal Squads that had to contend with them.

Daylight and night raids were lighter than those of recent days, consisting mainly of single aircraft instead of formations of bombers. This change in tactics was probably in response to the losses the *Luftwaffe* had suffered from the AA guns the previous night.

9. The Queen talking with women and children in the East End which had borne the worst of the first air raids in the Blitz.

10. Winston Churchill walking through a bombed street on his second tour of the blitzed city.

11. The King and Queen touring the streets of London, inspecting the bomb damage and talking to residents.

CLOSING PRICES

EVENING STANDARD. September 13, 1940

FINAL NIGHT EXTRA

Evening Standard

Amusements 8
Radio 8

Black-out: 7.48 pm, 6.4 am
Moon: Rises 5.49 pm : Sets 4.14 am

No. 36,201   LONDON, FRIDAY, SEPTEMBER 13, 1940   ONE PENNY

KING & QUEEN ESCAPE AS BOMBS HIT PALACE

City, Central London and Suburbs
Bombed in 4-Hour Day Raid
MANY FIRES STARTED

The Ministry of Information announced this afternoon that in to-day's air raid bombs were dropped on Buckingham Palace, and slight damage done.

The King and Queen were unharmed. Five bombs were dropped. One fell on the chapel and two in the courtyard.

They Raided London—Now Prisoners :
Exclusive Evening Standard Picture

This is the second time that the Palace has been damaged by bombs. A time-bomb exploded outside a few days ago.

The Palace was bombed to-day during a raid which lasted for 4hr. 10min.—London's longest daylight attack.

Bombs were dropped in many areas, including Central London and the City. At least four raiders were shot down.

After a 8½ hours night raid, the sirens first sounded in London at 7.37. The all clear was given at 8.32. The second warning was given at 9.47, and went on until 1.57.

Machine-gun bullets fell in Central London and repeated bursts of machine-gun fighting could be heard from above the clouds.

First Warning

In the first raid a small number of single enemy aircraft came in over south-east England, and a few air-planes came inland.

Several bombs were dropped out-side the London area.

At least two enemy airplanes were shot down in this raid.

One fell in a street in a South-West London suburb. The second, apparently a reconnaissance air-plane, was fired at by anti-aircraft batteries. Two rounds were fired, and the raider was seen diving with smoke pouring from it. Two airmen were seen baling out and the airplane broke in half. It is believed to have crashed in a park.

When one raider appeared in the London area, dodging in and out of the clouds, it was greeted with a salvo of shells from anti-aircraft batteries. The airplane dived down to 5000ft. and then quickly shot back into the clouds and disappeared.

Second Warning

After the second warning German four-engined bombers, flying singly, raided the London area for a number of hours. One of the raiders, flying at 1000 feet, was seen from the banks of the Thames with the puffs of anti-aircraft shells bursting around it.

This airplane dropped bombs on a mansion block and scattered in-cendiaries near public buildings. As raiders flew over London the full anti-aircraft barrage opened up.

Many high explosive and incen-diary bombs were scattered over a wide area. Some people were killed and others injured. At a college there were casualties. Bombing was indiscriminate, and it was therefore to be expected that there might be a considerable number of casualties at certain points.

All London firemen and A.F.S. men stood by to deal with the dozens of incendiary bombs which the raiders (Continued on Back Page Col. Four)

This exclusive Evening Standard picture shows you some of the German airmen who have made their last attack on London. The two above are being marched from their blazing machine. It was shot down by a Hurricane on the South Coast while returning from a daylight raid on the Metropolitan area. (Other pictures on PAGES TWO, SIX, and the BACK PAGE.)

The King Sees Wrecked Chapel at the Palace

Five bombs were dropped on Buckingham Palace to-day.

Two of them fell in the inner quadrangle, the third wrecked the private chapel in the south wing of the Palace, and the others fell in the roadway between the Victoria Memorial and the Palace gates.

The King and Queen afterwar visited the chapel to inspect t damage.

Incendiary Bombs

A reporter who had just left the Palace s..w a twin-engined airplane diving from the clouds. As it came over the Palace the pilot appeared (Continued on Back Page Col. Three)

to cut out his engines; then came the whistle of bombs, and the explosions threw the reporter to the ground.

A few passers-by scrambled to shelter as the airplane restarted its engine and climbed into the clouds again.

Two large craters were made in the quadrangle ; a water main burst, and many of the windows of the south wing of the Palace were shattered and the walls scarred.

Two members of the staff whose shelter was near the chapel were slightly injured. They were treated by members of the palace ambulance staff.

The two bombs which fell in the

SHELTERED IN TUBES

Platforms Packed

Hundreds of people used Tube stations as air raid shelters in to-day's big raid. From Earl's Court to Leicester-square, for example, every platform was lined with people sitting on newspapers and leaning against the wall.

Few appeared to make any effort to catch the trains, although the services were still running.

At Leicester-square the platforms and subways were packed. People were sitting on the steps.

London's Banks

London banks which had been closed all through the raid, opened afterwards within a few minutes.

The general policy, it was stated was to remain open until clients had been dealt with

Londoners Like Their Water Bus

Londoners like their steamboat ser vice between Westminster and Woolwich.

They turned up in hundreds when the first boats began to run to-day.

For 9d. return—7d. workmen's return—they can travel between Westminster and Woolwich in any-thing from one to two hours with-out troubling about traffic lights or other diversions.

People arrived at Westminster Pier continuously to take their places in the boats, which left every 40 minutes.

Beginning on Monday, the boats will run every 20 minutes.

The boats, which started running at 6.30, hold from 180 to 250 people. All were well filled. Railway season tickets and bus and tram return tickets were available on the boats

SEPTEMBER
13 Friday

In the morning the sirens sounded at 9.45 a.m. and the All Clear did not come until nearly 2.00 p.m. During this long daylight attack Buckingham Palace suffered significant damage from an explosive bomb. This bomb proved a boost to Londoners and the nation's morale. There had been rumours that the King had been booed on his tour of the bombed areas on Monday the 9th. The Queen remarked, 'I'm glad we've been bombed. It makes me feel I can look the East End in the face.' Indeed, the bombing of Buckingham Palace helped to encourage a feeling of solidarity between all Londoners.

The bombers returned again at night, although they were not escorted by fighter planes to protect them. The damage and casualties in London were much lighter than on the first few nights of the Blitz.

12. The King, Queen and Winston Churchill viewing the cleaning-up operation after Buckingham Palace had been damaged by a bomb.

13. The King and Queen beside the bomb crater.

14

15

SEPTEMBER
14 Saturday

Two daylight raids on London were fairly successfully contained by RAF fighter squadrons and caused little damage and few casualties. Despite favourable weather, the night-time raids were less frequent, lasting only about two and a half hours in total. Again, the *Luftwaffe* bombers were unaccompanied by a fighter escort, giving rise to speculation that they were being rested for a more massive onslaught.

14. A bomb which had fallen in the road outside Buckingham Palace in Friday's attack exploded later leaving this crater and damaging the Palace railing.

15. Nurses clearing up and salvaging in a wrecked ward.

16. Firemen busy after a bomb had caused a gas main fire. Often gas explosions occurred hours, even days, after the original bomb damage was sustained.

17. A bus in ruins after being hit by a bomb.

SEPTEMBER
15 Sunday

The reason for the *Luftwaffe*'s 'resting' of fighter aircraft and pilots on the previous few nights became apparent in a massive attack by around 600 aircraft during the day. After two major daylight attacks on London, the BBC announced in the evening that 185 German aircraft had been destroyed by the pilots of RAF Fighter Command and the gunners of the AA batteries. This is now thought to be an overestimate of the true number of *Luftwaffe* planes shot down but nevertheless it was a crucially important victory. The raids were believed to be a final blow prior to an attempted landing and invasion of Britain.

British success in fending off these daylight raids was seen as part of the reason for Hitler deciding, on 17th September, the indefinite postponement of 'Operation Sealion' – the codename for his invasion plans. The 15th September became known as 'Battle of Britain Day'. Despite their daytime losses, the *Luftwaffe* mounted a series of further raids throughout the night which lasted until 5.00 a.m. the following morning. They created a great deal of damage right across London.

18. Salvaging belongings the day after a raid.

19. Despite the almost total destruction of this home, the living room remains almost undisturbed – even the vases remain unbroken on the mantelshelf.

20. Carrying what they can, Londoners leave their wrecked homes behind them.

21. People salvaging their furniture and belongings from their wrecked homes.

Evening Standard

Amusements 8
Radio 8

BLACK-OUT : 7.41 pm to 6.9 am
MOON : Rises 7.4 pm. Sets 7.24 am

No. 36,203 — LONDON, MONDAY, SEPTEMBER 16, 1940 — ONE PENNY

185 Down—a Record: 4 London Warnings To-day

DOVER IS SHELLED AFTER BRITISH BOMBARDMENT

Fighters Break Up Raiders on Coast

The London area had four raid warnings to-day, but the first rounds in the day's battles were fought near the coast.

SHELLS FELL ON THE DOVER AREA, AND BIG FORMATIONS OF GERMAN AIRCRAFT WERE BROKEN UP BEFORE THEY HAD PENETRATED FAR INLAND.

The German guns, which fired four salvoes across the Channel, were replying to a bombardment of the French coast by British long-range artillery which had fired about two dozen rounds.

The German bombardment began at 11 a.m. while Dover's main streets were crowded with shoppers. People ran to shelters, but the shelling ended after ten minutes.

Eleven people were injured by the shelling, but no deaths have been reported.

The first big attacks by the German air force to-day—after their overwhelming defeat of yesterday in which they lost 185 airplanes—were made by two waves of bombers which crossed the South-East Coast heading due north.

One of the formations was of 30 bombers and the other of 34, each with the usual escort of about twice as many fighters.

CHASED AWAY

The formations were split up by anti-aircraft fire, and six of the airplanes turned back over the sea, met strong formations of Spitfires which chased them for a considerable distance out to sea.

Some of the raiders used new tactics.

One formation of nine Dorniers was packed so tightly together that their wing tips seemed almost to be touching. The remaining bomber force was spread out in groups of three.

But the experiment could not beat the fighters. Within ten minutes the main bomber force were scurrying across the Channel.

SMOKE RINGS

Later a large number of big purple and blue smoke-rings were seen over a S.E. coast town when a formation of enemy airplanes, flying very high, was broken up and driven away by fighters. No bombs were dropped.

The first three London warnings were from 9.57 a.m. to 10.32, from 10.53 to 11.35, and from 12.10 p.m. to 12.49.

The fourth began at 2.9.

Anti-aircraft fire was heard over the London area shortly after the third warning.

A single enemy raider flew low over a Thames Estuary town during this period. It was making its way towards London, and was met by heavy anti-aircraft fire.

There were no reports of any damage after three warnings. It continued on Back Page, Col. Three.

Mothers Safe To-day After Hospital Bombing

During the night three more hospitals were bombed. One of them is in South-East London, where these mothers and babies are pictured to-day. The maternity ward was damaged, but there were no casualties.

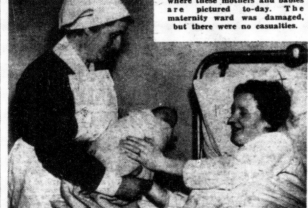

This is Mrs. Flynn, one of the mothers who came smiling through the ordeal. Her baby was born yesterday.

On 13th Fairway

Evening Standard Reporter

One of the 185 German machines brought down yesterday was destroyed over a Kent golf club. The pilot baled out, but his parachute failed to open, and he crashed on the thirteenth fairway.

Mr. R. A. White, the club professional, told me to-day: "The Messerschmitt was brought down by a Spitfire. Play was stopped while we watched the fight.

"We saw the German pilot leap from his airplane. His legs and arms were whirling about. He did not seem able to pull the rip cord of his parachute.

"He was a young officer of about 18 or 20 and was wearing the Iron Cross and other decorations. His Messerschmitt crashed two miles away.

"I was two down when we broke off our game to watch the fight, but I was so exhilarated by the success of the Spitfire that I then shot four birdies in a row and won my match."

Shelter Just in Time

The erection of an Anderson shelter for a family of five at a South-East town was completed only yesterday evening. When a raid started the family took refuge in it, and a few hours later a bomb fell and demolished their house. All were in the shelter, and this too, was placed safely on the edge of a crater and all escaped injury.

TIME BOMBS CARRIED TO PALACE LAKE

Details became known to-day of the third bombing attack on Buckingham Palace on Sunday.

Two time bombs fell during the lunch-time raid and did not explode.

The first bomb fell on the north-west wing of the Palace near to the Royal apartments. It crashed through the roof and landed in a bathroom.

Palace A.R.P. workers, police and military removed the bomb, which was carried to the edge of the Palace lake.

Similar action was taken with the second bomb, which fell on the Palace lawn some little distance from the building, and this too, was placed near the water's edge.

Small incendiary bombs fell at the same time in the Palace grounds, and some of them started small fires on the grass which were quickly got under control.

The King and Queen were not in residence at the time, and only a skeleton staff of servants and others were in the basement shelters, and there were no casualties.

London's Bomb Dispersal Squads.—PAGE THREE.

Bomb Down Stairs As Nurses Ran Up

ALL PATIENTS SAVED

Evening Standard Reporter

Twenty-three minutes after a bomb had crashed down the well of the main staircase of a London hospital last night and exploded at the bottom, several hundred patients from the surrounding wards, unhurt, were installed in another part of the hospital, having been carried down the fire escapes by nurses, doctors and medical students.

Although two bombs fell on the hospital within a few seconds of each other and considerable damage was done, the only casualty is a young doctor, who received a slight scalp wound.

"The first bomb fell at the back, blowing out all the windows on that side," the hospital superintendent told me to-day.

"As the nurses made for the main staircase to reassure patients the second bomb dropped plumb through the glass dome over the stairs, fell five floors through the well and exploded at the bottom.

"The nurses nearest to the doors were blown clean across the room and under the beds at the far side.

Many of the patients were victims of previous air raids. They were being evacuated to other hospitals to-day.

Two other London hospitals were hit during the night.

One bomb fell on a building used as kitchens and mess rooms. The hospital A.R.P. squad dealt with it; no great material damage was caused. The maternity home near by was untouched.

Big Fires on French Coast

Evening Standard Reporter

Two fires, which were started on the French coast last night, were still burning to-day.

One, in the direction of Calais, left a cloud of black smoke over the sea. The other, a smaller one, was in the direction of Boulogne.

Flying Boat Clare Safe

The British flying-boat Clare is safe, it was learned authoritatively in London to-day.

The Clare was on her third flight from America to England, and had been reported missing.

Bale Out— Knock Out

Evening Standard Reporter

When a Dornier bomber was shot down near a South-East town yesterday four men baled out and were taken to a police station.

Three of the men were quiet and decent, but the pilot, a short, stocky man, was very truculent and spat in the police sergeant's face.

He did not recover consciousness until late in the afternoon.

Merchant Ship Gets a Raider

The Admiralty announce this afternoon that the British steamer Port Auckland, which was sailing down the Thames during one of the raids on London yesterday, shot down an enemy bomber.

A shell from the Port Auckland's A.A. guns burst close under the German bomber, which caught fire and crashed in flames on the bank of the river.

One of the bomber's crew was seen to bale out.

The Port Auckland (8789 tons) is registered in London and belongs to the Port Line.

Channel Weather

Heavy rainfall to-day broke the spell of fine weather which has prevailed off Dover for many weeks.

The sky over the Straits was overcast, with low, grey clouds, and there was mist over the sea, but the French coast was silhouetted clearly against the pale horizon.

SEPTEMBER
16 Monday

As the clear-up from Sunday's severe bombing continued, there were a number of minor raids during the day throughout the London area. One large-scale attack in the early morning was successfully repelled by RAF fighters. At night bombing was widespread across most Metropolitan districts but damage and casualties were not heavy.

22 and 23. Two views of a huge bomb crater in the Strand, left after Sunday's incredible air battle over London.

No enemy aircraft reached London during daylight hours but during the night, and especially in the early hours of Wednesday the 18th, a number of bombs landed in Central London. The Oxford Street stores of John Lewis, Bourne and Hollingsworth and D.H. Evans were among the casualties. A small bomb scored a direct hit on Marble Arch subway, killing 20 of those sheltering there when the blast ripped the tiles from the walls. A high explosive (HE) bomb could penetrate up to 50 feet into the ground.

Four views of damage caused by raids on the night of Tuesday 17th.

24. A street in Stepney, much of which was terrorised by the use of parachute mines – a new form of bomb only just being introduced by the Luftwaffe.

25. Lambeth Walk.

26. Bond Street.

27. Burlington Arcade.

TEN LONDON FIREMEN KILLED IN RAIDS

THREE AT STORE IN OXFORD ST.

Ten firemen were killed during last night's raids.

Five were killed when a high explosive bomb dropped between two trailer pumps on their way to a fire in a south-east district.

Three firemen are believed to have been killed, and many more injured, fighting a fire which broke out after incendiary bombs had fallen on the premises of John Lewis, in Oxford-street.

One fireman was killed as he arrived in a tender. Apparently one of the bombs fell in his path, blowing in the front of the vehicle.

Trapped in Car

The bodies of two A.F.S. men and two civilians were recovered from a garage in the West End which was hit by a bomb.

Rescue squads were trying to extricate a civilian who was sitting in a car covered by the debris.

Two fire pumps and two cars were buried in the ruins.

Women and Babies Escape

A civilian who was sheltering in the basement of the building, told the Evening Standard:

"After the crash we made for a side door. Led by a girl who knew the way, we broke out through adjoining premises. The girl smashed windows with her shoe heel and using a table as a ladder, we scrambled through.

"Among those who escaped with us were two women with babies."

"No Footlights"

"It's a job that has got to be done, and we don't want any footlights," said a member of a bomb disposal unit of the Royal Engineers after a bomb was exploded on a Kentish heath.

The bomb had been brought on a lorry four miles from where it first fell.

Several of the unit are survivors from Dunkirk.

STILL AT YOUR SERVICE

THE
Elizabeth Arden
SALON

The Elizabeth Arden Salon has weathered the storm! Still at your service are Miss Arden's personally trained assistants: still available the treatments for which Elizabeth Arden is famous the world over—Face, Hair, Manicure, Figure. Show that crises leave us undaunted! Will you phone Mayfair 8211 for an appointment.

25 OLD BOND STREET

Party of Four

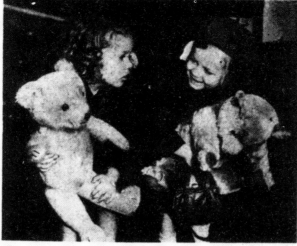

Two little girls, and two teddy bears . . . . picture at a London station as children from the more heavily bombed districts of the Metropolitan area waited for an evacuation train.

Raider Machine-gunned Women and Children
ON THEIR WAY TO SHELTER

Women and children on their way to shelter during a surprise night raid in the North-West of England were machine-gunned by German airmen.

This district had its heaviest casualties of the war. Exact details are not yet available but the casualties include a number of auxiliary firemen who were on duty at a suburban post which received a direct hit.

In view of the number of explosives dropped the loss of life and the amount of damage was comparatively light, but once again working-class homes took the main force of the attack.

Bombers suddenly swooped over the district and dropped a large number of incendiaries and high-explosives.

They were met by intense anti-aircraft fire from ground batteries.

A heavy formation returned to the attack later dropping more high-explosives.

House Left "Hanging"

One bomb landed obliquely in the cellar of a house, leaving the building precariously balancing over a crater.

A number of casualties were taken to a cinema for protection and treatment.

One bomb which fractured a water main in a street narrowly missed a tenement dwelling.

A public shelter received a direct hit, but, although the roof was lifted, no one was hurt.

Shelters again stood up to the bombing, and several houses were demolished while the tenants were safe in their shelters.

Railwaymen Defied Bombs Beside Line

After a recent air raid it was discovered that unexploded bombs were buried near an L.M.S. railway line in such a position that they threatened considerable damage.

A train of empty wagons was driven and left on one line, providing a screen between the bombs and two adjacent lines.

The whole of the staff concerned then volunteered to take the trains through, and the service was continued during the whole of the danger period.

Shot Servant Did Not Use Real Name

The Oxford coroner to-day opened and adjourned an inquest on Irene Sherry, an Oxford domestic servant, who was found shot late on Monday night, and in connection with whose death Private Edward George Beesley, of the R.A.S.C., is in custody.

Walter Sherry, her stepfather, said that for the past 20 years she had used the name of Sherry instead of Edwards, which was her real name.

A doctor said that death was due to haemorrhage from a bullet wound in the heart which could not have been self-inflicted.

Shelters Stood Fast

German bombs wrough this scene of havoc and destruction in a South London street . . . the surface shelters stood fast.

13 BOMBS FELL, NOT A HOUSE WAS DAMAGED

Industrial premises were damaged between the Thames Estuary and London during the night.

Houses were damaged in several Essex villages, but no fatal casualties have so far been reported.

Some cattle were killed in Thames-side fields.

Oil bombs causing fires were dropped on a town in South-East England. Men of the fire services worked all night putting them out.

In another south-eastern town a raider dropped 13 bombs. They fell in a residential part of the town but not one house was hit and the only damage was to some large huts and a tennis court.

One bomb hit a road and burst beneath the concrete. The road surface was forced up in a huge bulge but it held the blast and the windows of adjoining bungalows were not even cracked.

New Defence Against Bomber is Planned
EXPERIMENTS WITH SECRET SYSTEM

Evening Standard Air Correspondent

Concentrated experiments are going on daily to develop a method of bringing down German aircraft which so far has proved successful in defending small, vital sites—a method that was not in use at the beginning of the war.

For security reasons no hint can be given of the nature of the device, but I have seen it and know that it has not failed to bring down German bombers in certain circumstances.

It is not a gun, and it is not a ray. It has nothing to do with balloons. There is no question of an aerial minefield.

But this much can be said. It is so simple that the Germans, when eventually they learn the secrets of it—we hope, after the war—will kick themselves for not having thought of it before.

It Seems Likely

If it can be developed (and it seems likely that it can be), then the defence of the whole of the London area, and all our principal cities, will be immensely strengthened.

One of its best qualities is that it does not require a large number of men for efficient operation. It is also comparatively cheap to manufacture and operate.

Raid "Casualty"

Until last night this wax display model adorned the window of an Oxford-street store—one of the three damaged in the ten-hour raid. To-day, with many others, she was carried away from the danger zone.

Bunks for Babies in Shelters

Bunks for babies are planned for Stoke Newington's air raid shelters.

"It is necessary to provide somewhere for the babies to sleep that will not take up too much space, so we have planned a sort of nest of bunks, tier upon tier, where the children can sleep," an A.R.P. official said.

"If the experiment is successful similar bunks, on a larger scale, may be provided for adults.

"Men will have first call on these, because they cannot make up their sleep in the day, as many women can, so for once it will not be 'ladies first.'"

Australian Air Chief

MELBOURNE, Wednesday.

The death is announced of Group Captain T. A. Swinbourne, O.B.E., Director of Organisation at R.A.A.F. Headquarters.

Captain Swinbourne was Assistant Air Liaison Officer at Australia House from 1933 to 1935, and Assistant Chief of the Australian Air Staff from 1938 to 1939.—Reuter.

SEPTEMBER
18 Wednesday

Fire-fighters spent the day hosing down the smouldering remains of Oxford Street, while as many as 800 *Luftwaffe* aircraft were involved in daylight raids on London, sometimes singly, sometimes in formation. Amazingly, no real damage was caused but the prime objective was probably to harass Fighter Command's defences. Smaller numbers of aircraft in intensive raids from 9.00 p.m until 5.00 a.m. the following morning caused much greater damage, killed more than 200 people and injured many more.

Parachute mines were in evidence again. They had appeared only recently and were proving to be a significant problem. Instead of a high explosive bomb or incendiary device, the *Luftwaffe* would drop a mine attached to a parachute. Rather like an unexploded bomb, it was the uncertainty about when or what would cause the mine to explode that made it frightening.

28. and 29. Two views of Oxford Street on the morning of Wednesday 18th after the night's bombing. Fire-fighters are still hosing down the smouldering buildings.

LONDON ALTERS RHYTHM OF ITS LIFE TO COPE WITH RAIDS

Hours of Work, Bedtime, Travel, Changed

Evening Standard Reporter

London's homeward rush-hour has changed from six o'clock to round about five.

With the ready adaptability that is typical of them, the people have revolutionised their habits within a fortnight to meet the time-table of Goering's bombers.

Work has been speeded up, office hours have been changed, shops are closing early so that the great mass of the people go home an hour earlier than usual.

8 p.m. Bedtime

All London wants to get safely home and allow time for a peaceful meal before the night raid begins.

Many thousands are in their shelters, with clockwork regularity, by eight o'clock—bedding down for the night at a time when they would normally be going to the cinema or the "local."

An official of the London Transport told me to-day:

"The peak traffic-time has made a big switch over, and we have altered our rush-hour arrangements to meet the new situation as well as we can.

"Time-tables which would normally come into operation in the winter black-out are working now."

Shops Close Earlier

The big stores, which used to stay open till six o'clock, now close at five. Many City offices are doing the same.

Essential services are being maintained, in spite of earlier closing times.

In the office of a great petrol company, for example, girls work through the lunch hour, munching the sandwiches which they bring from home, so that they can finish the office work an hour earlier.

"Our system is flexible," I was told by a representative of this company. "The work has to be done, and if it cannot be completed in time for the staff to get home safely, they are accommodated on the premises for the night.

"In many departments, however, they are able to speed up their work so as to leave early."

The rush-hour crowds are going home in an orderly fashion. This great trek is no mad scramble for safety.

Lifts Home

Many motorists, following the advice of the Minister of Transport, halt at bus stops, offering lifts.

"It would simplify matters if passengers held out notices to indicate their destinations," one motorist told me. "I waste a lot of time and petrol stopping for bunches of people who are not going my way after all."

A few people are already doing this.

Homegoing typists, at the risk of laddering their silk stockings, scramble into lorries which stop to give them a lift home.

Some are fitted with rough seats for the passengers. One seen to-day had a footboard, with ropes dangling from the roof for straphangers.

Sit-down 'Strike' In Husband's Car

A new kind of sit-down strike was staged by Mrs. Nellie Kaminsky, of Philadelphia, when she parked herself in her husband's car and announced that she would stay there until he agreed to pay 10dol. (£2 10s.) a week to support her.—British United Press.

Daughter for M.P.

The birth of a daughter to Mrs. Marion Graham, wife of Captain Alan Crosland Graham, Conservative M.P. for Wirral, Cheshire, is announced to-day.

Mrs. Graham is the daughter of Mr. and Mrs. C. N. du Plessis, of Capetown, where the birth took place. She was married last November.

From Americans

Americans have given 870 tons of milk for evacuees in the Wayland, Norfolk, rural district.

Another West End Store Hit

To-day's picture of the damage outside Peter Robinson's after last night's raids over the Central London.

Check on Crowds in the Tube Shelters

Evening Standard Reporter

The Ministries of Transport and Home Security and the London Transport Board were to-day examining police reports and the reports of their own observers on the use of Tube railways as dormitories.

These state, it is understood, that there was "no trouble of any kind" last night and recommend that the public should be allowed to continue as before.

The reports follow an appeal made yesterday by the Ministries to the public, and "particularly the able-bodied men," to refrain from using Tube stations as shelters except in case of urgent necessity.

Free for Travel

The authorities are anxious to keep the tubes as free as possible for normal traffic and transport. Special police were posted at the tube entrances and platforms to see that train services were not impeded.

There were just as many people sleeping on the platforms of tube railways, especially in the East End, last night as on previous occasions.

The police, I understand, will inform the authorities that the people who seek shelter in the tubes in no way interfere with the running of the services.

One thing which the authorities wish to avoid is the overcrowding of stations, which would prevent passengers from getting through the corridors on to the platforms.

It is understood that there will be no question of banning the tubes for use as dormitories. Sleepers will be allowed to continue using them unofficially, but in controlled numbers.

The number at any station will be left to the discretion of the police and the station officials.

Sanctuary in the Tube, by Patricia Ward—See PAGE FIVE.

Son For Wife of Somaliland Governor

Mrs. Vincent Glenday, to whom the birth of a son in Nairobi is announced to-day. Mr. Glenday was Governor of British Somaliland until the evacuation of the territory a few weeks ago.

Bicycles are in Big Demand

Londoners are rapidly becoming bicycle-conscious, and dealers in many districts report a big increase in the sale of new and second-hand models.

Hundreds of Londoners have found bicycles to be one of the most convenient means of getting to work now.

"There is a particular demand for second-hand bicycles," the manager of a large dealers said.

"Our great difficulty is to obtain sufficient supplies. It is chiefly war workers, and factory workers in general, who want bicycles, but we have had a number of City clerks in black coats and striped trousers among our customers.

"Men and women members of the civil defence services are also buying bicycles. In some instances whole families have become bicyclists."

£12 For a Light

For a black-out infringement a householder was fined £12 at Dereham, Norfolk.

25 Reasons

There were 25 reasons why the marriage of Mr. William and Mrs. Della Besser did not work, their attorney explained to the divorce court at Tulsa, Oklahoma, recently. He said that there "was too much controversy over the children."

So the court allowed Mrs. Besser to take her seven children by a previous marriage and go to live with her relatives, while Mr. Besser and his 18 children by Mrs. Besser were allowed to remain on their 50-acre farm home.—Reuter.

"Open Doors" Plea

Beccles, Suffolk, Council have passed a resolution asking the townspeople to open their front doors when the warning sirens are sounded so that people in the streets may take immediate cover.

Leaving Hongkong

HONGKONG, Thursday.

Nearly 70 women and children will sail for Australia at the end of the week.—Reuter.

Soldiers and Nurses Stopped Hospital Fire

Nurses and soldiers during the night successfully fought the fire when an incendiary bomb which fell on the roof of a municipal maternity hospital in an East London district, in which there were 50 mothers and babies.

At a nearby hospital an high-explosive bomb extensively damaged the laundry buildings, but there were no casualties.

The district was heavily bombed with high explosives and incendiaries, and a number of houses was razed.

The known death roll is low—the latest figure being nine—but it is probable that other people are trapped beneath fallen houses.

About 30 incendiaries fell in the grounds of a grammar school without causing damage.

Stole Boots in Air Raid

For stealing a pair of military boots and an Army mackintosh from a demolished building while an air raid was in progress, Matthew O'Neill, 58, labourer, was at Bromley to-day fined £2, with one guinea costs.

It was stated that he had his life's savings, more than £40, on him when arrested. He was employed at a camp.

AIR-RAID VICTIMS WANT HELP NOW!

Camp-beds, blankets, clothes and soap; hot food, shelter, cash for personal necessities and fares to the homes of friends; a few pence to buy sweets for the children—these and many other things are wanted *at once*.

The casualties need nursing and comforting; their treatment requires bandages, lint, splints, swabs.

Everywhere—in London, Liverpool, Birmingham, Portsmouth, Dover, in all the big cities—the Red Cross and St. John are grappling day and night with the task of providing air-raid victims with these things, immediately after the bombing, while the carefully planned measures of State and municipal relief are brought into operation.

The Red Cross and St. John are on the spot wherever the bombs fall.

Give them your support, you who are mercifully safe, for the sake of the men, women and children who have been smitten.

Send your gift of money towards the cost of this work **now**.

DONATION FORM

To **The Lord Mayor, The Mansion House, London, E.C.4**

Here is my gift of £ ____ s. ____ d. ____ *for the*
Lord Mayor's Red Cross & St. John Fund

Name _____

Address _____

Make cheques and P.O.'s payable to the Lord Mayor's Red Cross Fund. Envelopes should be marked 'RED CROSS'.   42

SEPTEMBER

19 Thursday

Daylight raids were much lighter than of late, due mainly to poor weather. Night-time raiding was widespread and although it caused little damage a number of deaths occurred in incidents at Stepney and West Ham when no air raid warning was given.

20 Friday

During the day a large formation of about 100 German aircraft was turned back by RAF fighter planes. The German aircraft were mainly fighters, suggesting that the attack's main purpose was to wear down Fighter Command's defences. Nevertheless, a few bombers reached South East London and dropped their loads but damage and casualties were light.

Night raids caused more extensive damage to power and communications – principal targets for the bombers. Stepney Gas Works and the railway bridge at Southwark were hit, as were other rail links.

30. Peter Robinson's at Oxford Circus, hit when the *Luftwaffe* returned to the West End again.

31. Wreckage of buildings in Bruton Street.

32

33

34

SEPTEMBER

21 Saturday

A day and night of much reduced German activity – mainly fighter planes and single bombers trying to engage and penetrate RAF fighter and AA battery defences.

22 Sunday

RAF Fighter Command's quietest night since the beginning of the Blitz, with little activity by the *Luftwaffe*, though there were, as ever, some damage and casualties from the raids that did occur.

23 Monday

A large formation, mainly of fighter planes, was driven off before reaching London during daylight hours.

Night-time saw much more activity than over the previous weekend. Raids were widespread across London, causing considerable damage to road and rail links and many more deaths than in recent days.

32 and 33. Damage to County Hall – fallen masonry on the terrace.

34. Damage to the back of Selfridges store in Oxford Street.

35. Rescue parties working among wrecked Anderson Shelters in the East End.

36. East Enders queuing up to enter public air raid shelters.

SEPTEMBER

24 Tuesday

No large-scale attack was able to penetrate RAF and AA battery defences during the daylight hours, but at night there were a large number of raids throughout the London area.

In view of the air attacks upon London and Britain generally, the King announced that a new medal – 'The George Cross' – was to be awarded 'for valour and outstanding gallantry' on the home front.

25 Wednesday

A day of minor German sorties across London was followed by a night of widespread raids until the early hours of Thursday 26th September.

37. London carries on – a shop in Regent Street.

38. Business as usual in Lambeth Walk.

39. *'I think it is wonderful that they should carry on doing their job after losing their homes and spending nights in the shelters,' said the Queen yesterday, when she paid a visit to the London Hospital. She was referring to two women over 70 who are cleaners at the bombed hospital and were bombed at home as well.* Daily Mail, 24th September 1940.

CLOSING PRICES

EVENING STANDARD September 27. 1940

FINAL NIGHT EXTRA

Amusements 8
Radio 8

Black-out 7.16 p.m. to 6.27 a.m.
Moon Sets 4.28 p.m. Rises 2.4 7 a.m.

No. 36,213   LONDON, FRIDAY, SEPTEMBER 27, 1940   ONE PENNY

Evening Standard

They Crash in Dozens All Round London In a Day of Battles: Daylight Bombs
32 ARE SHOT DOWN!

Some of the places where planes fell:—Chislehurst, Orpington, Kingston, Richmond, Dorking, West Wickham, Esher, Cheam.

Woman Led Singing Class in Lifeboat

AXIS AND JAPAN: 10-YEAR PACT
Mutual Aid Pledged Against New Enemies

At least **32 raiders** were destroyed to-day in great **battles** which raged over and around **London** and in South-East England.

LONDON HAD THREE RAIDS. BOMBS WERE DROPPED IN CENTRAL, SOUTH AND SOUTH-WEST LONDON AND IN SURREY.

22 LONDON GIRLS DIE IN SHELTER

Direct Hit in To-day's Raid

Twenty-two girls, aged 16 to 30, were killed when a bomb scored a direct hit on their underground shelter at a factory in South-West London during the first raid to-day.

When the sirens sounded the many hundred girls employed at the firm went to cover. Ten minutes later one of the shelters in the forecourt of the building was struck. The entrance caved in.

They were buried beneath debris and masonry. Besides those killed, many were seriously injured. Office workers from other shelters helped rescue workers to clear away the debris. The last casualty was taken to hospital after 20 minutes.

The Queen's 'How Are You?'

Surprise for Woman Patient at St.Thomas's

Evening Standard Reporter

Mrs. Wise, of Lambeth, an air raid casualty lying in the basement ward of St. Thomas's Hospital, had a surprise to-day.

Just after she had finished lunch the King and Queen walked into the ward. "Well, how do you feel?" asked the Queen as she approached her bed.

"Oh, I'm fine now, your Majesty," replied Mrs. Wise.

The Queen talked to her for some time, asking about the air raid in which she was injured, and then moved off to another ward with the King, where they talked to other patients.

There are now only 12 patients in the hospital, which has been hit by high explosive bombs and which is carrying on with emergency wards underground. It can still accommodate 50 patients.

Channel Calm

A slight mist covered the calm sea in the Straits of Dover to-day. The sun shone brightly from a cloudless sky and the wind had swung round from north-east to north-west.

In the first raid attacks were made by 100 German aircraft. Formation after formation was split up and driven off.

Raiders crashed at places all round London—including Chislehurst, Orpington, Kingston, Richmond, West Wickham, Dorking, Esher and Cheam.

Four more raiders were brought down in a terrific air battle over a South-East Coast town.

Two more are believed to have crashed on another part of the South-East Coast.

Over the Thames

Three more bombers were shot down over the Thames Estuary. One pilot was seen to bale out.

Later another battle developed in this area and two German fighters were shot down.

Yet another raider crashed on the beach at Porlock, Somerset.

Three German airplanes came down in flames over a Kent village. Three men were seen to bale out.

An Air Ministry bulletin issued at 12.50 p.m. stated:

"Preliminary reports of this morning's engagements show that 18 enemy aircraft have been shot down by our fighters over South-East England. Two of our fighters have been lost, but the pilot of one is safe."

Down in Flames

Four of the raiders were destroyed in a south-west district, where one came to earth in flames. Another is believed to have been brought down in the eastern part of London.

Five other enemy airplanes were sent crashing at Chislehurst and Orpington, on the south-east outskirts of the capital.

There was a terrific battle over South-East London when German

Continued on Back Page—Col. Four

Miss Mary Cornish, who took charge of the children, resting after arrival.

Evening Standard Reporter

" I'd like to correct the impression that I'm any sort of a heroine."

That is what Miss Mary Cornish, only woman of the 46 City of Benares survivors brought in a destroyer to a Scottish port last night, told me to-day.

Soft-voiced, unassuming, 41-year-old, by no means a strong or athletic woman, she has returned from eight days' exposure in an open boat in the gale-swept Atlantic with nothing except a slight cold.

"I'm a bit stiff, too," she admitted. "There were ten of us huddled all the time in the bow of the boat, with a bit of canvas over our heads.

"There was no room to stand up and there was no room to lie down. We just huddled there, suffering terribly from cramp.

"It would have been bad enough on just bare boards, but when those boards have knobbles of iron on them it becomes even less comfortable."

Miss Cornish looked after six children—evacuees who were going to Canada. She was the only woman in the boat.

She teaches music at Luckley School, Wokingham, and is well used to taking singing classes.

"But I have never led such a singing class as we had in that lifeboat," she told me. "We sang all the time to keep up our courage.

"Those six little boy evacuees

Continued on Back Page—Col Three

R.A.F. BOMB PORTS AGAIN

The R.A.F. last night made further heavy attacks on Channel ports, including Ostend, Calais, Boulogne and Le Havre, where particularly heavy damage was observed, stated the Air Ministry to-day.

Kiel and other military objectives in North-West Germany were also successfully bombed.

One of our aircraft is missing.

According to watchers on the English coast, the attacks on the French coast were the fiercest yet made.

Bomb after bomb was seen to be dropped at different points, particularly at Calais and Cap Gris Nez, where the German long-range guns are supposed to be in position.

GERMANY, ITALY AND JAPAN SIGNED A TEN-YEAR MILITARY, POLITICAL AND ECONOMIC PACT IN BERLIN TO-DAY.

The terms of the pact were announced by the German propaganda news service as follows:

(1) Japan recognises and respects the leadership of Germany and Italy in the "new order" in Europe.

(2) Germany and Italy recognise and respect Japan's leadership in the "Greater Asiatic living space."

(3) Germany. Italy and Japan agree to support each other if any one of the three is attacked by a country which is not at present engaged in either the European conflict or the Sino-Japanese war.

(4) They agree to appoint immediately technical commissions composed of members appointed by the three Governments to establish details for joint co-operation and consultation.

(5) Germany, Italy and Japan solemnly declare that this agreement will in no way affect the political status existing at present between any one of the three countries on the one hand and the U.S.S.R. on the other.

(6) This three-Power pact comes into effect to-day and is to remain in force for a period of ten years from this date. If any one of the three parties should desire it, reasonable notice before expiry must be given for discussion regarding an extension.

The ceremony, which took place in Hitler's new Chancellery, was stage-managed

As each Nazi dignitary and each Italian and Japanese representative stepped into the hall, his name was announced with a flourish of trumpets and a roll of drums.

The Evening Standard Diplomatic Correspondent writes: This pact

(Continued on Back Page—Col. One)

Whitehall to 'Carry On'

Unless there is a real risk of Government offices being bombed, civil servants are to carry on with their work.

Instructions to this effect were issued to-day. All Government departments are asked to conform with new arrangements which have been made in the light of recent experience.

It was stated in Whitehall to-day that the national staff side are in agreement with the official view that it is essential to reduce to a minimum any loss to the national effort as a result of air raid warnings.

To-day's picture of three of the boys in a Scottish hospital. Left to right: Harry Steels, Derek Capel and William Cunningham Short.

SEPTEMBER

26 Thursday

Although there was a large number of raids across the country during the day, London escaped any serious incident.

After dark, raids began at about 8.30 p.m. and continued all night until about 5.00 a.m. on the morning of Friday the 27th. The night's raids caused a greater amount of damage than of late – the Houses of Parliament, the docks and some rail links all suffered to various degrees.

27 Friday

During daylight hours, the *Luftwaffe* mounted several large-scale raids but they were broken up by RAF fighters. In one attack, only 20 of a formation of 300 aircraft reached Central London. The Germans' losses were almost as large as on September 15th. But despite these daytime losses, the *Luftwaffe* were able to mount attacks on London throughout the night until 6.00 a.m. the following morning.

During the day, Government officials set about a pilot scheme for distributing ear-plugs to Londoners tormented by the noise and lack of sleep from the bombing, sirens and guns of the AA batteries. They were to prove unsuccessful, as most people felt they would rather hear the noise and know what was coming than remain in peaceful ignorance.

40. *The telephone worked but the conversation is not as private as it would be in peacetime. A minor inconvenience of air raids on London. Daily Mail, 28th September 1940.*

41

42

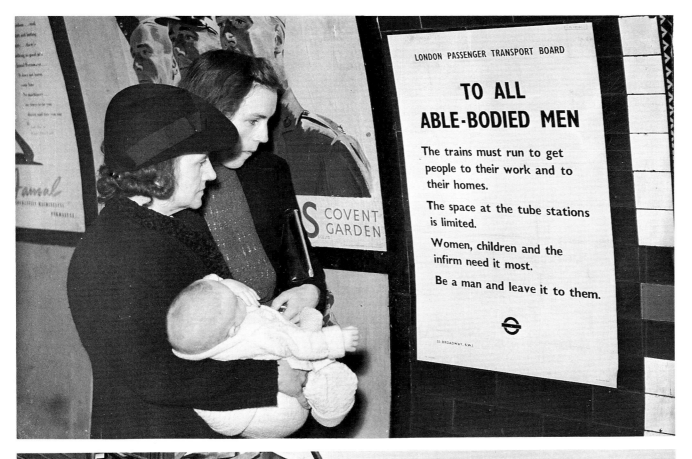

LONDON PASSENGER TRANSPORT BOARD

TO ALL ABLE-BODIED MEN

The trains must run to get people to their work and to their homes.

The space at the tube stations is limited.

Women, children and the infirm need it most.

Be a man and leave it to them.

SEPTEMBER

28 Saturday

Daylight raids by the *Luftwaffe* were becoming more obviously unsuccessful. After the heavy losses on Friday the 27th Saturday's attacks again failed to reach their targets, only a few bombers evading defences to drop their loads close to the Thames.

Night raids were more successful and on the night of the 28th, through until the early hours of Sunday the 29th, bombs were dropped London-wide. Many incendiary bombs were used, starting a large number of fires.

29 Sunday

During daylight hours, the *Luftwaffe* only attempted small-scale attacks. At night, raiding was by single aircraft. The total number of aircraft raiding London fell far short of the average 163 per day and damage and casualties were slight compared to other days in the Blitz.

41. Londoners asleep in an Underground station – the steps of the escalator becoming their pillows.

42. Road blocks scattered over the roadway after a bomb had exploded at Westminster near the Houses of Parliament.

43. Despite official rejection of using the Tubes for shelter, the public overrode them and by the end of September official announcements like this one showed that the authorities had decided to accept the Tubes as shelters and make them as organised and functional as possible.

44. Rescue workers in Lambeth Walk.

45

46

SEPTEMBER
30 Monday

The *Luftwaffe* mounted a number of major daylight attacks on London but very few bombs reached their target. German losses were heavy, with about 46 aircraft lost and a number damaged, to say nothing of the deaths of and injuries to skilled pilots and air crew. Night-time raids were more successful, with a number of German aircraft reaching Central London.

45. Looking across London Bridge after an air raid.

46. Londoners salvaging furniture and belongings from their bombed-out homes.

47. Damage caused by a bomb in Aldersgate Street is surveyed by a fireman.

48. Damage to the Houses of Parliament – Richard the Lionheart's sword is bent by the blast from a German bomb.

49

50

SEPTEMBER

The last major daylight battle between the
Luftwaffe and the RAF had been fought on
Monday, 30th September. German casualties
had proved too great to maintain the same
level of daylight attacks for the rest of the Blitz.
While daylight attacks would continue through
October and half of November, they would be
on a much reduced scale and after November
even lighter still.

Meanwhile for civilians in London, life had
taken on a new routine. After work at home,
office or factory, people would head in the
evening for the shelters whether or not the
Alert sounded. There, they were growing
accustomed to sleeping amid the din of the
night raids, ready to emerge next day for work.
Absenteeism, even during these early days,
was remarkably light – it was almost a matter
of pride to carry on as normal a life as
possible.

49. Salvaging from bombed-out Oxford Street
stores – even the dummies are taken to a place of
safety!

50. 'Pegasus Flies' – Pegasus, which topped the
Tower of the Temple Library, flies off as demolition
work progresses after the Library was bombed on
19th September.

51. The King talking to women whose homes were
bombed in the very first raids of the Blitz.

52. A view of the Tate Gallery after it had been hit
by a bomb – the empty frame once housed John
S. Copley's 'Death of Major Pierson at St. Helier'
but it, together with all the other works of art, had
been evacuated to safe storage at the beginning of
the war.

CLOSING PRICES

EVENING STANDARD, October 1, 1940

FINAL NIGHT EXTRA

Evening Standard

Amusements 8
Radio 8

BLACK-OUT 7.7 p.m. to 6.34 a.m.
MOON sets 6.35 p.m., rises 8.7 a.m.

No. 36,216   LONDON, TUESDAY, OCTOBER 1, 1940   ONE PENNY

FIGHTERS BEAT TO-DAY'S RAIDERS

Dive-Bomber Machine-Guns London Train and Streets

THEN SHOT DOWN BY HURRICANE

A German raider was shot down near Redhill, Surrey, to-day, 10 minutes after a train had been machine-gunned by a bomber in a South-East London area.

IT IS BELIEVED IT MAY HAVE BEEN THE SAME MACHINE.

Later a German reconnaissance airplane was fired at over the London area, and R.A.F. fighters routed a formation of about 15 raiders which crossed the South-West coast.

Three of these raiders were seen to fall out of the formation to the northward of Poole.

TWO BOMBS

The raider which attacked a train near London was a Junkers bomber —the rearguard of the German night raiders.

It dropped two bombs in a residential part of a town in the South-East London area, which caused some casualties.

The train which was attacked had just left the station of the same town when passengers heard a dog fight going on overhead as British fighters engaged the raider.

A railway worker said that the *Continued on Back Page—Col. Three*

Bomb Blows A.R.P. Lorry Over House

An A.R.P. lorry was hurled over the roof of a house, crashing into a garden, when a heavy bomb exploded in a South-West London district during the night. The four people in it were killed.

Other members of the squad were injured. One, Johnny Peters, well-known London boxer, is in a grave condition.

Houses on both sides of the road were demolished by the explosion. A number of people who had not taken cover in their shelters are believed to have been killed.

In one Anderson shelter five people were trapped for an hour under the wreckage of two houses.

Mrs. A. Hoare told the Evening Standard: "I never expected that we should be released alive. The weight of the wreckage on top seemed to be getting heavier all the time as the shelter gradually sank into the ground."

Twenty-two people were rescued from wreckage in this street after squads had worked all night.

Seven Die in Bungalows

A bomb scored a direct hit on two bungalows where 12 people were living in north-west London. Seven people were killed, including two little children.

R.A.F Shot Them Down

These German airmen were certainly seeing London—but only as prisoners. They were shot down in recent air battles and were being taken to an internment camp.

LORD WOOLTON APPEALS TO COFFEE STALLS

To Help to Feed Shelterers

Evening Standard Reporter

Lord Woolton, the Minister of Food, wants to mobilise a great army of London coffee-stall keepers to help in a big campaign to feed Londoners who spend the night in public shelters.

"Many of these coffee-stall keepers have gone out of business owing to the black-out," he said to-day. "I am anxious to get hold of them again.

"If they come forward I will get them petrol and other necessary supplies and arrange which shelters they are to go to."

Lord Woolton, in co-operation with voluntary organisations, has already got canteen vans in attendance at various times of the night, and particularly at 6 a.m. to sell to people leaving their shelters meals at reasonable prices.

"To-morrow," he said, "I am
(Continued on Back Page, Col. Two)

5-Hour Raid on Berlin

The R.A.F. gave Berlin its longest raid during the night, and again battered the French coast between Boulogne and Calais.

Other targets in Germany were also attacked, it was learned in London to-day.

In their raids on the invasion ports, the British bombers were concentrated in the region of Calais.

After one wave had let go their bombs a fire broke out which increased to tremendous size. The flames were reflected on the sea almost to the English coast, and like a huge beacon it blazed away without any diminution for over six hours.

Heavy Barrage

The Germans have increased their defences along this stretch of the French coast considerably.

It is also reported from the Dover area that 25 long-range guns are now known to be mounted along the French coast between Calais and Boulogne.

The raid alarm in Berlin lasted five hours and ten minutes. Activity was mainly concentrated on the outskirts, where are most of the industrial buildings.

The Berlin correspondent of the New York Times, quoted by Reuter, says there was little anti-aircraft firing in the city. Not a shot was heard from the New York Times office.

The correspondent adds though, that only one bomb is reported to have fallen actually in Berlin.

Air Raids at 101

Mrs. Sarah Ward, Luton's oldest woman, 101 to-day, refuses to get excited over such things as air raids.

"I eat well, drink well and sleep well," she observes.

Well Conducted

Bottle for the baby, administered by a conductor whose bus took mothers and children from London to a reception area in the country to-day.

George Cross for St. Paul's Bomb Men

3 WOMEN GET MEDAL

THE FIRST THREE AWARDS OF THE GEORGE CROSS, WHICH RANKS NEXT TO THE VICTORIA CROSS, WERE ANNOUNCED TO-DAY.

They were made to:

Lieutenant Robert Davies, R.E., and Sapper George Cameron Wylie, R.E., of the squad which removed the time-bomb from the vicinity of St. Paul's Cathedral, and Thomas Hopper Alderson, part-time worker (detachment leader), rescue parties, of Bridlington.

Three women have been awarded the George Medal, which is for wider distribution. The official announcement of the awards says of Lieutenant Davies, who was in charge of the bomb disposal party:

"So conscious was this officer of the imminent danger to the Cathedral that, regardless of personal risk, he spared neither himself nor his men in their efforts to locate the bomb.

"After unremitting efforts during which all ranks knew that an explosion might occur at any moment, the bomb was successfully extricated.

"In order to shield his men from further danger, Lieutenant Davies himself drove the vehicle in which the bomb was removed, and personally carried out its disposal."

The actual discovery and removal of the bomb fell to the lot of Sapper Wylie, adds the announcement. His untiring energy, courage and disregard for danger, were an outstanding example to his comrades.

Mr. Alderson received the award for his "consistent gallantry, enterprise and devotion to duty during enemy air raids."

(Other awards—PAGE SIX.)

Lieut. Davies.

Want to Fight Nazis With Bows

In the Ogoja Province of the Eastern Provinces of Nigeria live about 40,000 clansmen of the Afikpo tribe. They are sturdy and warlike though their "armaments" consist largely of flint locks, bows and arrows, spears, matchets, javelins, slings and stones.

They make up in enthusiasm what they lack in equipment. Recently an Afikpo deputation handed to the District Commissioner the following resolution:

"We agree to give one-sixth of our surplus funds to the King to help him in his war with Germany. If the King needs more money we can help him. All we ask is that he beat the Germans properly this time. Why cannot we fight, too?"

Dogs Showed Light

Miss Rhoda Smith, of Chalfont St. Giles, fined £1 at Beaconsfield to-day for showing a light, blamed her dogs, who, she explained, pushed their way into the house leaving open the door.

Shelter Dictator For London

ADMIRAL EVANS

Admiral Sir Edward Evans to-day became London's shelter dictator. He will have the power to marshal all the available shelter resources, to create new ones, and to see that every Londoner has a safe and reasonably comfortable refuge when the bombers come.

He is one of the two London Regional Commissioners for Civil Defence.

"He continues in that appointment," I was told by the Ministry of Home Security, "but from now on he is to concentrate entirely on London's shelter problems. He is to be 'O.C. Shelters.'"

The Admiral's first job will be to cut down the red tape which surrounds the problem of opening deep shelters in business premises by night as well as by day. Already some of these have been opened, but there are still far too few.

Admiral Evans.

Injured Doctors Tended Injured

Three large bombs falling on North-East London suburb during the night damaged houses and made many people homeless.

Doctors and nurses in a first-aid post were hurled off their feet, and ceilings fell on them. Ignoring their own cuts and bruises, they were soon administering aid to the injured.

Rescue parties were to-day still searching for three trapped people.

Straits Are Choppy

Weather in the Straits of Dover to-day was cold and cloudy. The wind was still in the north-east and the sea was choppy. Visibility was excellent and the view of the French coast was exceptionally clear.

OCT

1 Tuesday

A few minor attacks were launched by the *Luftwaffe* during the day but none penetrated as far as Central London, although a single aircraft bombed and machine gunned Croydon. Night raids were heavier than by day and resulted in some damage but fewer deaths (about 30) than on recent nights.

2 Wednesday

Daylight raids were again only minor but German aircraft managed to penetrate the defences and drop bombs around Woolwich, Camberwell and Lewisham.

The night was the quietest since the first day of the Blitz, 7th September, but there were still raids almost continually from dusk on the 2nd until dawn on the 3rd of October.

53. She Saved the X-Ray Apparatus: Yesterday's Daily Mail *picture in Central London after the night raids. The girl, a doctor's assistant, was carrying off part of an X-ray apparatus salvaged from the ruins in a famous street* [Harley Street] *which received a direct hit.* Daily Mail, 2nd October 1940.

OCTOBER

3 Thursday

Poor weather conditions meant there were no formation raids during the day but a few single aircraft dropped scattered bombs throughout London. The pattern of raids by single aircraft continued through the night but in no great numbers. Casualties and damage were both slight.

4 Friday

Again overcast weather conditions limited the scale of the *Luftwaffe*'s attack. By day and night, raiding was carried out mainly by single aircraft, although at night the single aircraft followed one another in rapid succession – on average about one every two minutes.

54. This Anderson Shelter saved the lives of three people in South West London in a raid in early October.

55. Some of the staff of John Lewis in Oxford Street sorting goods salvaged from the store after September's bombing.

56. Many children had been evacuated in September 1939 but had drifted back home when no bombing had come. More children were evacuated or re-evacuated at the beginning of the Blitz a year later, but many families decided that they would rather face the bombing together and children were often to be seen playing in the damaged, rubble-strewn streets and bomb sites.

EVENING STANDARD, October 5, 1940

FINAL NIGHT EXTRA

Evening Standard

Amusements 8
Radio 8

Black-out 6.58 pm to 6.40 am
Moon Sets 9.10 pm, Rises 1.4 pm

No. 36,220.   LONDON, SATURDAY, OCTOBER 5, 1940.   ONE PENNY

EAST LONDON BOMBED TO-DAY: 10 SHOT DOWN

Three-hour Battle in South-East

SEVENTY PLANES ROUTED BY R.A.F.

TEN RAIDERS ARE REPORTED TO HAVE BEEN SHOT DOWN TO-DAY IN BIG BATTLES OVER SOUTH-EAST ENGLAND.

A force of seven raiders penetrated to Central London during a daylight alert. Two bombs were dropped in East London.

At least five raiders were destroyed when about 70 German bombers and fighters crossed the Kent coast. They were attacked by R.A.F. fighters and a three-hour battle followed. Three of the raiders were seen to dive into the Channel.

Two Heinkel bombers were shot down on the South Coast—one near Battle, and the other in the sea off Newhaven.

Three enemy bombers were shot down in flames within five minutes over Ashford, Kent.

Over London British fighters attacked the enemy, and machine-gun fire was heard.

One of the bombs dropped in East London fell in a churchyard, making a crater about 20 feet across.

The bomb barely missed the church. Many of the stained glass windows were blown out and the walls were chipped by flying earth and stones. Windows and roofs of houses were also damaged, but there were no casualties.

The second bomb, which fell in the same district, caused casualties, some of them fatal.

Guns in Action

When anti-aircraft guns opened fire on the London raiders, which were flying at a height of 15,000 feet, turned off in a north-easterly direction. Practically on their tails were British fighters manœuvring for the attack.

Three airplanes flew high over Central London while guns were in action. Bursts of anti-aircraft fire were seen near a barrage balloon.

Other German bombers were attacked by British fighters over an East London district, and the raiders turned tailed.

About 70 German bombers, and fighters equipped with light-calibre bombs, tried to make a dash for London from the Kent coast.

They were split up by anti-aircraft fire, and then British fighters went into action. The enemy were turned back before they reached London and fled in an easterly direction.

Twenty German bombers crossed the Kent coast near the Straits of Dover and headed towards London.

Flying in three groups, tightly packed together, the bombers swept out of high clouds over the sea with the sun behind them.

Anti-aircraft guns put up a fierce barrage, and shell puffs appeared all round the raiders, which kept in formation as they flew inland.

Fifteen bombers, heading inland at more than 20,000ft. were in open formation as A.A. guns blazed away. Then R.A.F. fighters were heard, apparently in contact with the enemy.

Three bombers raided a South Coast town at different times to-day. In the last raid there were some casualties when bombs fell in a shopping street, damaging a public-house.

The raider was chased over the sea by British fighters.

Bombs were dropped on two South-East towns.

There were a number of casualties.

(Continued on Back Page, Col. Two)

STEPNEY'S DICTATOR

The Borough of Stepney—one of the worst-bombed districts in London—is now ruled in civil defence matters by a "dictator" appointed by the Government, Mr. J. K. Arnold James, the Town Clerk.

Two orders, one by the Ministry of Home Security and the other by the Ministry of Health, have been issued under the Defence Regulations giving him all civil defence powers formerly exercised by the borough council and the emergency committee.

Stepney is the first borough in the country since the intensive air attacks began in which the Government have used their powers under the Defence Regulations to nominate a civil defence "dictator."

Under the new scheme Mr. James will be able to take quicker and more direct action than had been possible to deal with difficulties due to air raids.

Before going to Stepney in January of this year he was Town Clerk of Finsbury.

BARLEY-SUGAR (2 TONS) FOR RAID WORKERS

Two tons of barley sugar have been ordered by the London County Council for distribution to air raid marshals, firemen and other air raid workers under the council's authority.

The consignment marks an extension of the policy of recommending barley sugar for children and others under the care of London's medical officer of health.

Channel Gale Drops

The south-westerly gale which had been sweeping the Straits of Dover dropped during the night, and the wind veered round to the west.

The sea was calmer to-day, but visibility was still limited by mist. The sky was overcast by high cloud formations.

President and Katherine Hepburn

Here is an out-of-the-ordinary picture from New York to-day. It shows two famous people as table companions—President Roosevelt and Katherine Hepburn. The actress was the guest of Mrs. Roosevelt at her cottage at Hyde Park, New York State, with other stage folk, writers and artists to discuss a national radio show in support of the New Deal.

TWO TRAINS BOMBED

Two trains were bombed when they were stationary in a South-Eastern town at about midnight last night. The passengers were badly shaken but there were no casualties.

Weather Stops R.A.F. Night Raids

It was learned in London to-day that as extremely unfavourable weather conditions over enemy territory have continued, our bombers carried out no operations during the night.

Father of Triplets

A verdict of accidental death was returned at the Romford inquest on George Wilson, 43, of Gordon-road, Rainham, Essex — the father of triplets—who was knocked down by a bus in the black-out near his home.

Duke's Daughter Weds

Mr. Stephen Vernon and Lady Ursula Filmer-Sankey, elder daughter of the Duke of Westminster, after their marriage to-day at Caxton Hall.

Cinema Prices Up To-morrow

Evening Standard Reporter

West End cinemas within half a mile of Piccadilly-circus will to-morrow raise prices to 1s. 10d., 3s., 4s. 6d., 6s. 6d. and 8s. 6d.

Increased entertainment tax and higher costs are making cinema seats dearer throughout the country..

In London suburbs and the larger provincial towns, prices, starting to-morrow in cases where cinemas are open, will be 9d., 1s., 1s. 2d., 1s. 6d., 1s. 10d. and 2s. 6d.

At country cinemas where charges are now 6d., 9d. and 1s., the new prices will be 8d., 1s., and 1s. 2d.

"Dopey" is Dead

Eddie Collins, the comedian who inspired the character of the Dwarf "Dopey," in Walt Disney's "Snow White" film, has died at Hollywood, reports Reuter.

Collins, an old-time vaudeville star, was selected for the role of "Dopey" after Disney saw his act in a burlesque theatre.

For a year, at Disney's request, Collins visited the "Snow White" studio twice a month so that his facial expressions and actions in various situations in which the cartoonist wanted to portray "Dopey," could be photographed.

Eddie Collins

Two Nazis in Thames

The bodies of two German airmen were washed up in the Thames Estuary to-day.

SNUG NIGHTS FOR MILLION IN LONDON

Admiral Evans on His Winter Plans

Evening Standard Reporter

Shelters for one million Londoners to snuggle down in comfort this winter is the aim of Admiral Sir Edward Evans, who to-day outlined his plans to me.

His task is to find sleeping accommodation for the 1,000,000 who cannot safely spend the night in their own homes.

The Admiral had an interview with Mr. Winston Churchill when he was appointed O.C. Shelters, and, on the instruction of the Prime Minister, he is losing no time in tackling the problem.

"The German blitzkrieg against London is not going to succeed," he said to me. "The way in which we shall beat the Germans is by providing snug shelters for our people.

"While the Germans are shivering this winter, even the poorest of our people will be able to sleep in reasonable comfort.

Special Heating

"To ensure this it is essential that all our public shelters should be properly heated.

"I intend that there shall be electric stoves in every shelter that otherwise might be cold or damp. One of the big electrical firms has already been put to work on a big scheme of shelter heating."

A system of admission by ticket only to many of the big shelters is being arranged.

"This will insure that the right people will get into the right shelters, and will eliminate the queues," Admiral Evans told me. "My proposal is that the admission cards should be something like railway season tickets.

Mothers First

"Mothers with young children will be given absolute priority when space in the shelters is allotted. Working men and women will come next."

In the Tubes bunks are to be provided only in those stations and tunnels that are not used for traffic.

"Anderson shelters and communal surface shelters are to be bunked, and they can easily be made homes from home. Before we have finished they will all be properly lighted and heated.

"I should be quite happy to snuggle down for the winter in a properly-built Anderson shelter. Actually, I sleep under the kitchen table."

New Underground Station As Shelter

During a tour of inspection of a nearly completed underground station at Bethnal Green to-day, Mr. Herbert Morrison, Minister of Home Security, said: "I intend to use every existing deep shelter in London for the safety of the public during air raids."

The station which Mr. Morrison inspected is 65 feet beneath the ground and can accommodate thousands of people.

Although workmen have not yet completed building operations, and no lines are laid, the building is considered absolutely safe by experts of London Transport who have examined it.

Mr. Morrison, who was accompanied by Admiral Evans, arrived as the guns were blazing at one of the tip-and-run raiders.

OCTOBER

5 Saturday

RAF and AA defences kept the daylight attacks, mounted by the *Luftwaffe* in view of the improved weather conditions, from Central London. The weather also brought many more night-time attacks, with the Germans employing both formation and single aircraft raids until the early hours of Sunday the 6th.

6 Sunday

Very poor weather conditions made this one of the quietest days and nights of the early Blitz. During the night raids no casualties were reported and damage in and around London was slight, although Northolt Aerodrome suffered some damage when a single aircraft bombed it during the day.

57. A section of the Tower of London was damaged and a Yeoman Warder killed when the North Bastion received a direct hit by a bomb on 5th October.

58. Pedestrians stop to view the damage to the Tower.

100 DISTRICTS BOMBED LAST NIGHT

Evening Standard Reporter

Raiders operating in bigger forces than ever and flying in groups bombed more than 100 areas in London, the Home Counties and the South last night.

Hundreds of incendiary bombs and high-explosives of a light calibre were dropped on suburban areas, causing widespread damage to houses and business premises.

The raid lasted nearly as long as the previous night—the longest so far.

Most of the aircraft used in last night's attacks were Messerschmitt bomb-equipped fighters. The first waves approached the London area from all directions, but later they mainly came in from the South-East and the South-West.

After circling the London area at a great height, dodging the fierce barrage, they dropped incendiary bombs and flares. One raider dropped a stick of high-explosive bombs while the flares were still burning and caused damage to many buildings.

The salvo was followed by a terrific outburst of gunfire, which lit the sky for miles around.

Several fires were started in one suburb, where raiders dropped a Molotov bread-basket, followed by high-explosive while A.R.P. workers dealt with the fires.

Bomb Sets Loose Barrage Balloon

One bomb burst near a barrage balloon post on a London common during the night. The blast loosened the balloon, which broke away.

Wardens hearing the swish of the cable through the air and a number of bright flashes caused by its coming in contact with trolleybus wires turned out to deal with incendiaries.

While hundreds of firemen fought fires in another London district, some of their colleagues acted as spotters, when raiders returned to drop high-explosive bombs round the flames.

A doctor's wife was in her London home when she heard the whine of a bomb. She rushed out to join her husband and a staff of four in their shelter.

The bomb demolished the doctor's house and a garage.

Every window in one London street was smashed. "We had only just put our windows back after a previous bombing," said a resident.

In one district an auxiliary fireman returned from duty to find that his home and four other houses had been razed.

NAVAL V.C. VISITS HIS OLD SCHOOL

Cheers for Lieutenant R. B. Stannard, V.C., when he visited his old school, the Royal Naval Merchant School at Wokingham, Berks. Lieut. Stannard was awarded the V.C. in August for saving his ship and many men during bomber attacks at Namsos, Norway.

Fire Services Showed 'Utmost Efficiency'

THIS communiqué was issued by the Air Ministry and Ministry of Home Security at 8 a.m.:

"Late yesterday evening enemy aircraft made attacks on several towns in South and South-West England. Only slight damage was done, but some casualties were caused, several people being fatally injured.

"One of the enemy bombers was shot down, bringing the total of enemy aircraft destroyed yesterday to eight.

"Last night the enemy's attack was directed mainly against London and the suburbs.

"Bombs were also dropped in several other places in South-East England and a few scattered and intermittent attacks were made in some other parts of the country.

Essex Town Raided

"In the London and suburban areas several fires were started, but the fire services again showed the utmost efficiency and brought them all under control.

"Damage was done to a number of houses and industrial premises. Full reports of casualties are not yet available.

"It is feared that some may have been caused in one building in London which was struck by a high explosive bomb and partially demolished, but the indications are that the casualties generally have not been heavy.

"In a town in Essex a number of houses were damaged and from several other places there have been reports of damage to houses but not to any extensive degree.

"Though there have been a small number of fatal injuries, reports show that the total number of casualties has been slight."

Incendiaries on Hoppers' Camp

Fire bombs rained on a hoppickers' camp in a south-east area. Several huts were set on fire.

In a district in the West Country a high explosive scored a direct hit on a public shelter. Five people were killed and several injured.

Bullets from an enemy airplane set fire to a piggery in a south-east rural district. Most of the pigs were rescued by the farmer.

Affairs of "Founder of Pelmanism"

Mr. William Joseph Ennever, aged 71, of Carolene-terrace, Sloane-square, who said he was the founder of Pelmanism, admitted liabilities of £16,092 and no assets when his public examination was held at London Bankruptcy Court to-day.

He attributed his failure to his liability for arrears of income and surtax made against him several years ago.

Torpedoed in the North Atlantic

The Mackay Radio in New York quoted by British United Press reports having intercepted an SOS from the British steamer British General (6989 tons, British Tanker Co.), stating that she had been torpedoed in the North Atlantic.

Raider Crashes Into Haystack Near London

This Messerschmitt 109 crashed into a haystack when it was shot down outside the London area.

GASSED RESCUE SQUADS CARRIED ON IN RELAYS

Eight people were killed and others injured when a bomb scored a direct hit on a shelter in a London recreation ground during the night.

There were 150 people in the shelter, including a warden, who suffered severe shock but was otherwise unhurt.

Rescue gangs worked throughout the night to release people trapped in the debris.

Another bomb damaged a block of mansions opposite the recreation ground; and two women, a man and a boy were trapped.

Rescue squads had to work in relays because of escaping gas. Eight members were overcome, three were revived only after long treatment.

The rescuers tunnelled a passage through the debris and found the trapped people all in an upright position. They talked to them while a doctor was sent for to administer morphia.

The two women and the boy died.

Thirteen almshouses attached to an old parish church were bombed and three old people were trapped beneath the debris. Rescue workers extricated 89-year-old Thomas Main and two elderly women.

Shot His Best Friend

At the inquest at Lewes to-day on Trooper Andrew Morgan, of Edinburgh, his best friend, Trooper Alfred Lane, explained that Morgan was bending down attending to his boots when he (Lane) picked up a rifle lying against a form and touched the trigger.

Someone had released the safety catch and the rifle fired.

The Coroner said he was satisfied that the two men were the best of friends.

Raid Relief Fund Saved From Wreckage

NURSING HOME HIT

In the wreckage of municipal offices bombed in London during the night was found a safe containing thousands of pounds collected for the relief of raid victims. It was undamaged.

The public baths in this district were damaged, too.

Towards midnight the intensity of the attacks started to decrease. Single fast-flying raiders sped across the capital, dropping sticks of bombs.

Bomber Which Machine-gunned Train Shot Down

Damage in last night's raids outside London was widespread.

The attacks on Southern England extended as far as the south-west. There were several reports from the south-east of streets being machine-gunned.

At one South-East Coast town a single airplane raked the streets and a passenger train.

Three people were killed and nine injured.

Bombs were dropped near a hospital and in the grounds of the A.R.P. headquarters.

The raider was later brought down by A.A. fire. The crew were killed.

In one district more than 40 people narrowly escaped when a high-explosive dropped a few yards from a public shelter. The door of the shelter was blown off, but there were no casualties.

In another suburb a nursing home was set on fire. Patients were moved while the fire was got under control. There were no casualties.

Bombs fell in the centre of another district, one of them within 100 yards of the town hall. It killed several horses in a bakery's stables.

RESCUE IN DARK

Two houses were wrecked, several people being injured and four killed.

Three houses were demolished in another street, where seven people were killed. A.R.P. rescue squads worked in the dark to rescue two people trapped in the debris. One man died just before he was freed.

A London doctor was visiting a woman who was suffering from shock after a raid earlier in the day. A bomb flung his car, parked outside the house, over a six-foot wall.

Two bombs fell within 100 yards of each other near a London market. Five public houses were hit. One, almost demolished, was the only one closed to trade. No one was inside.

The licensee of one public house said: "My family and some friends, a party of seven, were in the vaults. I ran down when the bomb fell and found them playing cards. The explosion hadn't even been heard down there, but the window of the bar was blown in."

Buildings damaged in this area included the licensed premises of a wine company, which were hit for the second time within 12 hours.

Addresses: Army Warning

Eastern Command orders state that letters which disclose the addresses of military units are reported as being sent to foreign countries by members of H.M. Forces.

"Disclosure of such addresses," state the orders, "are a grave breach of security instructions, and commanding officers are to ensure that all ranks are made aware of it."

Empire Air Training

An Empire air training contingent of 700 R.A.F. personnel arrived at Bulawayo to-day, to occupy Bulawayo air training school.

They were welcomed by the Rhodesian Minister for Air.—Exchange.

OCTOBER

7 Monday

An improvement in the weather meant the *Luftwaffe* seized the chance to mount a number of large-scale attacks, both by day and by night.

Daylight raids were much larger than they had been for several days but they were not very successful. Night raids were again heavy and caused much greater damage and casualties.

8 Tuesday

Another day and night of large-scale attacks caused significant damage and casualties – approximately 200 people killed and 400 injured. Churchill addressed the House of Commons summing up on the month of Blitz. He pointed out that improved shelter facilities and accurate air raid warnings had cut the death toll to one tenth of what had been estimated before the war, but 'the destruction of property has, however, been very considerable. Most painful is the number of small houses inhabited by working folk which have been destroyed, but the loss has also fallen heavily upon the West End, and all classes have suffered evenly, as they would desire to do.'

9 Wednesday

Churchill had remarked in his speech to Parliament the day before on the easing in the intensity of the Blitz in the first days of October. The previous night's bombing, and raids during the day and night of 9th October, marked a new offensive. Damage and casualties were increased.

59. Rescue squads tear away at the debris to reach trapped victims after raids on Tuesday the 8th.

60. Cleaning up after Tuesday's raids had hit lines into Charing Cross Station. This picture was not passed for publication by the Press and Censorship Bureau until 8th March 1944.

61. *The stage was the platform. The 'auditorium' was an electric railway line which a couple of weeks ago would have meant death to a human being. But Aldwych Tube Station is now an air raid shelter and members of ENSA brought music, song and comedy to the shelterers last night. Daily Mail, 9th October 1940.*

CLOSING PRICES

EVENING STANDARD, October 10, 1940.   FINAL NIGHT EXTRA

Evening Standard

Amusements 8
Radio 8

BLACK-OUT 6.46 p.m. to 6.48 a.m.
MOON, Sets 2.7 a.m.; Rises 4.20 p.m.

No. 36,224.   LONDON, THURSDAY, OCTOBER 10, 1940   ONE PENNY

ST. PAUL'S HIGH ALTAR WRECKED BY A BOMB

CHEERING BOY V.C.

R.A.F. comrades cheering 18-year-old Sergeant John Hannah as he left Buckingham Palace to-day after receiving his V.C. from the King. Story and another picture on the BACK PAGE.

More Waves of Raiders Routed Over Coast To-day

"During a recent attack on London an enemy aircraft dropped a bomb on St. Paul's Cathedral, piercing the roof at the eastern end of the cathedral, and destroying the High Altar.

"THE MAIN FABRIC OF THE CATHEDRAL WAS NOT AFFECTED NOR WAS THE CHOIR DAMAGED AND NO ONE WAS INJURED."

This statement was issued by the Air Ministry and Ministry of Home Security to-day.

To-day, after the longest night raid of the war, formations of German aircraft tried to reach London from the East and South.

They were beaten back in big battles with British fighters. About 80 enemy airplanes passed

DE GAULLE IN CAMEROONS

Welcomed by the Governor

DUALA, Cameroons, Thursday.

GENERAL CHARLES DE GAULLE, LEADER OF THE FREE FRENCH FORCES, LANDED HERE YESTERDAY, RAISING THE FREE FRENCH STANDARD ON FRENCH TERRITORY FOR THE FIRST TIME.

He landed from the gunboat Commandant Duboc, which took part in the Dakar expedition, and embraced Governor-general le Clerce, kissing him on both cheeks.

The two then reviewed native soldiers and sailors and French troops of the Cameroons garrison on the pier.

A great cheer went up from members of the expedition as a burly driver of the Cameroons garrison shouted:

"You'll find yourselves at home here, for there's plenty of Pinard."

Pinard is the red wine which is served to French soldiers.

Wild Cheers

As the Commandant Duboc touched the pier of the capital of the former German colony, three ranks of black troops came smartly to attention. In front of them were grouped Governor-General Le Clerc and his staff.

For a moment there was silence. Then the crowds surging on the pier broke into wild cheers.

While the members of the expedition were disembarking, General de Gaulle drove through the densely-packed streets of the beflagged city to the Governor-general's palace, where local officials and native chieftains were presented to him.

Many of these had come from Senegal, Dahomey and the Ivory
(Continued on Back Page. Col. Two)

GERMAN DESTROYERS BOMBED

Aircraft of the Fleet Air Arm, operating with the Coastal Command, bombed shipping, naval quays and workshops at Brest during the night.

Hits were registered on enemy destroyers. One of our aircraft has not reported to its base.

Winston Churchill, Junior

MRS. RANDOLPH CHURCHILL

Mrs. Randolph Churchill, wife of Mr. Randolph Churchill, M.P., only son of the Prime Minister, gave birth to a son to-day.

The boy, the Prime Minister's third grandchild and second grandson, is to be christened Winston.

Before her marriage a year ago, at the age of 19, Mrs. Churchill was the Hon. Pamela Digby, daughter of Lord and Lady Digby.

Mr. Winston Churchill's other grandchildren are the son and daughter of his daughter, Mrs. Duncan Sandys.

The New Aristocrats

"The poor people are an aristocracy of heroes.

"They have shown it by the way they have behaved in London and in all places where they have been bombed."—The Archdeacon of Lewes, the Ven. F. H. D. Smythe, at Brighton to-day.

The Duke of Northumberland's £1,446,489

The Duke of Northumberland, Lieutenant, Grenadier Guards, of Alnwick Castle, Northumberland, who died on active service on May 21, left unsettled estate of the gross value of £1,446,489 with net personalty £1,092,538 (Estate Duty £193,883).

The Duke of Northumberland—the ninth Duke—was 27 years old.

He left, if he were governing director at his death of Alnwick Estates, Limited, 1000 Ordinary shares in the company to his successor in the title and appointed him governing director, and all other his property to the trustees for the holder of the title.

In 1936 the ducal estates in Northumberland were turned into a private company.

During the war the estates of bankers in the fighting forces who are killed on active service are exempt from Estate Duty. In the case of officers the first £5000 of the estate is exempt. This amount the Estate Duty is assessed in the normal way and then discounted. This discount is based on the officer's normal expectation of life.

"I Started Fires to Guide Planes"

16-Year-Old Boy's Alleged Confession

"I sympathise with Hitler, and I started fires during air raids to guide his bombers."

This confession was alleged to have been made by a boy of 16, who was committed for trial by a London juvenile court to-day on charges of assisting the enemy.

Mr. H. A. K. Morgan, for the Director of Public Prosecutions, described the boy as a traitor who had deliberately set fire to houses damaged in raids.

The district formed vigilance committees to try to solve the mystery of frequent fires, said Mr. Morgan, and he referred to the fine work of two detectives who had patrolled the locality night after night.

They arrested the boy when he was bicycling near a house which had just been fired.

At his home they found a copy of Mein Kampf, a photograph of Hitler and a peaked cap similar to that worn by Hitler.

"Shone a Torch"

In an alleged statement the boy said that he went to houses which had been damaged, set fire to curtains and then watched wardens and firemen fighting the fires.

At one house he "started a big fire," and after it had been put out he started another a few doors away.

The statement continued: "I had often shone a torch into the sky to guide the German airplanes, but that was too risky for me, so I set fire to the houses to cause a glow which the raiders would see."

"Rationing Without Coupons" Inquiry

Mr. Robert Boothby, Parliamentary Secretary to the Ministry of Food, states in a written reply that various schemes of rationing with and without coupons are now being investigated.

A Cup of Tea

Mr. and Mrs. Young and their son, William, having left their garden shelter to make a cup of tea, were in the kitchen when a bomb fell and wrecked their London home. Mother and son were killed. Mr. Young was extricated badly injured.

Their shelter was undamaged.

The High Altar.

over the Essex coast and up the Thames Estuary in three formations. They were turned back by the barrage and were chased away by fighters.

One formation was met by British fighters high above the clouds. The raiders turned during a terrific dog fight and made off to the north-east.

Another formation arrived some
(Continued on Back Page. Col. Three)

More Nazi Troops For Rumania

Officials in Berlin to-day, says the British United Press, declared that it is to be announced officially that several German units will be despatched to Rumania to protect her important industries.

Several German instruction units to help Rumania's armed forces to maintain the guarantee Germany has given to Rumania have also been sent, these officials said.

Several groups of fighter airplanes are to be sent.

Foreign Powers friendly to Germany have been informed.

It was added that the troops will stay in Rumania "only for a limited time as long as circumstances necessitate."

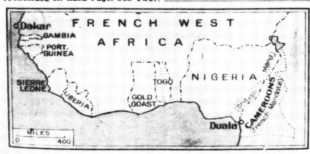

FRENCH WEST AFRICA

Dakar
GAMBIA
PORT. GUINEA
SIERRA LEONE
LIBERIA
TOGO
GOLD COAST
NIGERIA
CAMEROONS
Duala

MILES 0   400

OCTOBER
10 Thursday

Around 6.00 p.m. a bomb pierced the roof of St Paul's Cathedral and destroyed the High Altar. During the rest of the day and night, there was an almost constant succession of raids by single and small formations of aircraft.

Late in September and into October, the *Luftwaffe* had developed methods of evading RAF and AA defences. Using Messerschmitt 109s, originally a fighter aircraft, carrying one 250 lb bomb, the pilots would fly at high altitudes of around 25,000 feet. These aircraft could be over South London within 17 minutes of the first radar warnings. Spitfires took 22 minutes and Hurricanes 25 minutes to reach 25,000 feet from 'scramble' orders. The only way to counter these high-flying Messerschmitts was for RAF Fighter Command to mount a round-the-clock airborne patrol over Southern England – putting great strains on both manpower and equipment.

62. Damage to St Paul's High Altar. A new High Altar was consecrated in 1958.

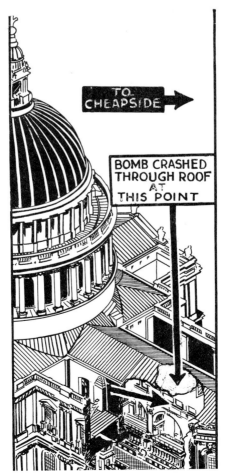

TO CHEAPSIDE →

BOMB CRASHED THROUGH ROOF AT THIS POINT

OCTOBER

11 Friday

The *Luftwaffe* made increasing use of the bomb-carrying Messerschmitt 109s, especially during the day, but few managed to reach Central London. At night, although fog probably reduced the number of raiders, nearly 300 people were killed or injured by the bombing.

12 Saturday

Attacks during the day and night followed a similar pattern to Friday 11th, raiding ending around 2.30 a.m. in the early hours of the following day on both occasions. Similar casualty figures were reported.

63. Cleaning up at St Matthew's Hospital near City Road, after it had been bombed.

64. Another concert in a Tube shelter. The pattern of daily life in London was now, for most people, to head in the early evening straight from work or home to the shelters before even waiting for the siren to sound, so used were they to the constant air attacks.

65. Damage to *The Times* Newspaper Building.

66. A bombed house in Hackney. This picture was earmarked to be used for an Appeal in the overseas *Daily Mail.*

OCTOBER

13 Sunday

Although the British Air Defences had some success in repelling *Luftwaffe* attacks by day, many of the German Messerschmitt 109 fighter-bombers slipped through to drop their bombs. Night raids were heavy and continued throughout the night until 6.00 a.m. on the morning of 14th October. These night raids coincidentally hit several communal shelters including a Tube shelter. The death toll for this day reached nearly 400.

During the evening of Sunday 13th October, Princess Elizabeth, with her sister Princess Margaret beside her, gave her first broadcast when she spoke to British children everywhere. Throughout the war, the Royal Family, including the two princesses, remained based in London and refused to evacuate to what were considered 'safer' areas.

14 Monday

Despite the best efforts of RAF Fighter Command and AA artillery, many *Luftwaffe* aircraft penetrated defences, especially at night when the death toll equalled Sunday's. Sixty-eight deaths alone were caused when a bomb hit Balham High Street Station where about 600 people were sheltering. Damage, too, was considerable.

67. The Monument to the Great Fire of London in 1666 photographed on 14th October 1940 amid the debris of the Luftwaffe bombing.

68. Fire-fighters damping down the smouldering ruins of St James's Church in Piccadilly, hit during a night raid on 14th October.

69. A trolley bus wrecked by a bomb.

70. On the night of the 14th, Winston Churchill, seen here inspecting bomb damage early in the Blitz, escaped injury while dining in the basement of 10 Downing Street when several bombs landed in Whitehall.

DOCTORS AT SHELTERS

Ministry Discuss Rota Scheme

Evening Standard Reporter

One of the plans for safeguarding the health of people forced to spend their nights in air raid shelters, which the Ministry of Health have discussed with the British Medical Association, is for a rota of local doctors, who will visit public shelters in every London area.

A Ministry of Health official said: "Measures will be taken to safeguard the health of people congregated in shelters. So far there is cause for watchfulness, but not for pessimism."

Influenza figures are normal for the time of year, and it is denied that paratyphoid has increased as a result of the increased use of public shelters.

Games in Shelters

Westminster City Council hope soon to be able to provide games and books in all their big air raid shelters, including Aldwych tube station.

The Council have 40 shelters with accommodation ranging from 500 to 600 persons in each.

"We intend to fit the shelters with shelves and cupboards to store games and books, and the shelter-marshals will be responsible for them," an official of the council said.

"We also intend to extend the system of shelter concerts."

Hot and cold running water and canteens are to be installed in the largest shelters.

More Women Police

Women police, up to 10 per cent. of the county force, are to be enlisted in Buckinghamshire.

Bombed Church Carries On

A priest fixing a notice, "Hitler does not stop us," on the door of a Roman Catholic church in London which is maintaining "Services as Usual" despite damage.

100 Shelters Cannot be Used: No Bolts

Willesden Borough Council have 100 Anderson shelters lying in their yard, it was revealed by the mayor, who said that the shelters cannot be erected, although they are required urgently, because the bolts are not available.

Shortage of supplies of concrete is delaying the completion of other shelters in the district.

Weygand in Tunis

ROME, Wednesday.

General Weygand has arrived in Tunis by air, according to a despatch received by the Stefani Agency.—Reuter.

THE NEW SIREN SUITS ARE BRIGHT

By Corisande

Siren suits are fashion news again. Dressmakers are combining to make them bright and attractive.

Furs, too, have a particular interest this week. Many firms have arranged for fur coats to be sold at bargain prices before the purchase tax is imposed on October 21.

Peter Robinson's, Oxford-circus and Regent-street, are rapidly clearing up the damage done in a recent air raid.

New Quarters

Some departments are being shifted to new quarters. "We hope," I was told, "to announce the date of the reopening of the store very shortly now."

When the largest fur organisation in the country arranged to remove valuable stocks from various districts, Gooch's, 63-85, Brompton-road, Knightsbridge, decided to take over the stocks, and they are offering them at sale prices this week.

It is not only inexpensive furs that are being asked for.

Canadian mink coats at 29 guineas are finding plenty of buyers. It is the sort of price that will not be heard of again for a very long time.

Harvey Nichols, of Knightsbridge, are featuring some simple, practical clothes that are both attractive and warm.

Coats are important. Some tweed models for the country have a cosy detachable hooded cape in plaid material, very good for slipping on for shelter wear.

Next best to a fur coat is one that is fur trimmed.

Coat Week

A black coat with the back and front of the bodice made from Persian lamb, with pockets also of fur, proves that there is nothing

smarter than a fur-trimmed coat, provided that the fur is well-placed.

Fur week, with fur coats and furs of all kinds at special prices, at Marshall and Snelgrove, Oxford-street, is being followed by coat week (winter wraps at attractive prices) beginning on Monday.

Apart from these, the firm are paying special attention to shelter clothes and comforts generally.

The newest shelter suit is a ten and a half guinea model (an extra guinea for outsize) lined throughout with fur. Other suits start from two guineas.

Prison Warning to Raid Hooligans

When a 16-year-old boy was fined £2 at Bromley Juvenile Court to-day for obstructing the police in an air-raid shelter, the chairman said to him:

"I want to tell you, and others like you, that people found guilty of these offences in future will be sent to prison."

P.-c. Gunner said that while he was arresting a violent prisoner in the shelter the boy jumped on his back and he had to release his hold.

Detective Mullin said the boy was one of a gang of hooligans from a London district who came into Kent every night for shelter.

Free Plants

Surplus bedding plants will be distributed free of charge at the London County Council's parks and gardens next Saturday, between 9 and 11 a.m.

Personal application should be made to the officers-in-charge. Plants will not be given to children under the age of 14 unless they bring a note of authority from a parent, teacher, or other other responsible person.

Hundreds of Pets Abandoned

"LEAVE THEM WAY TO ESCAPE"

Hundreds of stray dogs and cats are being "picked up" by the police every week in the more heavily bombed areas of London.

People forced to leave their homes by bombs are often in such a hurry to get away that in numbers of cases they either forget their pets or cannot find them.

Mr. E. Keith Robinson, secretary of Our Dumb Friends' League, who patrols his Hampstead neighbourhood each morning after the Raiders Passed signal, collecting homeless animals, stated to-day:

"Pet owners should leave a window or back door open during raids, so that their animals can escape, if necessary.

"Animals have a far keener sense of danger than we have, probably due to their 'sixth sense'—their protective sense.

"People who have lost their cats or dogs should make a point of returning to their homes within 24 to 48 hours. If the animals are still alive—which they usually are—they will probably be waiting for them."

Casualties to animals in air raids have been far lower than any of the animal welfare societies had expected.

Park Flower Shows

The London County Council's chrysanthemum shows in certain of their parks are to be held as usual. The shows will open shortly at Finsbury Park, Battersea Park and Victoria Park, and will remain open for about three weeks.

At some parks, where shows cannot be held, the flowers growing under glass will be cut for distribution to hospitals.

OCTOBER

15 Tuesday

A fairly regular pattern of the Blitz was the concentration of massive attacks in the middle of the month, often assisted by a full or bombers' moon. (There was also a reasonably regular pattern of heavy attacks at the end of the month.) October the 15th matched that pattern and during a night of full moon, 410 German aircraft dropped a total of 538 tons of high explosive (HE) bombs on London and a number of parachute mines.

Again, the death toll was high, over 400, and nearly 900 people were seriously injured. Nine hundred fires were started and thousands of people, especially in East London, were made homeless. All rail traffic into and out of London was stopped. The Fleet sewer was breached and its waters poured into a railway tunnel at King's Cross. Three large water mains were also breached, depriving many areas of water – a not unusual occurrence, but in this case a larger area than usual was affected and it took longer to restore supplies. Battersea Power Station, Beckton Gas Works and even the BBC at Portland Place were all damaged by bombs.

16 Wednesday

While the homeless and others cleared up after the previous night's raid, daytime attacks on the capital were slight – fog hampering German operations.

Night-time activity by raiders was much less than on recent nights but London still suffered death and destruction from the bombs that did fall.

71. Mid-October saw the start of a massive clear-up operation. The picture here shows some of the 5000 men of the Auxiliary Military Pioneer Corp refreshing themselves with buns and tea provided by the Salvation Army before returning to the work of salvage and clearing the debris.

OCTOBER
17 Thursday

Maintaining their strategy of using fighter aircraft carrying single bombs flying at high altitude to evade defences, the *Luftwaffe* managed to bomb London both by day and by night, although with far less severity than the raids earlier in the week. London Transport put out a call to the regions for buses to replace the many familiar red double-decker London buses damaged in the Blitz. Reinforcements in a variety of colours came from across the whole of Britain.

18 Friday

During the day, *Luftwaffe* activity was slight and night fog made flying difficult. Nevertheless, there were still some raids throughout the night, causing about 45 deaths and some damage.

72. The damage to the ancient Elizabethan Dining Hall in the Middle Temple – the hole was once the carved wooden screen supporting the minstrel gallery.

73. As part of the clear-up campaign, the Pioneer Corps salvages this piano from a wrecked home before the debris is cleared away.

74. Soldier volunteers from the Army Pay Corps clearing up bomb damage in Harley Street.

75. This daylight bomb falling on 18th October was heard by a cameraman who was on the scene in less than a minute to find the police taking charge of events. Even on days when German activity was intermittent, the destruction continued.

Evening Standard

Amusements 8
Radio 8

Black-out : 6.27 p.m. to 7.4 a.m.
Moon rises 7.52 p.m., sets 11.21 a.m.

No. 36,232   LONDON, SATURDAY, OCTOBER 19, 1940   ONE PENNY

First of Million Shelter Bunks Fitted

SHELTER SPEED-UP: STATE WILL PAY

GUNS BEAT OFF GLIDE RAIDERS

Hit-and-Run Plan Tried

CLOUDS WHICH BLAN-KETED LONDON AND THE OUTSKIRTS HANDI-CAPPED ANY PLAN OF A MASS ATTACK BY GERMAN RAIDERS DUR-ING THE NIGHT.

The first arrivals, flying singly and at great height, were facing the barrage in the outskirts soon after the first of the night's two Alerts sounded.

They did not try to break through, but flew over the out-skirts, backwards and forwards, as if lost.

Most of the airplanes engaged were bomb-equipped Messer-schmitts.

They adopted tactics which they had tried before—flying high and at great speed, shutting their engines off, and then trying to glide through the barrage to their objectives.

But ground batteries, the advantage of the weather with them, detected the enemy craft as soon as they were in range. The barrage in the outskirts was as intense when raiders were in the vicinity as on any peak night.

Harassed by the heavy guns, the first two raiders were heard to falter in their flight as if struck by the blast of bursting shells. They did not wait about to face more gunfire. They dropped their light calibre bombs and fled, followed by fierce gunfire.

Weather Cleared

Later when the weather cleared a little, larger forces tried to break through. The barrage became more intense and the enemy pilots, apparently unable to see the flashes of the guns, split up and tried hit-and-run tactics.

They bombed parts of the out-skirts blindly, their bombs dropping through the mist on
(Continued on Back Page, Col. Three)

Health Squad at Work in London

A new measure to speed up the building of air raid shelters, and a promise by the Government to pay the whole cost in future were announced to-day by Mr. Herbert Morrison, Minister of Health.

BUT THE LOCAL COUNCILS WHO BUILD THE SHELTERS MUST PRACTISE REASONABLE ECONOMY IF THEY ARE TO BE REIMBURSED.

Two other steps have been taken for the welfare of people who use public air-raid shelters in London. These are:

1—The Ministry of Health have appointed a medical vigilance squad of three doctors to tour the large shelters.

2—The first of the million bunks which the Ministry of Home Security are providing for shelters were delivered in certain districts to-day.

"Free to Act"

In explaining his speed-up measure, Mr. Morrison said a letter was being sent this week-end to all local authorities notifying them that in future the Government would reim-burse them for the whole cost of future contracts for the construction and equipment of shelters.

"The Ministry of Home Security," said Mr. Morrison, "is now playing an increasing part in the direction
(Continued on Back Page, Col. Four)

The Bombs Fell as They Played Darts

Evening Standard Reporter

Rescue parties, working through the night raids and the rain, saved 15 people trapped in the debris of a public house in a London suburb hit by two heavy bombs.

The sirens had sounded, but

To-day's picture of the daughters of Mr. McLaren. The one on the right was unhurt. Her sister, who is a civil defence worker, was not at home.

the bars were crowded. It was still early in the evening.

Soldiers on leave, A.R.P. workers off duty, business men home from the City, and the usual collection of local bar "characters" were drinking their beer, playing darts over a leave-ha'penny and talking over the day's events in a warm haze of tobacco smoke.

Then the bombs crashed down. Mid-day to-day the bodies of more than twenty people had been extricated from the wreckage. One of the twelve injured taken to hospital was the landlord's wife.

The landlord was among those killed, but one of his daughters escaped unhurt. Another daughter
(Continued on Back Page, Col Five)

Murder Hunt: Arrests Are Expected Shortly

Arrests are expected shortly in connection with the murder of Miss Gwendoline Cox, the manageress of the off-licence adjoining the Alexandra Tavern, in High-road, Wood Green, who was shot by one of three young men when she refused to hand over the till.

People who saw a group of young men leave the tavern attended an identification parade at Harrow police station to-day.

Three young men were interviewed at Scotland Yard last night. It is believed that they were able to help the police

Duce Discusses "Important Questions"

ROME, Saturday.

A number of "important questions" were discussed at a meeting of the Italian Cabinet under the presidency of Mussolini, says the official Stefani news agency.—Reuter.

Returning Raiders Crashed, Admit Nazis

Two German airplanes returning from the raids on Britain on Thurs-day night crashed on return, it was stated by Nazi officials to-day, and one other airplane was shot down in night fighting.—British United Press

Mother Takes Twins Away

One grave, the other gay . . . smiling Mrs. Digby, a London mother and her twins, Trevor and Phyllis, as they waited to leave for a safer area to-day.

HAMBURG AND KIEL BOMBED

Aluminium Works Set On Fire

An Air Ministry communique issued this afternoon states:

"Bad weather, low cloud and severe icing conditions hampered the operations of our bomber air-craft last night.

"Nevertheless, the shipyards at Kiel and Hamburg were bombed and fires were started by attacks on the aluminium works at Lunen, a factory at Dortmund and on the wharves at the inland port of Duisberg.

"Railway and goods yards were attacked at Schwerte, Osnabruck, and Dortmund.

"All aircraft operating last night returned safely, but one is missing from a reconnaissance carried out yesterday."

Mr. Chamberlain's Nephew Killed

One of Mr. Neville Chamberlain's nephews, Flying-officer Ralph Hope, of the R.A.F., was killed as a result of enemy action this week.

His machine was shot down three weeks ago, but he escaped and afterwards visited Belfast on leave. He was married there a year ago.

Not Quite Every Day

The Goebbels political review broadcast from all stations, was busy making excuses to the German people to-day.

"Not every day can a British battle-ship be sunk," the announcer said "The British giant cannot be destroyed in a few weeks, or even months. It took centuries to build up this colossal empire.

"But not one day passes without the British suffering losses."—Associated Press

Trench Capes and Steel Helmets for Home Guard

Sir Edward Grigg, Under-secretary for War, announced to-day that, as there was a great demand for great-coats, a trench cape had been devised for the Home Guards. It would be of a material proofed against rain, and there would be a large issue in the near future.

Every Home Guard should have his battle dress, either in denim or serge, in the next few weeks.

Sir Edward, who was speaking at the opening of a new training school for Home Guard commanders and instructors, said it had been decided not to compromise with the many forms of mild steel helmets and to issue nothing but hard steel helmets to the Home Guard. They were being received at a considerable rate every week.

The training school is in a country house and men from the Home Guard will go there from all over the country. They will spend a fortnight at the headquarters and will receive messing and lodging free.

The Bomb Disposal Squad at Work

Evening Standard Reporter

To-day, I saw Acting-captain R Davies, G.C., and his bomb dis-posal squad of the Royal Engineers, deal with two delayed action bombs in a London street.

The bombs fell during a night raid —one in the basement of an office, the other in a basement of a shop on the opposite side of the road.

Acting-captain Davies and his men have inspected the bombs daily and to-day disabled and removed the one from the office and then went over the road to deal with the second.

The first bomb had fallen through part of the building and was in an upright position against a wall.

More Tube Stations to be Open in Raids

London Transport announced to-day that it has been found pos-sible to make arrangements whereby the following Underground stations will not now be closed, as previously, during air raid Alerts:

Arsenal, Green Park and Hyde Park-corner (Piccadilly Line); Chancery-lane and Marble Arch (Central Line); Old-street (Northern Line), and Maida Vale (Bakerloo).

Woman, 93, and Six Daughters Trapped

A woman of 93, her six daughters, and a maidservant were trapped in the cellar of their large detached London house, which was brought down by a direct hit during the night.

When they were rescued, two of the daughters were dead.

Raiders To-day

Enemy airplanes were believed to be in the vicinity of two South Coast towns in daylight to-day.

OCTOBER

19 Saturday

Only one daylight raid was launched against London but in the early hours of darkness a heavy attack was mounted by the *Luftwaffe*. Bombing, often by single aircraft, was widespread throughout the region and casualties were greater than on the previous three days.

20 Sunday

Formations of Messerschmitt 109s flying at high altitude attacked London during the day but little damage was done. Raiding continued during the night, fairly heavily until midnight and then with less intensity until 6.00 a.m. the following morning. In the past week, thousands more had been made homeless. Many of these people found new homes with relatives or people willing to open their homes to Blitz victims. Others went to Rest Centres. For the 250,000 people by now made homeless in the Blitz, the Rest Centres were supposed to be temporary – a 'resting' place for a few hours before being moved on to be rehoused. However, this was seldom the case and many people spent weeks in Rest Centres, usually in school buildings, which were not really designed for long stays.

Overcrowding, inadequate washing or toilet facilities, lack of furniture and a basic and repetitive diet were endured with amazing calmness by many rest centre inhabitants. There was still much clearing up to be done before many of the homeless again had homes of their own.

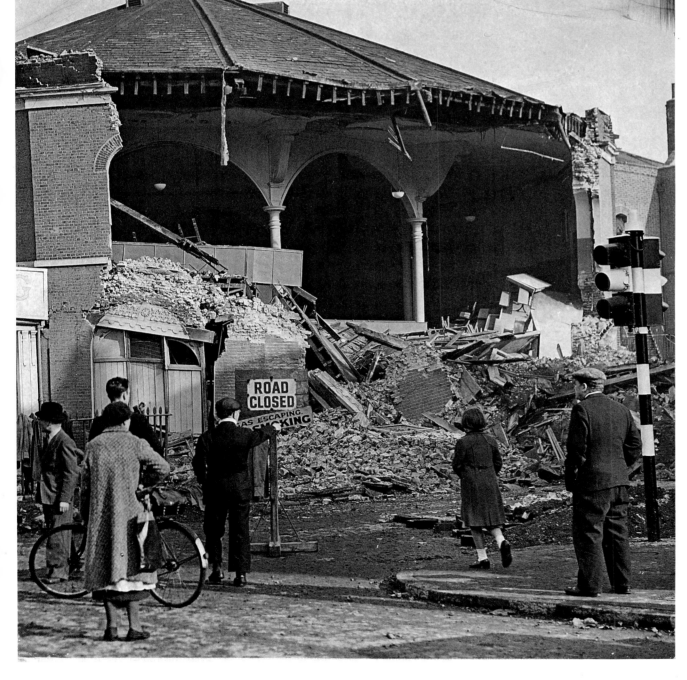

76. A policeman tests for gas leaks from this damaged lamp standard by the 'sense of smell' method.

77. Two bombs fell on this sports stadium – The Ring at Blackfriars – on Saturday 19th.

OCTOBER

21 Monday

Early-morning fog and low cloud over Britain enabled the *Luftwaffe* to take advantage of the cover for a number of attacks on London by day and night, but casualties in the capital were not as severe as other Blitz nights – around 50 deaths.

22 Tuesday

A fairly quiet day and night as German operations were hampered by fog over the South of England.

Two views of Leicester Square showing
78. Damage to Thurstons 'home of billiards' and
79. The Automobile Association.

Leicester Square was bombed on the 17th but the Press and Censorship Bureau did not allow publication of these pictures until later in October. There was a great deal of debate in Government about how much information should be released, for two reasons. First, accurate information about the extent of the destruction would give the Germans useful data when targeting their raids. Secondly, and what caused most debate, was the extent to which scenes of devastation, especially of landmark sites, would lower public morale, as against the damaging effects of rumours which circulated in place of no, or obviously inaccurate, information.

80 and 81. Pictures of children carrying on with their lessons in shelters during air raids. 80. A drawing lesson at a boys' school in North West London. 81. A shelter knitting lesson in progress at a girls' school in the same area.

82

83

84

85

OCTOBER

23 Wednesday

The poor weather conditions continued to work in London's favour, although the few raids that were mounted still managed to evade British air defences.

24 Thursday

Slightly better weather conditions brought more raiders but there was very little damage. Casualties, at less than 100 killed or injured, were slight by comparison with other Blitz days.

25 Friday

Further improvements in weather conditions meant much heavier attacks by day and night and bombing was widespread throughout London. Casualties were very much greater than during the last few days of fog and low cloud – more than 100 deaths. At night, the RAF bombed Berlin and Hamburg in a 'reprisal' raid. It was Berlin's second major raid in four days. On the 21st, the RAF had attacked in a single raid lasting four hours.

82, 83 and 84. The salvaging of jewellery and other valuables from the Chancery Lane Safe Deposit which was bombed in September. Despite the wreckage and debris, most treasure in the vaults was in perfect condition.

85. A bomb crater in Seymour Street by the side of Euston Station.

86. Bomb damage to the Regent Palace Hotel.

87. Salvaging goods in the silverware department of William Whiteley's in Bayswater.

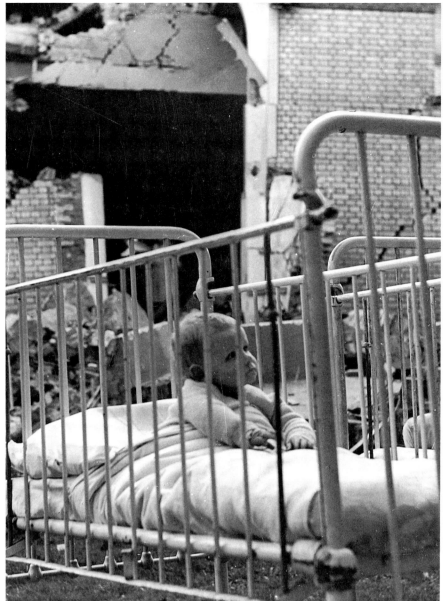

OCTOBER
26 Saturday

RAF Fighter Command had some success in turning back some formations of Messerschmitt 109s during the day but at night many single aircraft managed to evade British air defences and reach their targets.

27 Sunday

Despite many of the *Luftwaffe*'s aircraft being deployed in daylight attacks on RAF aerodromes, a return to the tactics used early in the Battle of Britain, some raids were also successfully mounted against London.

At night raiding was over a very large area of the London Metropolitan District and wider into the Home Counties.

88. This child surveys the wreckage of his orphanage from his cot. The Children's Home was bombed in a night raid on 27th October.

89. The scene in Queen Victoria Street, Blackfriars, where the District Railway carried on operating despite the fact that a bomb had blown away the roof of the tunnel. The pictures were not allowed to be published until April 1941.

90. A damaged trolley bus in Blackfriars Road, hit during a daylight raid.

91. Inside the burnt out library of Holland House where a number of valuable books were destroyed when it was fire-bombed by the Luftwaffe.

92. The damaged Court Room in Stationers' Hall bombed on 15th October.

Those Onions: All Sorts of Prices Now

Evening Standard Reporter

Women want to know why, having fixed the retail price of onions at 4½d. lb., the Ministry of Food does not impose it.

"Legal authorities are drafting the order," I was told by a Ministry official.

Meanwhile shops continue to charge a strange assortment of prices.

In one shop onions cost me 6d. a pound, and in another near by I was asked to pay 10d.

A provision store has made a cut in the price of tripe from 9d. (the official maximum price) to 6d. a pound "Just so that the housewife will not have to pay an impossible price for tripe and onions," the manager told me, smilingly.

Plaice Down to 1s. 8d.

"Offal is fairly plentiful this week. There are good supplies of English pig's liver, which is one of to-day's best "buys."

The demand for butcher's meat has lessened in many districts, with the result that butchers still have plenty left in their cold storage rooms from last week.

Fish is down in price. It is more plentiful to-day, too. This morning I was able to buy herrings and kippers which have been almost unprocurable during the past few weeks.

The herrings are small—the fishmonger described them as "glorified sprats."

Plaice has come down from around 2s. 6d. a lb. to 1s. 8d.—a drop of 33⅓ per cent. Cod is 1s. 4d. and 1s. 6d., and whiting is 10d. and 1s. a lb.

It has been suggested to the Ministry of Food that in view of the difficulties of deep-sea fishing and the commandeering of trawlers for naval purposes, fresh-water fish should be bred in ponds.

"There is a prejudice against them because of their 'earthy' flavour," a Ministry official said, "but this can be overcome by careful preparation and cooking."

£20 for a Light

Charles Babb, of Farnborough Park, Kent, was at Bromley to-day fined £20 or two months for showing a light.

THE ENGLISHMAN'S

A "Morrison" (Concrete) Shelter Inside and Safety Rooms Built Like Tables

Evening Standard Reporter

Fortress homes throughout London and the Home Counties;

Strong rooms in private houses;

Safety "floors" in big business premises;

A "Morrison" shelter which can be erected inside a house.

These are some of the possibilities arising out of a speech by Miss Ellen Wilkinson, Parliamentary Secretary to the Ministry of Home Security, to her Jarrow constituents.

Get-You-Home Service Starts

ASK ME FOR ALTERNATIVE ROUTES

Information booths to help the travelling public are being set up in London and around the suburbs. This woman was inquiring to-day at the "Get-you-home" booth at Wimbledon.

They are the recommendations of a group of experts attached to the Ministry, and are the results of their investigation into the safest kind of buildings during air raids, and of the causes of casualties in certain types of shelter. They have placed their findings before the Minister, Mr. Herbert Morrison.

I understand that the first result will be that the Government will take over many large buildings in London and the Home Counties.

These are being divided into two classes:

A "first-class" type, which is the reinforced concrete frame building, and a "second class" type, which is the steel frame building.

It is estimated that there are available one first class building in every ten square miles in London.

The idea is to make these buildings into fortress homes for homeless people. They will be divided so that each section is a self-contained flat.

Safety floors will be on the first or second tier, which will be bricked in with blast walls as protection against glass splinters.

Experience has shown that the heaviest calibre bomb will not penetrate to these floors in the first-class buildings. People in the "fortresses" will be sheltered on these floors in preference to the basements.

Arch-Shaped

For private houses the recommendations are two-fold:

One is that special strong rooms should be built.

This, in effect, would be a gigantic table with its top near the ceiling and the legs on each corner, with perhaps another support in the centre.

Windows would be bricked-up, and the room would be built where possible in the middle of the house.

The other idea is the installation of an indoor shelter. It would be like the Anderson shelter, but made of concrete instead of steel.

One design which is being considered by the Ministry of Home Security shows curved concrete blocks which fit into each other to make a parabolic arch. This shelter could easily be fitted in a kitchen or passage of an ordinary-sized house.

Safer Than Basement

I understand that the reason the new shelter is to be of concrete is that there are now ample supplies of cement and that the difficulty of transport has been overcome. This news follows to-day's announcement that brick and cement controls responsible to the Ministry of Works and Public Buildings have been set up.

Office safety floors will be a further recommendation. Experience has shown that in some cases of direct hits on big buildings people in basement shelters have been in greater danger than those on the lower floor.

Where first floor and second floor rooms have been strengthened against blast and falling debris the margin of safety has been increased. There may be a general extension of this policy.

"Brilliant Light": Woman Sent to Prison

Mrs. Rose Lewis, of Green Wrythe-lane, Carshalton, was sent to prison for a month at Mitcham to-day for allowing what was described as a brilliant light to stream from her bedroom window during an Alert.

It was her second offence.

The Roof

"When a roof has to be repaired, it has to be repaired," said a builder to-day in the King's Bench Division.

Mr. Justice Wrottesley—Do you think that proposition still obtains to-day? I should like to know; I am interested personally.

"Yes, it does," replied the builder.

HOME HIS FORTRESS

Safe in Their Shelter

A bomb dropped in the South-East during the night and demolished four cottages, one the home of Mr. and Mrs. Heath —seen here to-day. They were safe in their shelter.

GIRL POSED AS M.T.C. OFFICER, COURT TOLD

Gertrude Anne Carbotton, aged 20, a companion help of Hoop-lane, Golders Green, was charged at Hendon to-day with doing an act calculated falsely to suggest that she was acting in the performance of essential services with the Mechanised Transport Corps.

She was also accused of obtaining by false pretences an officer's uniform value £10 9s.

It was alleged that the girl represented herself as a member of the M.T.C. on leave. She ordered the uniform and asked for early delivery because she had to attend a funeral.

She told the police, "I wanted lodgings, but had no money. I was foolish to say that I was in the M.T.C. but I have tried to join. I am fed up with civil life."

Both charges were referred to Bow-street.

Camouflage More Buildings, Urge Select Committee

The camouflaging of vital industrial points should be speeded up, declare the Select Committee on National Expenditure in their report to-day.

Other recommendations are:

The four existing camouflage departments should be united in a single organisation with its own research staff and administered by the Ministry of Home Security.

Greater use should be made of the experience and knowledge of the non-departmental members of the Camouflage Committee than has been made in the past.

Owners of industrial undertakings, who, though not required by law to camouflage their concerns, yet desire to do so, should be encouraged to seek official guidance.

Fur Trimming for your Winter Coat

by Corisande

A woollen coat trimmed with fur is going to be the solution of the winter wrap problem for a great many women this year.

Sketched is one example from the collection in the Small Women's Department at Debenham and Freebody, Ltd., Wigmore-street.

The material is dark green bouclet, the trimming a bow made from shaded beaver fur.

Two points to remember about this department are that there are ample stocks of all kinds of fur-trimmed coats, as well as frocks, suits, dinner dresses, and so on, available. These are not subject to the Purchase Tax; that new deliveries of fur-trimmed garments will be subject to the tax, which will be one-third of the cost.

Sketch by DOROTHY THATCHER

Light up—and smile!

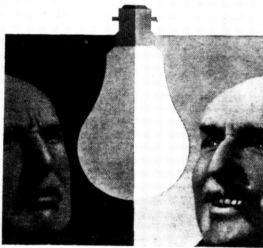

Get this clear — dim lighting does *not* rest your eyes (unless you're going to sleep). It only strains them, adding to the fatigue and nervous tension of the day. Rest your eyes, rest your nerves, and renew your vitality by having good, bright, well-diffused lighting in your home. Darken your windows by all means, but not your spirits. Get bright, reliable lamps that will give you *all* the light you pay for — Get Osram.

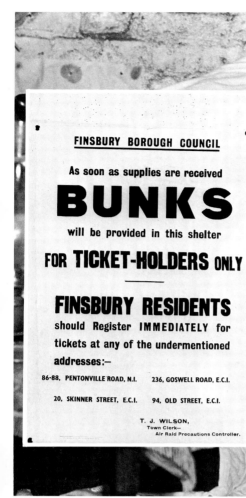

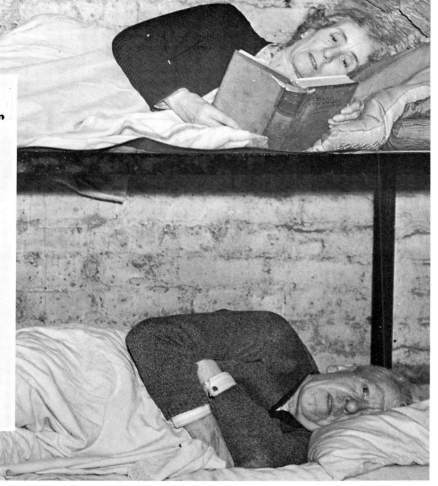

94

97

OCTOBER

28 Monday

None of the German attacks mounted during the day reached Central London but raids after dark continued as usual, although none was severe.

29 Tuesday

As on Sunday 27th, the *Luftwaffe* used much of their energies attacking RAF aerodromes during the day and although London was raided many bombs were dropped in the Home Counties. There was a suggestion that the Germans were training a large number of pilots and so, by and large, avoided the tried and tested skills of London's air defences.

30 Wednesday

A day and night of light raiding by the Germans meant there were few deaths and only slight damage in the London area.

31 Thursday

Again, a day of only slight activity by the *Luftwaffe*, operations being hampered by rain and winds. Nevertheless, for Londoners the presence of any German aircraft spelt danger and millions of people took to their shelters for the fifty-fifth night of unbroken attack. Time in the shelters was now part of everyday life. Wherever people sheltered, things were beginning to be more organised than in the early days of the Blitz. In public shelters, sanitation had been improved, some sleeping bunks installed, even entertainment and canteens provided. Rules and regulations (often unofficial) now governed the behaviour expected in shelters.

93. Shelter notice.

94. In late October, Westminster Council began providing bunks for the basements of private houses in the area.

95. These lightweight shelter bunks were the brainchild of a racing bicycle designer. They opened to provide 3 sleeping beds and closed to take up only 4 inches of space.

96. Conditions of issue on reverse of Westminster Shelter tickets.

97. Issuing shelter tickets.

Gale in Channel Stopped Night Raids on London

SOME BASES FLOODED

The much lighter raids on London and Britain during the night were due to bad weather conditions over Northern France, which, though enabling the German light bombers to take off, made it difficult to land.

The south-westerly gale which lashed the Straits of Dover dropped during the night, when the wind swung round to the north-west. A few raiders then took off.

The Germans admitted to-day that "extremely unfavourable weather greatly restricted the possibility of offensive action."

The advanced striking airfields of the enemy are not only being waterlogged, but are being continually attacked by the R.A.F. who are trying to drive back these bases until the bombers' flight to Britain becomes longer and longer.

After the usual early Alert in London last night, the Raiders' Passed signal was given in about two hours.

More Guns Used

Few districts heard the raiders during the first Alert. They flew into a barrage that was not affected by weather conditions over here There seemed to be a wider variety of guns in use

Early to-day the raid flared up again. For a time it seemed that there was to be another mass attack. But the big barrage broke out again and split up the small formations.

Damage in the London area and the Home Counties was slight. A hospital in one South-East district was slightly damaged.

Land girls were machine-gunned by a raider which dived low out of the clouds in a Midlands town. Bullets penetrated a roof and sprayed a car park.

A north-east Scotland district had a comparatively heavy raid. A number of houses and business premises were destroyed.

The 'Under Fives' are Leaving

A London mother registering her two "under fives" to-day for evacuation to a safer area.

Bombs On London, East Anglia and Town in Midlands

The Air Ministry and Ministry of Home Security communique issued at 7.40 a.m. to-day was one of the shortest since the mass night raids on London began eight weeks ago. It said:

"There was a further diminution in the enemy's air activity over this country last night.

"A few bombs which are reported, mainly in East Anglia, London and a town in the Midlands, caused little damage and few casualties.

"A few bombs were also dropped with little effect at one point on the north-east coast of Scotland."

"Where are you going to?" they said to him to-day as they compared their destination labels.

He *Slept* Beside a Time-Bomb

A heavy bomb had made a deep hole in a London recreation ground and had not exploded. The Bomb Disposal Section were making ready to explode it when a policeman asked if he could look down the hole.

As he walked towards the edge one of the R.E.'s shouted, "Hi !— Mind you don't kick any dirt down that hole because my mate's down there having a sleep."

And the beams of a torch shone into the hole revealed a soldier actually sleeping by the side of the biggest bomb the policeman had ever seen.

Bombed From Shop and Home

A Wests End antique dealer, asking at Westminster County Court to-day to be allowed to pay a debt of £60 at 10s. a month, said that his stock was destroyed by bomb blast.

"All my best pieces of china and glass were in the window and were all smashed," he said.

Five days later his house was damaged by blast an dhe was now out of work but had been offered a job at £3 a week.

When a solicitor suggested that £10 a month could be paid, and that it was a business that did not need a shop, Judge Austin Jones said: "That may be so, but it is not the kind of business that is flourishing just now."

An order to pay £4 a month was made.

Boys' Shelter Hit —Three Killed

A public surface air raid shelter in London was hit by a bomb and a section of it demolished during the night.

About a dozen boys, aged 14 to 16, occupied the section which was wrecked. There were killed, several injured. Women and children in an adjoining section escaped unhurt.

Climbed 60ft. Escape To Rescue Woman

Climbing a 60ft. fire escape during the night, an A.F.S. man rescued a woman from the wreckage of her London home on the top of a block of flats. The top floor had been shattered by a bomb. The fireman was attracted by the woman's shouts

3 Die Playing Cards

One of several bombs dropped in a London district during the night pierced the roof of a surface shelter. Blast killed three youths who were playing cards inside

"Very Inquisitive Person" in a Tunnel Shelter

Wilfred Ivor Goodsall, 35, debt collector, of Kingscliffe-gardens, Southfields, S.W., was at Ramsgate to-day fined £5 for attempting to obtain information of military importance.

Goodsall, who slept in the town's tunnel shelter when he came to Ramsgate to make inquiries for a hire purchase firm, admitted that he questioned a soldier and a Home Guard regarding A.A. defences. He alleged that a soldier to whom he was introduced by a woman was actuated by jealousy.

It was stated that the police were satisfied that Goodsall, who was described as a very inquisitive person, had acted from indiscretion. The Mayor advised him to hold his tongue in future.

They Drove Blazing Vehicles to Safety

Night workers drove blazing vehicles out of a London garage early to-day after an oil bomb had crashed through the roof and exploded. Several vehicles were destroyed.

A.F.S men had the outbreak under control in an hour

Brother Saved Her

Eleven people, including a three-year-old boy, in an enlarged Anderson shelter in London, were buried when a bomb demolished it during the night.

Mrs Ada Jordan, who was with her husband and son in the next shelter, which was only slightly damaged, said to-day : "My daughter, who was in the large shelter, was the last to be rescued. She was buried for three hours. My 17-year-old son Leonard went on digging for her although the barrage was so heavy.

"This is the second time Leonard has rescued members of his own family."

DRIVE TO EVACUATE LONDON CHILDREN IS MAKING PROGRESS

Evening Standard Reporter

The Ministry of Health's drive to complete the evacuation of children from London is well in hand. Hundreds of the homes of the 279.000 children who remain in the London region were visited to-day by teachers and welfare workers, who stressed the advantages of sending the children away.

The London County Council official in charge of evacuation in a North London borough, said to me :

"The callers began their work on Wednesday.

"The expert knows she has only about three minutes to spend on each visit, and does not stay to gossip.

"We are in great need of volunteers, but they must be patient, tactful and persuasive

"The sort of visitor who will become involved in doorstep argument will do more harm than good.

"We want the good-tempered people to volunteer.

"Church and social workers would be most helpful."

Danger to Health

Mothers who refuse to send their children away are told first about the dangers to health of winter nights in shelters.

The second plank in the interviewer's platform is education

Parents are warned that unless the child is given uninterrupted schooling in a comparatively safe district, future chances in life will be seriously hampered.

Although a number of mothers have been persuaded to send their children away o rto go with them under the family evacuation plan, some parents refuse to be convinced by words.

"The only argument that will finally convince the parents will be provided by Hitler," one official said.

"It is a bomb near the house. Thousands of parent, will continue to keep their children in London until that happens."

Education Problem

The education of children left in London is also worrying the authorities.

Many schools have either been bombed or have been taken over as rest centres, and hundreds of children are roaming the streets instead of getting on with their studies.

The Minister of Health, Mr. Malcolm MacDonald, has pointed out that some mothers refuse to take their children to the country because there is an aged or sick relative in the house who cannot be left alone.

Thousands of these old or infirm people have already been evacuated separately, under a special scheme.

A further batch are to leave London for the country in an ambulance train.

Among them will be a blind man and his wife, and a bedridden man of 84 who has been bombed from his house.

Time Bomb Saves Six Families

A time bomb has saved the lives of six families evacuated from their homes in London a few days ago.

Last night, while they were sleeping in nearby rest homes, a high-explosive bomb fell in front of their homes, demolishing them Slabs of concrete were hurled into the air, one piece crashing on top of an Anderson shelter, driving it into the ground.

Another bomb fell on lock-up garages in a neighbouring district—wrecking 20 cars.

A.F.S. Dormitory Hit

Three auxiliary firemen were injured, one seriously, when a bomb directly hit their dormitory in London during the night.

The one seriously injured was still pinned down by heavy debris to-day. A doctor administered morphia to him.

Girl Dug Out Three From Debris

When a bomb struck an Anderson shelter in a London suburb last night a family of three were flung ten yards and buried beneath debris and concrete.

They were Mr. and Mrs. Percy White and their seven-year-old daughter Doreen.

Miss Violet Varley, 21, an ambulance driver, who lives next door, said to-day : "I heard the whistle of a bomb and ducked under the table. Then I ran out. Doreen's hand was sticking out of the earth, and I was able to free her.

"Two huge pieces of concrete were pinning down Mr. and Mrs. White." All three were taken to hospital.

TWO DICTATORS

CHARLES SPENCER CHAPLIN and Adolf (Schickelgrüber) Hitler were both born in the same week of 1889, but Chaplin is really the better comedian. There has been a strange similarity, too, in the pattern of their lives. In Picture Post this week four pages of pictures from the new Chaplin film, 'The Dictator,' show how easily Chaplin could have assumed the major role although it is doubtful whether Hitler could have starred in "City Lights" or "The Shop Walker" with the same success.

Rebecca West writes the text for the pictures — a brilliant study of the two characters.

NOV

1 Friday

German attacks on London were heavier than on the previous few days and nights but not classed as severe, although over 300 Londoners were left dead or injured. The *Luftwaffe* were still employing Messerschmitt 109s as fighter-bombers flying at high altitudes to try to outrun RAF defences.

2 Saturday

Casualties after another day and night of attacks amounted to 100 dead or injured in the London area. Damage was classed as slight, although the raids, as was invariably the case, left some road and rail communications blocked and a serious fire at Barkers of Kensington.

3 Sunday

This was the first night since 7th September that no bombers attacked London. Extremely bad weather made flying impossible, so the capital escaped with only a few bombs dropped in daylight hours.

98. *Back from Berlin – to this. A Pilot Officer DFC looks over the ruins of his home, bombed while he was 'over enemy territory'. Daily Mail,* 2nd November 1940.

99. *A German bomb dropped in Leicester Square recently. The first pictures of the damage were released yesterday. This one shows the wreckage of a line of taxi cabs. Daily Mail,* 1st November 1940.

FLARES LIT SKY AS GUNS SHOOK RAIDERS

Another London Hospital Hit: 5 Bombs In One Road

The first raiders over London during the night dropped dozens of flares which lit up the sky for miles.

For the first few hours heavy bombers and Messerschmitt-bombers flew in towards London at regular intervals. The guns in the outskirts were in action almost continuously.

Early in the raid a breadbasket of 10 bombs fell near and on a hospital. One bomb crashed through the roof. Patients were in a shelter. No one was hurt. A fire was quickly put out.

Near by a high explosive fell near an underground shelter. There were a number of casualties.

Diners in a London hotel were shaken when a high explosive fell in a street near. The windows of the hotel were blown out. Dinner was continued.

People were trapped when a high explosive hit a basement shelter in another London district. The bomb fell on a building above the shelter.

There were also casualties when a public-house in another district received a direct hit.

Five bombs fell in one street, doing considerable damage to buildings and fracturing gas and water mains. One man was killed running to shelter.

Other bombs fell on a wardens' post and a church. There were a number of casualties at the wardens' post. The church was severely damaged.

Damage Was Not Heavy During Night

The Air Ministry and Ministry of Home Security communiqué at 7.40 a.m. to-day stated:

"The attacks on this country which were resumed shortly after darkness last night were widespread and on a fairly heavy scale.

"Bombs were dropped in many places in England and Scotland, but, according to reports so far received, casualties were not anywhere numerous and damage was relatively slight.

"London was again the main objective, but bombs also fell in two towns in the Midlands, on Merseyside and at a number of places in South-East England, the Eastern counties, and Scotland.

"The attack on the London area continued throughout the hours of darkness and bombs were dropped at many points. Although some damage was done, reports received up to 6 a.m. show that the number of people killed and injured is small.

"The main attack on the Midlands and Eastern and Southern Scotland ceased shortly after midnight.

"In these areas damage was not heavy and there were not many casualties."

Bombed Goldfish

A pond in the front garden of a house in London, containing more than a dozen goldfish, was destroyed when a bomb scored a direct hit on it last night.

How Officers Crossed A River

This is how Australian infantry officers in training crossed a river. They tied up their kit in waterproof sheets and swam over wearing their steel hats and pushing their bundles in front

80 Canteens and 1000 Waitresses for 200,000 Tube Shelterers

Evening Standard Reporter

Improvements to air raid shelters, including the provision of bunks, first-aid posts and canteens, are now being effected at a rapid rate.

Local authorities and Government officials have been asked to work at top speed to convert every all-night shelter into a model rest centre before severe weather sets in.

Here is a summary, compiled from official sources, of what has actually been achieved to date.

BUNKS.—Orders have been placed for 1,750,000, and deliveries are now coming in fast. Dormitory accommodation has been provided for hundreds of thousands.

TICKETS.—Most local authorities in the bombed areas have begun the issue of tickets. When the Ministry of Home Security decides which system of reserving and allocating shelter accommodation proves most satisfactory, a standard ticket will be issued for general distribution.

Doctor to Every 500

MEDICAL SERVICES. — Doctors and nurses are already in attendance at some of the big shelters.

The aim is to provide a sick bay and a dispensary at every shelter accommodating more than 500 persons.

SANITATION.—Ministry of Health inspectors are now going round to give their advice. Lavatory and washing accommodation has been installed in a few shelters, and will soon be available in many more.

It is claimed that sanitary arrangements have already been "completely transformed." Twice-daily cleaning is now usual in the big shelters.

CANTEENS.—Many have been installed, and voluntary workers are coming forward in large numbers to serve meals and refreshments.

Red Cross Nurses

A refreshment service has been provided at two Underground stations—Holland Park and Shepherd's Bush.

There will eventually be canteens in 80 stations, and 1000 women will be engaged in catering for the 200,000 people who shelter in the Tubes.

A survey is being made to decide how much space can be allocated to bunks, and these will be installed as soon as the survey is completed.

First-aid posts with Red Cross nurses have now been provided at South Kensington, Gloucester-road and Paddington stations, and other stations will soon have trained nurses in attendance.

Card Sharpers at Work in the Shelters

Evening Standard Reporter

Complaints are being made to local authorities and the police about the increase in gambling in air raid shelters.

In some cases it is believed that card sharpers are operating in public shelters.

Shelter wardens and police have received instructions to keep a close watch for men who are known to the police for their gambling activities.

It is believed that one gang are visiting different shelters each night and so avoiding attracting attention by constant visits to one place.

One man who was caught by a gang of card-sharpers told me:

"I was watching three men playing three-handed solo whist. They invited me to join them and I did not realise that in a public shelter you were not permitted to play for money. They allowed me to win one night and invited me to join them the next night. I lost all my money to them and have not seen them again."

BLAST SCENTED THE AIR

Scattered Perfumery

A bomb in one London district during the night did the authorities a good turn.

When some old houses were wrecked in a previous raid, one corner section was left in a perilous state. The authorities planned to demolish it. Last night one small bomb razed the remaining walls.

Passers-by sniffed the air on their way to business to-day. Blast had blown in the windows of a shop and scattered perfumes and cosmetics.

His Night Off

As he was off duty last night, Mr. Bert Smith, a member of a stretcher party in one London district, slept in his kitchen with his wife and two daughters, aged 21 and 16.

A bomb, falling in the road, wrecked his own and several other houses.

Although covered with debris Mr. Smith and his family were saved by a partition wall. After getting his wife and daughters safely out, Mr. Smith went back to assist four people trapped in the house next door.

He later helped to extricate dead and injured.

Among buildings damaged were premises formerly used as a nurses' home and now a rest centre for bomb victims. Thirteen people, mostly women and children, sheltering in the basement were led through the wreckage unhurt.

7 A.R.P. Men Killed

Seven A.R.P. men in a school used as a depot in one London district were killed when a bomb pierced the roof and exploded during the night.

NOVEMBER

4 Monday

If any Londoners had hoped that Sunday the 3rd's cessation of night-time bombing was to last they were disappointed. After some minor attacks by day the night raiders returned. Bombing was fairly severe during the early hours of darkness and although the severity of the bombardment later eased, the raid continued until after dawn on the morning of Tuesday the 5th.

5 Tuesday

London was on Alert from dusk until after dawn on Wednesday the 6th, after a day with no reported casualties. Despite the lengthy Alert, bombing was not severe, nor were damage or casualties.

Winston Churchill addressed the House of Commons after the second month of the Blitz: 'Fourteen thousand civilians have been killed and 20,000 seriously wounded, nearly four-fifths of them Londoners.' But he went on: 'None of the services upon which the life of our great cities depends – water, fuel, electricity, gas, sewerage – not one has broken down. On the contrary, although there must inevitably be local shortages, all the authorities concerned with these vital functions of a modern community feel that they are on top of their job.'

6 Wednesday

Again, minor attacks during daylight hours were followed by heavier raids in the early hours of darkness, with much lighter bombing sustained until dawn the following day.

100. Pensioners from the Royal Hospital at Chelsea washing crockery salvaged from the damaged building.

EVENING STANDARD November 9, 1940.

FINAL NIGHT EXTRA

Evening Standard

Amusements 8
Radio 8

Black-out 5.48 p.m., to 7.41 am
Moon rises 3.14 pm, sets 3.6 am

No. 36,250   LONDON, SATURDAY, NOVEMBER 9, 1940   ONE PENNY

R.A.F. BOMBED MUNICH WHILE HITLER SPOKE

Waves of Planes Rained Fire and High Explosive Bombs for Hour and Half

MILAN, TURIN AND 18 AIRFIELDS RAIDED

R.A.F. bombers roared over Munich last night to bomb military objectives there while Hitler was making his two-hour speech to the veterans of the Nazi Party in the city's famous beer hall, the Loewenbraeu Keller.

In London to-day it was understood on reliable authority that strong forces of our bombers were over the Bavarian capital and that "operations began at a fairly early hour."

THE R.A.F. EFFECTIVELY PUT A STOP TO ANY BROADCASTING OF THE SPEECH TO GERMANY ITSELF, ARRIVING OVER MUNICH JUST ABOUT AN HOUR AFTER HITLER WAS DUE TO START SPEAKING.

MOST OF 35's CHOOSE THE R.A.F.

Evening Standard Reporter

If all those 35's (born between July 1 and December 1, 1905) who registered to-day are lucky enough to find their way into the Service of their choice, the Royal Air Force are going to get a lot of men.

Sixty per cent. of the men to whom I spoke at one labour exchange want to get into the R.A.F.—"if only for ground duties."

A good percentage of the balance were going to choose the Navy.

But there was one man who much

The bombers took off from Britain on their 600-mile flight as darkness fell.

The last bomber did not leave Munich until 10.10 p.m. (B.S.T.), about an hour and a half after arriving. During that time the R.A.F. bombed the railway communications of Munich most heavily. Tons of high-explosive and fire bombs were dropped by continuous waves of aircraft.

But that was not all. Several of the tail-gunners of the British bombers dropped bricks and other articles while the bombing was going on. Notes addressed to "Adolf" were tied to them.

And, it was learned in London, "one stick of bombs overshot its mark and hit the famous beer cellar, starting a large fire."

Most of the rail communications and shunting yards which the R.A.F. bombed are in the centre of Munich.

To-day's official German war communiqué admits: "British bombers obtained several hits in Munich, Stuttgart and a number of towns in Wurttemberg, causing slight damage.

ONLY ONE BOMB LAST YEAR

The U.S.A. broadcast of Hitler's speech—scheduled for 7.20 to 9 p.m.—was cancelled and the full broadcast to Germany was postponed until midday to-day. Only an abridged version was given to the Nazis last night.

But then there was another hitch. The broadcast to-day had to be postponed until this evening.

Many leading members of the Nazi Party were in Munich to hear Hitler.

The Loewenbraeu Keller is the beer hall which last year was partly wrecked by a bomb just after Hitler had made his annual speech there to commemorate the abortive Nazi putsch of 1923.

Hitler did not attend to-day at Munich Cemetery when members

(Continued on BACK PAGE)

C.Q.M.S. COE

wanted to get into the Army. He was Arthur Henry Coe. Coe volunteered for the R.A.S.C. in September last year, worked his way up to be a C.Q.M.S., went to France, and was one of the 2500 survivors out of 5350 aboard the liner Lancastria when she was sunk by bombs off St. Nazaire. That was during the evacuation from France.

"I shall never forget the hours we spent in the water with German aeroplanes machine-gunning us," he told me.

Coe was discharged from the Army
(Continued on Back Page, Col. Five)

London Daylight Bomber Shot Down Off Coast

Out of the clouds over one London district to-day glided a Heinkel. It dropped four bombs and flew away.

British fighters raced up, located the Heinkel, chased it to the Sussex coast and sent it crashing into the sea.

One of the crew baled out.

An Air Ministry and Ministry of Home Security communiqué this afternoon said: "Enemy activity over this country up to noon has been limited to a few flights by single aircraft."

There was no Alert when the London bombs fell. Three crashed through the roof of a building in which there were a number of clerks. A fire was started, but was quickly got under control.

There were a number of casualties, some believed to be fatal.

The first Alert in London sounded this afternoon.

Incendiary bombs were dropped on a North-East Coast district to-day by a Junkers 88.

Reports of night raids—PAGE SIX.

Railway Seasons Concession to People Under 18

Half rate season tickets for those under 18 which in the past were issued for a period of not less than one month, will in future be issued also for weekly periods.

They will be available for those earning less than 25s. a week—instead of 18s as at present.

It was announced to-day that the Minister of Transport has approved these concessions as recommended by the Railway Executive Committee.

The concessions will come into force on December 1.

Mr. Chamberlain

The condition of Mr. Neville Chamberlain, who, Mrs. Chamberlain announced last night, is gravely ill, is understood to be unchanged. He is at his country home in Hampshire.

The King and Queen visited Mr. and Mrs. Chamberlain recently and stayed about an hour.

Bus Curfew on Dogs

London Transport announce that on and from Monday, November 18, passengers will not be allowed to board buses, coaches, trams or trolley buses with dogs during black-out hours.

GREEKS HAVE ADVANCED SLIGHTLY

Six Miles from Their Frontier

THE GREEKS HAVE ADVANCED SLIGHTLY IN THE PINDUS MOUNTAINS SECTOR OF THE FRONT, IT WAS STATED BY MILITARY CIRCLES IN LONDON TO-DAY.

It is now reported that they

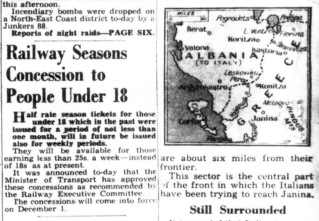

are about six miles from their frontier.

This sector is the central part of the front in which the Italians have been trying to reach Janina.

Still Surrounded

It is reported that Italian troops are still surrounded in this region—in the neighbourhood of Dystraton.

This Italian column was cut off when they advanced into the Pindus mountains, and the Greeks are said to be "mopping them up."

"We are counting the booty"
(Continued on Back Page, Col. Two)

"Our Separation is Permanent," Says Doris Duke

SAN PEDRO (California), Saturday.

Mrs. Doris Duke Cromwell, the tobacco heiress, admitted that she has separated from her husband, Mr. James Cromwell, former United States Minister to Canada, when she sailed from here to-day for Honolulu in the liner Matsonia.

"It is a permanent separation, and I have no plans for the future," said Mrs. Cromwell, according to the British United Press.

She said they had been estranged for four or five months, and that last met her husband on his birthday—June 4.

Lining up to register at the Westminster Exchange to-day.

NOVEMBER

7 Thursday

By day most of the *Luftwaffe*'s attacks were concentrated on coastal shipping, those in the Thames Estuary being the nearest the bombers got to London.

Under cover of darkness until around midnight, several bombs were dropped on London causing damage and blocking a number of railway lines.

8 Friday

More daylight attacks on shipping in the Thames Estuary. These increasing attacks were a peripheral part of the 'Battle of the Atlantic' in which German U-boats, surface ships and aircraft attempted to sink convoys bringing essential supplies of food and raw materials from the USA and the Colonies. Raids at night were widespread throughout the London area.

9 Saturday

A change in the pattern of attacks from the last two days saw the raiders attacking London during the day, although none of the raids was severe. Night raids were again fairly light.

10 Sunday

No daylight attacks on London and most of the raiding at night was before midnight. Casualties were larger and damage greater than on recent nights.

101. *A nun kneels among debris and fire-blackened beams to say her daily prayers. Around stand the gaping walls of the gutted building . . . symbolic picture in a bombed London church yesterday.* Daily Mail, 9th November 1940.

URGENT SHELTER ACTION URGED BY LORD HORDER

Epidemics Danger if There is Further Delay

Evening Standard Reporter

I understand that the Horder Committee, in their report on health and conditions in air-raid shelters, to be published in a White Paper on Tuesday, recommend:

More nurses, both Government and voluntary, in all public shelters;

More doctors on whole-time duty in the shelters;

Compulsory apportioning of shelter accommodation;

A census of shelter-users;

The issuing of tickets to all those users.

Other recommendations included in the report are additional sanitation in all Underground shelters, and permission for Anderson shelter owners to use public shelters in bad weather and yet retain their Andersons.

Speed Imperative

The committee are against compulsory measures in regard to gargling, inoculation and medical examinations in the shelters.

It is the opinion of Lord Horder and his entire committee that unless those recommendations are put into immediate operation the whole purpose of the report may be destroyed by an outbreak of those epidemics which the committee have been working to prevent.

"If there is much further delay there will be grave danger of a serious outbreak of the illness and disease which, by the setting up of the committee, it was hoped to prevent," I was told to-day by a member of the committee.

"The need for a speed-up in carrying out improvements is absolutely imperative."

Lord Horder and his colleagues broke all advisory committee speed records in the compilation of the report. They handed it to the Government less than a week after their formation, over six weeks ago.

8 Wardens Escape

Eight wardens were buried when the basement of a London school used as an A.R.P. post was struck last night.

All were got out alive.

Merseyside and Midlands Raided

"Last night, aided by clear moonlight, the enemy renewed his raids on this country," says to-day's Air Ministry and Ministry of Home Security communiqué.

"The attacks were on a fairly large scale and though London was the main objective, secondary and less persistent attacks developed against other parts of the country, notably the Midlands and Merseyside.

"In London, the first bombs were dropped shortly after nightfall and bombing continued at intervals throughout the night.

"Damage was done in many districts and it is feared that at several points a number of people lost their lives, but nowhere were the casualties large.

"The raids on the Midlands and Merseyside took place in the early part of the night and were not on a heavy scale.

"Bombs fell at several points but the damage done was slight and the number of casualties relatively small.

"Elsewhere, bombs were dropped at many isolated points in the Home Counties and South-East England.

"Reports at present received from these areas show that there were few casualties and the damage was slight."

Bombed Babies Listen to Nursery Rhymes & Music

Nursery rhymes to music at a mansion at Beaconsfield, Bucks. where babies from bombed districts are being looked after.

BOMB KILLS M.O. IN BATHROOM

A bomb dropped in a residential suburb of London last night and killed the Medical Officer of Health for the district.

He was in the bathroom when the bomb crashed through the roof.

His wife and daughter had left the house only a few minutes before.

Two Little Boys Killed in Sleep

Two blocks of flats on a London housing estate were badly damaged when bombed last night.

In one block two small boys were killed while asleep in bed, but in the other block there were no casualties.

An elementary school near the estate was damaged, as was another school some distance away.

A high-explosive bomb fell in the middle of a street, fracturing a gas main.

Denies Petrol Was Delivered

Mr. D. M. McIntosh, of Bromley, Kent, sued at Westminster County Court to-day by the Petroleum Board for £26, the price of 400 gallons of petrol, said that he never ordered it and never received it.

Henry Long, an officer of the board, suggested that the order had been duplicated. "We say that two lots of petrol of 400 gallons each were delivered on the same day. One was paid for and the other was not," he said.

Judge Austin Jones adjourned the case sine die, remarking that the parties ought to be able to settle the dispute between themselves.

SEVERAL DIE IN WRECKED SHELTER

Throughout the night in bright moonlight, and again to-day, rescue squads were toiling amid the wreckage of a London shop and house wrecked by a bomb last night.

Under that shop 75 people were sheltering in a bricked-up basement, most of them women and children.

The building above collapsed, blocking the shelter's escape exits.

The ceiling over one end of the basement held, but those at the other end were buried under debris. Several were killed.

"People we managed to get out quickly had been killed by the explosion," a rescue worker said to-day.

A surface shelter in a neighbouring district was struck early in the raid.

Several people were killed there, too.

Five people, including a girl of 16, were brought out alive, but the girl has since died.

One of five homes in a London suburb hit a brick surface shelter in which 14 people were staying the night. One was killed, and four injured.

Busmen's Canteen Hit: Girls Buried

A number of people are known to have been killed and more injured when a London building was directly hit by a bomb during the night.

Rescue work went on through the night. Attempts were still being made to-day to reach people thought to be trapped.

Most of the casualties were in a canteen in which busmen were sheltering. It was also believed to-day that two girls, working in another part of the building, were still beneath the wreckage.

Lumps of masonry were hurled about. Steel girders were flung yards by the explosion.

One hundred rescue workers were clearing the debris to-day.

She Betted With Post Office Money

Betting with Post Office money was said to have brought Mrs. Sarah Redford Bradbury, aged 52, into the dock at Derby Assizes to-day, when she pleaded guilty to charges of theft, fraudulent conversion and falsification of accounts while acting as sub-postmistress at New Mills, Stockport. She was sentenced to three years' penal servitude.

The amounts specified in the charges totalled £2300, and in further cases which she asked to be taken into consideration the amount involved was £1500.

Surgeon and Wife Killed

The deaths, by enemy action, are announced to-day of Mr. G. F. H. McCormick, surgeon and physician, of Thurloe-place, S.W., his wife and his father-in-law, Mr. A. G. Bloxam, a Fellow of the Chartered Institute of Patent Agents.

Mr. McCormick was 40 years old and his wife was 37.

Bomb Injures a Woman Bus Conductor

Evening Standard Reporter

At one period during the night heavy and light bombers were approaching London at a rate of one a minute. But few were able to break through the inner barrage.

Several buses were destroyed in one London area. A trolleybus was damaged by the blast from one bomb which burst outside a block of houses.

Three people were killed, including an ambulance driver who was getting off the bus. The bus driver, woman conductor and six passengers were injured.

Coast Town Streets Machine-Gunned

A Dornier 17 dived out of the clouds and machine-gunned streets in a South Coast town after bombing it last night.

Thousands of bullets were fired, but no one was hurt, and the damage to property was slight.

Another raider, flying at a great height, dropped a stick of 13 bombs on a south-east town. Most of the damage was to house property.

Five people are known to be dead and a number injured.

One bomb fell on a bowling-green at the side of a working men's club. Men and women in the club were injured by flying glass.

In the billiards room players dived under the table as they heard the bombs coming.

Surface Shelter Hit

A number of casualties, some fatal, were caused when Liverpool was bombed during the night after two days of quiet.

They were the first high explosive bombs to drop in the city for over a week. A number of houses were demolished and some people were trapped. A man, his wife and another woman were killed when a heavy bomb struck a small surface shelter at the back of their house.

Several people were rescued from the wreckage of three houses.

Only slight damage was caused by a raid in the West Midlands. High explosive bombs and an oil bomb were dropped in two roads in one town, demolishing a house and damaging another, but no fires or casualties were reported.

Gratitude

A barrister who was dug out of the debris of a bombed building appeared at the Essex Quarter Sessions at Chelmsford to-day to plead for leniency for the son of a fireman who saved his life.

The boy, aged 16, was charged with several other youths with breaking into a shop at Hornchurch and stealing cigarettes.

Mr. Frederick Levy, addressing the Bench, said:

"I have a personal interest in seeing that everything is done on behalf of the man to whom I am so much indebted. I will do what I can to assist this boy to keep straight."

The boy was placed on probation for three years.

SHELTER INFECTION

The Facts

MUCH HAS been written and said recently about the great dangers of "shelter life"—the possibilities of epidemics and widespread infection breaking out during the coming months. Don't be scared by these reports. These are the facts.

The chances of infection have somewhat increased—especially colds and sore throats — *but there is nothing to be alarmed about*. Even in normal times most of us spend a good deal of our lives travelling in crowded buses, trains and trams, or sitting in stuffy offices — yet we don't come to much harm.

Further, the likelihood of your picking up any complaints through spending the night in a shelter can be very much lessened by this very simple precaution: *use a good nasal spray regularly*.

The Milton Nasal Spray is a very good one indeed — because

This is the Spray referred to. It is available at chemists, price 1/4 and is not subject to Purchase Tax

the Milton method has a *double* advantage. Firstly, Milton is the most suitable antiseptic for use in nose and throat — where the air-borne germs first lodge when they are breathed in. Secondly, the Milton Nasal Spray can be used for sterilising and deodorising the air in Anderson and other small shelters and in refuge rooms.

You and your family will have little to fear from germs or shelter infection if you buy a bottle of Milton and a Milton Nasal Spray and use them regularly — before going to shelter and immediately after coming out.

Milton costs 8d, 1/4d., 1/11½d and 3/4d a bottle (including purchase tax), from all chemists. Many chemists still have tax free stocks available at the old prices (7d, 1/2, 1/9 and 3/-), but these are being rapidly exhausted.

NOVEMBER

11 Monday

Attacks by day resumed but only on a minor scale. Night raids lasted for just a few hours after dark.

12 Tuesday

Very minor German activity by day was followed by a night of regular bombing raids until around dawn the next morning. By this period of the Blitz everyone in London had adapted to life under continual threat of air attack. So much so that most people were able to get more than four hours' sleep at night, despite the sirens, AA guns booming, aircraft noise and bombs dropping. Some people even claimed to sleep through bombs dropping right outside their sheltering place, wherever that might be. A 'Shelter Census' had taken place in early November and found that on most nights, 4 per cent of London's population was sheltering in the Tubes, 9 per cent in public shelters and 27 per cent in domestic, mainly Anderson, shelters. Of the remaining 60 per cent, some would be on duty but many would be sheltering in cupboards, under the stairs or sleeping in ground-floor rooms.

13 Wednesday

A day and night of light bombing. Only 25 bombers raided London at night, dropping 28 tons of high explosive (HE), far short of the nightly average of 201 tons of HE and 182 incendiary bombs. Casualties and damage reflected the minor nature of the raids.

102. The Pioneer Corps salvaging furniture from a bombed house. They will go on to salvage bricks, timber and steel which can be reused in the building of air raid shelters.

103. Salvaging of a different kind! A Harrow schoolboy with some of his souvenirs – incendiary bomb fins which the boys swopped and sold among themselves.

These Are the Stories of the Raids

A STREET IN COVENTRY

100 FIRE BOMBS ON HOSPITAL

Nearly 100 incendiary bombs fell last night on a school in a London suburb which is used as an emergency hospital.

Thirty-eight pumps and two water towers were used in fighting the fire for three hours.

A large assembly hall, which was a hospital ward, was burned out, but nurses and A.R.P. men moved the patients to safety. There were no casualties

The roof of the main school building was destroyed, but the two wings were saved. Two incendiaries lodged in the chapel roof, but the fire was soon put out.

Airplanes continued to circle over head while patients were being evacuated, and while the flames were tackled by the members of the hospital staff and the fire brigade

A few more incendiaries were dropped, but no more high explosives

Air Hole Cut to Trapped People

Two women wardens were killed when a wardens' post was demolished in a London suburb late last night The post was in a large boarding-house The victims were Mrs Barstow, the proprietress, and Miss Keighley

Sheltering in a strengthened room of the boarding-house were a number of guests Rescue parties were still digging for them to-day

They made an air hole and calls for help could be heard.

The guests include business men and their families who have been bombed out of their London homes

A block of flats opposite was considerably damaged and three families are still unaccounted for.

Stuck to Post, 'Phoning SOS "We're on Fire"

Five firemen were killed and three more were to-day still buried after a bomb had partly demolished and fired a building in London last night.

The bomb hit a place used as recreation and mess-rooms. When it was heard falling some firemen scrambled beneath a billiards table in the recreation room.

It is believed that the three men missing were underneath the table.

The fire spread throughout the building, which was ablaze in a few minutes.

The officer in charge of the switchboard stuck to his post until he had reported the bombing to his superintendent .

Twelve other casualties were caused by two bombs which fell in the same road, damaging five shops.

Sought Quiet, is Killed by Bomb

A few days ago a young Manchester man, Walter Lazenby, arranged to stay at a house in the Home Counties as he could not sleep in London where he had lived for many years Early to-day the house received a direct hit The bedroom in which Mr. Lazenby was asleep was demolished and he was killed.

Three Wardens and Four Soldiers Die

In one London district three wardens, who were on duty, were killed during the night.

It was feared to-day that four soldiers were dead beneath the wreckage of a house.

Another house demolished was occupied by a doctor. His body has not been recovered.

Havoc and destruction in a Coventry street after the dusk-to-dawn raids on the town.

INJURED BOY UNAWARE FATHER WAS KILLED

Outside London the raids were on a minor scale during the night. Only one district in an East Anglian area received much damage. Houses were destroyed and the casualties were heavy.

A boy of 10 was rescued suffering from leg injuries. Questioned by A.R.P. workers, he said his father was with him in the kitchen and his mother had gone next door.

The father was dead It is feared the mother was killed, too

In another district in East Anglia a school and a church were destroyed

Extensive damage was caused to houses and shops in a North East Coast town.

Four heavy calibre bombs exploded in a thickly-populated area of a South Coast town It was feared to-day that there were a considerable number of casualties.

Houses and a school received direct hits, and soldiers assisted A.R.P. squads in extricating people buried in the wreckage.

A policeman named Ruffell, thrown from his bed by the explosion, rushed on duty although his face was bleeding.

Bomb Falls Into Baby's Cot

A school in the Home Counties had fire bombs rained on it early to-day. The masters and fire squads put out the fires before there was serious damage.

Fifty incendiary bombs fell in a neighbouring town and two houses were burnt out. In one a bomb dropped through the roof on to the cot of a six-months-old baby, who was severely burnt.

The mother wrapped a coat round the baby to put out the flames.

Soldiers forced their way into another house and rescued two elderly bedridden women.

Lord Stanmore and Sister Hurt by Bomb

Lord Stanmore and his sister, the Hon. Rachel Nevil Gordon, were injured when a house in which they were staying was partly destroyed by a bomb last night. They were taken to hospital.

A number of large bombs and six high explosive bombs were dropped in the district and five people were killed in houses

Lord Stanmore, who is 69, was Lord-in-Waiting to King George V. from 1914 to 1922.

Sorting Office Hit

At midnight a bomb hit a sorting office in a district on the outskirts of London. The only two members of the staff on duty—they were fire-watching—narrowly escaped

At daybreak the staff cleared the office, and the mail was sorted and distributed with less than an hour's delay.

Defied Gas and Fire

Six people were killed, including two railwaymen and two children, and five others were still buried to-day after a high explosive bomb demolished four houses in one London area during the night.

Rescue parties, handicapped by escaping gas and then fire, carried on.

Horses Trapped in Bombed Stables

Releasing one of the nine horses imprisoned in their stalls to-day after a bomb had struck some London stables in the night raid.

What's All This Fuss About?

When a bomb exploded outside one London house early to-day 63-year-old Mrs. Bambury, who was with her husband on the first floor, was left 15ft. above the ground as the front of the house collapsed.

There was danger that the floor might collapse, but Mr. Bambury went down the stairs, which were damaged but intact, and called wardens and police to help him to rescue his bedridden wife.

Mrs. Bambury was not worried. She greeted her rescuers with: "What's all this fuss about?"

She was taken to hospital.

Wholesale Looting

"While the bombs fall and everybody is taking cover, wholesale looting goes on upon every railway," said Mr Harry Ricketts, prosecuting solicitor, at Marylebone to-day.

George James Hanks, 28, railway servant of Canal View, N.W., was sentenced to nine months' hard labour for stealing from a railway depot goods valued at £15.

Mr. Ricketts added that railway policemen were nightly taking risks which they ought not to face to stop wholesale looting.

The Magistrate (Mr. L. R. Dunne) said that the only way to stop these thefts was by making an example of those who were caught.

Church Wrecked

A large bomb fell in a London district last night wrecking a Roman Catholic church and damaging two Methodist churches.

A local newspaper office was destroyed and a number of shops in one parade damaged. Twelve people were missing to-day.

Doctor Cuts Way Into Debris to Give Morphia

A doctor cleared away debris to administer morphia to a woman—one of two people buried—when three houses in one London district were demolished.

Brother and sister, John and Cecilia Tanner, aged five and two, were killed when their home in a London suburb had a direct hit early to-day.

Their mother was injured and is suffering from shock. The father escaped.

In another district a boy aged 10 was killed while sleeping under the stairs, and his mother and father, Mr. and Mrs. G. Dossell, were trapped in the kitchen. They were rescued and taken to hospital.

It is feared that at least eight people were killed in four demolished houses on the outskirts of London.

Two wardens were injured when an anti-aircraft shell crashed through the roof of their post in one district and exploded almost at their feet. They were Mr. P. Garcier and Mr. J. Johnson.

There were no casualties when a high explosive bomb fell in the courtyard of a police station.

Labour Camps for Denmark

Germany's occupation of Denmark has been followed by the introduction of labour camps, says the Associated Press.

The authorities have decided to spend £400,000 on building these camps, and any youth who has been unemployed for 100 days or more will be compelled to enter one.

NOVEMBER

14 Thursday

Despite a full or 'bombers' moon, London suffered no air attacks. Instead, the *Luftwaffe* struck a massive blow against Coventry. A total of 449 German planes dropped 503 tons of HE and 881 incendiary bombs. Of the 250,000 inhabitants of Coventry, 554 were killed and 865 seriously injured. The heart of the city, including its cathedral, was almost totally destroyed and the population left stunned and frightened.

15 Friday

After a daylight raid on the capital, the Germans launched a huge raid on London as a follow-up to Coventry's night of terror. The bombing was almost as severe as the attack on 15th October and the previous night's Coventry raid but casualties were lower, under 600 dead or injured. There was a great deal of damage to property – homes, factories, shops, institutions and railways.

Despite the severity of the attack, Londoners did not react with the stunned terror of the people of Coventry – they were too used to these attacks and besides, while the heart had been ripped out of Coventry, London was too big an area for the *Luftwaffe* to achieve the same there.

16 Saturday

Despite poor weather conditions, German aircraft managed to drop over 100 tons of HE throughout the night but damage was not too severe.

While the *Luftwaffe* were bombing London, the RAF were dropping 2000 bombs on Hamburg in a raid seen as a reprisal for the bombing inflicted on Coventry.

104. Silhouette of a London skyline illuminated by a blaze caused by a bomb. Bow Bells Church is the spire in the centre of the picture.

105. Wreckage outside the Carlton Club in SW1.

106. Civilian workmen and soldiers working on a deep crater in Charing Cross Road.

107

108

109

NOVEMBER

17 Sunday

As a further sign of change in tactics the Germans chose Southampton for a major attack. Despite poor weather, 159 aircraft dropped 198 tons of HE and 300 incendiary bombs on the dock area of Southampton. Over London, the weather conditions for flying were even poorer but a number of bombs were dropped in Central London and in districts close to the river.

18 Monday

A quieter day throughout Britain and although London was harried from just after dark until about 6.00 a.m. the following day, only about 5 tons of HE were dropped, causing little damage and few casualties.

19 Tuesday

At night, Birmingham was the principle target for the bombers and London suffered only a relatively minor amount of bombing.

107. Bomb damage to the National Gallery from a raid on the 15th.

108. Inspecting the damage to the Dress Circle caused when Drury Lane Theatre was bombed.

109. A crater alongside St Martin-in-the-Fields in Trafalgar Square. Some 500 people sheltering in the crypt escaped injury when the bomb fell during a raid early in November, but the pictures were not passed for publication until two weeks later.

110. Tours by the King and Queen to inspect bomb damage and to talk to the people were important in trying to maintain morale. This picture shows them visiting some of the new deep air raid shelters.

2nd WINTER: By Frank Owen

ON January 30 Herr Hitler made a speech at the Berlin sport palast. He addressed it largely to "Herr Churchill," who was still at that time first mate to Mr. Chamberlain as First Lord of the Admiralty.

We had then been at war for five months, and hardly a shot had been fired on the Western Front. People called it the Bore War. Herr Hitler said: *"We know what Herr Churchill has achieved in these past five months. We also know what France has done. But Churchill and Co. do not seem to know what Germany has done. These gentlemen appear to think that we have slept for five months."*

On May 15 six German "Panzer-divisionen" broke through the French defences at Sedan. Subsequently, ten or twelve of these heavily armoured divisions came into action. By June 15 the French armies were rolling back in hopeless rout west of Paris.

France at that time had two armoured divisions available. Britain had one, and it was not in France.

These German "Panzer-divisionen" are mechanised forces of approximately 14,000 men. They represent the acme of war machine power. Each of them has three echelons:

(i) A motorised battalion for reconnaissance, with 50 armoured cars, a motor-cycle infantry company and supporting artillery units.

(ii) A shock brigade of 450 tanks.

(iii) An "occupying" force of two infantry battalions in armoured cars, a motor-cycle battalion, an artillery regiment, with sappers, signallers, pioneers, and anti-tank units.

Altogether, each "Panzer - division" disposes about 3000 vehicles. It is commonly agreed that these troops annihilated the French resistance. After them came the ordinary motorised infantry divisions, which "mopped up," and still farther behind plodded the masses of "foot," who never got near the battle and who merely arrived in time to form the Army of Occupation.

◆ ◆ ◆

WHEN did the Nazis perfect this remarkable striking force which gave them the victory of June? **In the five months before January 30, "when Germany slept." In the four months before May, when Hitler was "missing the bus."**

Of course, the Germans had powerful mechanised forces before then. It was with tank plus the flying artillery of their aircraft that they overwhelmed the Poles in the world's first blitzkrieg. But it was in the sombre winter days and long nights of the "sitzkrieg" that the mighty "Panzer" army was built up to final strength.

How long and arduously the German workers toiled in the factories last winter, making tanks! How rigorously and ruthlessly the Nazis drove their captives of the highly technicalised Czech race to make them armoured cars and mobile guns in Skoda! And all the time the aircraft workers of the incorporated protectorates of the Reich bent to their task of piling up the Luftwaffe squadrons.

In those days France was turning out 300 airplanes a month, while our own aircraft production was only half of what it is to-day. (I get this figure with the aid of our Ministers, who have informed us that our aircraft production is now double what it was.)

In those days the shift in the German factories ranged from ten to twelve hours. A day off was an event, two days off a miracle. There was no talk of a Christmas by the fireside. There were no unemployed, and women were conscripted from sixteen upwards for industrial labour. A million Polish prisoners of war laboured in the fields.

As for Britain, we had 900,000 unemployed, and at Christmas some of the aircraft works shut for the week. Sundays and half-Saturdays were sacrosanct.

Last winter it was Britain who slept. We see now how we were aroused, at the very edge of annihilation. Only now do we realise the debt we owe to the men who came forward then, knowing all the fearful facts, and bade us pull ourselves together and fight on.

To-day this picture stands vividly before the eyes of the British people as they look back upon a grim but not inglorious year. Therefore we ask soberly now: What is this year's winter-set?

◆ ◆ ◆

AT crack o' dawn on those dry sunny days of May the vast fleet of German tanks used to surge forward irresistibly against the Allied lines. But it was not because the Boche got up early in the spring that he arrived on the Bay of Biscay by mid-June. It was because he (and she) had worked so late all winter.

The Boche is working late this winter. In shrouded factories in far Bohemia, new centre of German arms production, there are being forged the weapons of another spring's blitzkrieg.

What are they making, the industrious German and the enslaved Czech, the transplanted Dutchman and the French worker, toiling under the threat of shorter rations for his family and perhaps a heartrending appeal from a brother who is still a prisoner of war?

The answer is (I.) aircraft, (II.) submarines. Field-marshal Keitel has tanks enough for the moment.

There are still no unemployed in Germany. Moreover, they have added to their labour-power, not only the war prisoners of Poland, Norway, Holland, Belgium, France, but practically the whole industrial population of these countries. The entire economic effort of at least 120,000,000 people in the heart of Europe is directed into the channels of the Nazi war industry.

German loot has been on a giant scale. The stocks of ten nations have been carried off. It is true that these stocks are not inexhaustible and that the British blockade will ensure that they cannot be replaced. **It is certain, however, that they will last their present owners well beyond the coming spring. . . .**

The reputable Oxford Institute of Statistics notes that wages are pegged in Germany while they are rising here; that we are still spending heavily on the relatively more expensive business of laying down armament plant, while the Germans are simply turning out munitions. Setting these facts against the higher cost of Germany's *ersatz* products, the Institute calculates that the Nazis are exerting 30 per cent more energy than Britain on their war output. This disparity, if it is accurately assessed, is profound.

Nor do explanations of Mr. Ernest Bevin serve better than the explanations of Mr. Ernest Brown in allaying public concern that in the second winter of war we have still three-quarters of a million workers that we cannot find a use for.

◆ ◆ ◆

THE eye ranges over the battlefield of Europe, which stretches from the deep defiles of Greece to the high rollers of the Atlantic, and on all fronts it records that where we can come to grips with our enemy we have no need to fear the outcome.

But the vital question we have to face is quite another one: Are we beating the enemy at the lathe? For here, and not where the brave Evzone highlanders charge Alpini with the bayonet, is the real battle of cold steel.

Up and down the land we see huge new plants now coming or about to come, into production. Beyond the seas India and the Dominions are growing in industrial power and output. And in America we have the prospect of supreme supply in all the machines of war, safe from bomb and from bombardment, offering us a guarantee of ultimate victory.

◆ ◆ ◆

BUT between those days of future superiority and these present ones there lies this long night of winter. What is going to happen then?

Right now we are facing a new and double air offensive, directed with considerable force and complete ruthlessness against our factory front and its supply lines. First and most spectacular is the direct assault by night bombing. Hardly less formidable is the air attack against the Atlantic convoys.

It is certain that both the R.A.F. attacks on industrial Germany and the Royal Navy's ceaseless blockade by sea are more damaging than the German campaigns. But this advantage will be utterly cast away if at the same time we do not catch up and surpass the enemy in output. Airplanes and ships, and guns for both, are our priorities. After that tanks.

Therefore a few immediate proposals:

(i) **Real rationing.** We are bringing in too much food. The ship space is needed for vital raw materials.

(ii) **More food growing here.** It is not enough to plough—you must lime and manure the land. The farmers have not got the money. Give it to them. For the cost of one day's war (£9,000,000) you could multiply the fertility of your fields.

(iii.) **Signing-on.** Workers on the reserved list, engaged in war industry, should be required to sign-on and not sign-off and go elsewhere whenever they please. Pay and labour conditions as before. But if men walk out and won't work they should find themselves in a place which does not provide for these habits—the Pioneer Corps.

(iv.) **Stop calling up whole classes for service.** There are enough unequipped troops. France called up 5,000,000 men. She sent back 2,000,000 to the workshop, and had done better still if she had sent back as many more. We need ten workers behind each fighter.

(v.) **Take over the railways and be done with it.** War material should be consigned free. The R.A.S.C. don't charge for carrying supplies up to the line.

(vi.) **Pool private transport.**

(vii.) **Survey and register all housing space for billeting.** It can be done in ten days. The local estate agencies plus the constituency party agents know all the facts. Vital factory hours are being lost as one Ministry after another bumbles round looking for accommodation for personnel.

(viii.) **Dig up all the coal that can be raised.** What we don't need now we can dispose of when we relieve Europe.

(ix.) **Total mobilisation of India for war production.**

Before this war is done, this short programme may look like the old world dreams of an 1850 Whig. Meantime, let every man in Britain ask himself whenever he feels like taking life easy, "What have I done this winter day to win the war this spring?"

"'ULLO, YER LORDSHIP! WE WAS JUST TRYING TO INOCULATE SOME INVALIDS."

SHELTER HEALTH   Copyright in all Countries.

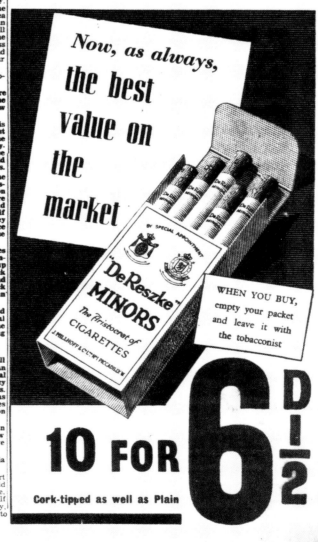

NOVEMBER

20 Wednesday

A very similar pattern to that of Tuesday the 19th. As weather conditions improved with darkness, Birmingham was the principal *Luftwaffe* target, with London in receipt of minor raids all night long during which a total of 48 tons of HE and 32 incendiary bombs were dropped.

21 Thursday

The City and Government buildings were, as on the two previous nights, the targets for minor raids from dusk until dawn.

22 Friday

Birmingham again received a major raid and the bombing of London followed the same pattern as on the previous few nights.

111. Firemen and ARP workers clearing debris from a London school building – used as a welfare centre and tuberculosis dispensary – that was bombed and destroyed by fire.

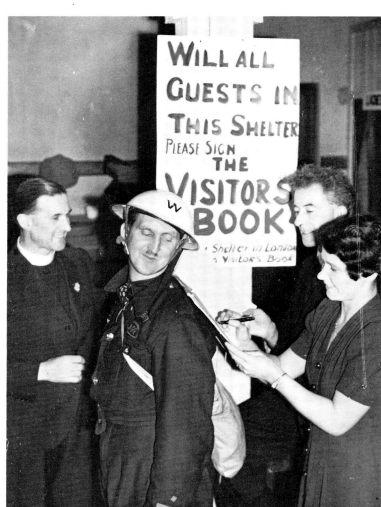

112

113

114

115

Torn repairs

Boarded Up

Shutters

Torn repairs

Patched Windows

During Air Raids this Store is only closed when there is danger overhead & is re-opened immediately our Roof Spotters give the "Danger Past Signal" —

Customers wishing to enter the Store during the danger period may do so by the Shelter entrance, located at the rear of the building, 58, Kingly Street.

Galeries Lafayette Ltd.

NOVEMBER

23 Saturday

During daylight hours some bombs were dropped on London. Among the aircraft involved in this attack were some from the Italian Airforce, the *Corpo Aèreo Italiano*. First striking from their base in Belgium at the end of October, they proved to be no match for the RAF fighters but continued intermittently to join *Luftwaffe* attacks on London, East Anglia and the South East.

At night Southampton was the principal German target and a minor attack on London again damaged the City and Whitehall.

24 Sunday

At night, a major attack on Bristol, with London in receipt of only a series of very minor raids.

25 Monday

Fog meant virtually no *Luftwaffe* activity and London had its first bomb-free day and night since the Coventry attack on the 14th.

26 Tuesday

The *Luftwaffe* were again limited by fog but a brief and minor attack was launched at London by night.

112. Signing the Visitors' Book at a London shelter!

113. The Savoy Hotel was bombed early in November. This picture shows the scars to the building after the bomb debris and rubble have been cleared away.

114. The Pioneer Corps sorting through wreckage.

115. Firemen at work on a fire in London.

116. This picture of Buckingham Palace on 23rd November showed that the King and Queen suffered the same fate as everyone else, trying to repair bomb damage – the materials for repair were simply unavailable.

117. This picture, taken in Regent Street, emphasises the 'business as usual' attitude. In fact, all the big stores were open as usual.

Reduce the risk of attack on *YOUR* train

Trains showing lights are targets for bombs and machine-gun bullets.

It is for YOUR protection that train lights are extinguished during Air Raids. There is sufficient light for reading during All-Clear periods.

For *your own safety* please see that blinds are kept down during black-out hours.

The enemy raiders have a maxim: "Where there's light there's life."

WE'LL BEAT HITLER BY HELPING ONE ANOTHER

BRITISH RAILWAYS

OPERA SINGER IS NOW AN ENGINE DRIVER

DARKER LONDON

by IAN COSTER

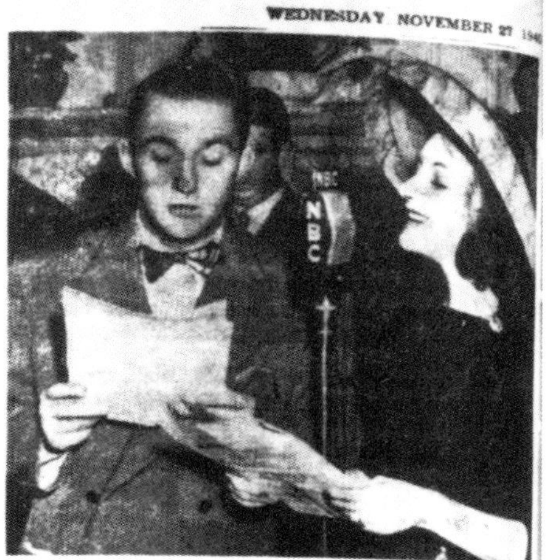

Bing Crosby and Mary Martin give a turn at Bing's Del Mar Turf Club.

OPERATIC baritone drives "Royal Scot" locomotive through raids and black-outs these nights. He's A. J. Lennardo, of Longsight, Manchester, L.M.S. express engineer.

He played Mephistopheles in "Faust" and sang in "Pagliacci" for British National Opera Company, and he's sung for the B.B.C several times He gets offers now but he turns them down because he thinks he's more useful to the country on the footplate than on the boards

Lennardo learned to be tough in the previous war: he was in the Suvla Bay landing.

THAT first song by Sarah Churchill, "I Give My Heart," has been bought by Francis, Day and Hunter She wrote words and music, and the firm thinks she's got a future as a song writer In fact, they intend to spend £500 on exploitation

ONCE ran bookstall in Caledonian Market, and later bookshop in St Martin's-lane, Peter Murray Hill, now appearing with Askey and Murdoch in "The Ghost Train" film. War closed his shop but he still goes on searching second-hand book shops, adding to his packing-case library One of these days he hopes to open a shop again, preferably in some country town

SOUND library at Shepherd's Bush studios is run by Glasgow-born Charles Tomrley It includes 13,000 sound effects, including "steam hissing," "Cornish express at speed," "water going down a plughole," "ship hitting sandbank," "clatter of rifle dropping," "teeth snapping," every kind of "human muttering" and all sorts of "footsteps"

Pride of the library is "noise of kick in the pants." Asked how he got it, Tomrley replies "Ask Charlie Naughton of the Crazy Gang."

ABOUT to celebrate eighth year of partnership, the Aspidistras, first-rate turn now in "Diversion" (Wyndham's) and at the Players' Theatre. They burlesque Victorian ballads delightfully

Two of the trio, Elsie French and John Mott, were in "The Beggar's Opera" when they thought of the idea of old-fashioned parlour songs for music-hall tour They were joined by Cornelius Fisher Their repertoire is so big that they haven't repeated themselves in six weeks

THOSE hobby horses will race again at Officers' Club, Grosvenor House, **Sunday, with Sutherland Felce, starter, steward and judge** It's to be grand **military handicap** with bottle of champagne **as prize.**

POPPED into town again Philip Ridgeway, who tried to beat the air raids with revue at the Criterion, lost money, gave it up His idea he tells me, was to get his ten-year-old "Parade" going again And in a week, he opened in Lancashire town with Irene, Helen Cherry, and people he'd been able to collect He couldn't get his band parts, so he had to hum all the tunes over to local orchestra until they knew them

But now the "Parade" is off again with several new discoveries, including 15-year-old Christine from Portsmouth, 21-year-old Betty Ann Royce 18-year-old Joan Bellinger, daughter of London C.I.D. officer, 16-year-old Jean Aspinall, described as "a young Sophie Tucker." Arthur Stott, who's been with him for ten years, has rejoined

And Ridgeway says the West End can look after itself from now on

Songs from "Veronique" on Radio To-night

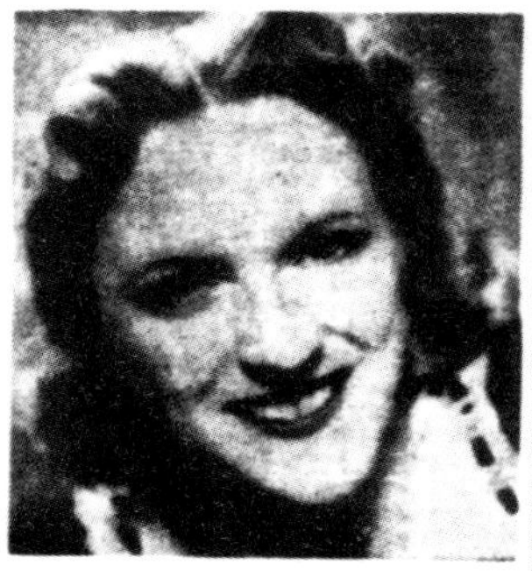

Lorely Dyer in songs from "Veronique"—Home 9.20 p.m.

Home Service

(203.5 M., 296.2 M., 391.1 M., 449.1 M. 48 82 M.)

3.0.—Joseph Lewis and his Orchestra **3.30.**—A narration based on account by Daniel Defoe, and on other writings of the Great Storm of November 27 1703 **3.45.**—Book of Folly A gramophone fantasy

4 15.—Hi Gang! (recording of Sunday's broadcasts), with Bebe Daniels Vic Oliver Ben Lyon **5.0.**—News and service in Welsh **5.20.**—Children's Hour

6.0.—News and Announcements **6.30.**—News in Norwegian **6.45.**—The World Goes By

7 15.—Gabrielle Brune in Young Lady at Large: Episode 4; with Frederick Burtwell Gwen Lewis, Ian Sadler Doris Nichols, Foster Carlin, Betty Astell Billy Milton; B.B.C Revue Orchestra **7.40.**—Christians in a World at War—4

8.0.—Symphony Concert, Part 2 Eva Turner (soprano), Parry Jones (tenor) Joyce Sutton (contralto). B.B.C Symphony Orchestra, conducted by Basil Cameron **9.0.**—Time, Big Ben News

9 20.—Songs from Veronique; with Derek Oldham Lorely Dyer, Bernard Ansell Gladys Ripley and Doris Gambell.

10.10.—The Bone of the Dinosaur: Problem in detection in two parts Part 2—Solution,

10.30.—North of the Tweed: Talk by George Blake **10.45.**—Gaelic Concert **11.0.**—Jonn Cruft (oboe), Taylor String Quartet **11.25.**—Jack Payne with his Band **12.0.—News.**

Forces

373.1 M., 41.49 M.

3.30.—Music of Billy Mayerl, played by Jack Wilson **3.45.**—Home Service **5.0.**—Richard Valery and his Orchestra **5.30.**—Aberystwyth Madrigal Singers, Aberystwyth University College Quartet **6.0.**—News in Dutch and French

6.30.—ENSA Underground: Admiral Sir Edward R. G. R. Evans, Regional Commissioner for London Civil Defence, introduces ENSA concert in a public shelter in London, with George Formby and Geraldo and his Orchestra.

7.0.—B.B.C. Northern Orchestra **7.30.**—Sports News from Canada **7.40.**—Edward O'Henry, theatre organ **8.0.**—Meet the Empire: Bill and Bob talk to some friends from Nigeria

8.20.—Send for Doctor Dick: with Dick Francis, Sonnie Hale, Patricia Leonard, Ralph de Rohan, Helen Clare, Jacques Brown, B.B.C. Variety Orchestra **9.0.**—News in German.

9.20.—Listeners' Requests played by B.B.C Military Band **10.0.**—Epilogue **10.15—11.0.**—Geraldo and his Orchestra.

Standard quiz

1. Which European statesman held the office of Prime Minister for a longer continuous period than any other?

2. The price of milk is going up on December 1. How much will it be per quart in London?

3. What are the colours of the ribbons of:

a. *The George Cross* b. *The George medal?*

4. Who popularised the word "jitterbug" in this country, applying it to alarmists? When?

5. A CALUMET is:

A kind of verse, an Indian tobacco pipe, a shawl, a musical instrument a plumber's tool, an American cigarette?

Key on PAGE ELEVEN.

BALLETS AND OPERAS

ARTS, Leic.-sq.—1-2 2.15-3.15 3.30-4.30 Stalls 1/ LUNCH AFTER-LUNCH & TEA BALLET

THEATRES

HARROW COLISEUM.—(HAR 2383.) 2.30, 6.30. Revue SH——I KEEP IT DARK Billy Thorburn

THRESHOLD (Bay 1551) Daily at 2 THE SCARLET PIMPERNEL, with Robert Eddison

WYNDHAM'S (Tem 3028) Daily 2.15 sharp A Mixture devised by Herbert Farjeon **DIVERSION** Edith Evans, Walter Crisham, Joyce Grenfell, Dorothy Dickson, Irene Eisinger, The Aspidistras

CONTINUOUS REVUE

WINDMILL, Picc.-cir.—9th Yr. **REVUDEVILLE**, 138th Ed (5th wk.) Cont. dly from 11 15 a.m

PICTURE THEATRES (WEST END)

ASTORIA, Charing Cross-road. Continuous 11 to 7. 'TIL WE MEET AGAIN (A): 11.10, 2.15, 5 15 Pop Always Pays (U): 12.45 3.50 etc

CARLTON THEATRE, Haymarket, Whi. 3711. CECIL B DE MILLE'S **NORTH-WEST MOUNTED POLICE** in TECHNICOLOR (A) ONE SHOW DAILY AT 2.30 p.m only. Sats and Suns at 2 o'c & 4.30 p.m Seats are Bookable. 1/10, 3/-, 4/6, 6/6, 8/6

EMPIRE Leic.-sq.—From 10 a.m Vivien Leigh Robt Taylor Waterloo Bridge (A) 2nd WEEK

GAUMONT, Haymarket —Con. 10 to 7 Jon Hall KIT CARSON (U) 10.40, 12.50 3.5 5.20

LONDON PAVILION.—Continuous from 10 a.m. OUR TOWN William Holden, Martha Scott (A)

PICTURE THEATRES (WEST END)

MARBLE ARCH PAVILION.—Continuous 11 to 7 RONALD COLMAN GINGER ROGERS in LUCKY PARTNERS (U): 12, 2 40, 5.20

METROPOLE.—VIC 4673 MARYLAND (A), in Technicolor The Boys from Syracuse (A).

ODEON, Leic.-sq.—Cont from 10 a.m. 2nd Week HIRED WIFE and SLIGHTLY TEMPTED (A)

PLAZA.—BING CROSBY, MARY MARTIN, BASIL RATHBONE RHYTHM ON THE RIVER (U)

REGAL, Marble Arch —Cmg 11 a.m. Brian Aherne. THE LADY IN QUESTION (A) 1.5 4 5, 7 o'c

RITZ, Leic.-sq.—10 a.m. to 7 p.m. GONE WITH THE WIND (A) 42nd WEST END WEEK

ROYAL, Marble Arch.—E. Bergner, CATHERINE THE GREAT (A) Rbt. Donat. The 39 Steps (A)

WARNER, Leicester-square. Ger 3423 **KING OF THE LUMBERJACKS** (A) with JOHN PAYNE, GLORIA DICKSON STANLEY FIELDS. Also GAMBLING ON THE HIGH SEAS (A) Programmes commence 10 0, 2.10, 4.30

PICTURE THEATRES (SUBURBAN)

ELEPHANT TROCADERO.—Hitchcock's FOREIGN CORRESPONDENT (A) The Saint Takes Over (A)

KILBURN GAUMONT STATE.—Nelson Eddy, Jeanette Macdonald NEW MOON (A) Zanzibar (A)

SWISS COTTAGE ODEON.—NEW MOON (U) Jeanette Macdonald Down West McGinty (A)

WATFORD GAUMONT.—Maureen O'Hara, DANCE GIRL, DANCE (A) SAINT TAKES OVER (A)

WEST NORWOOD REGAL.—Hitchcock's Foreign Correspondent (A) Bested by a Beard (A)

RESTAURANT ENTERTAINMENTS

CAFE DE PARIS.—Ger 2462. Open for Lunch Tea Dansant and Dinner daily

FISCHER'S RESTAURANT, Bond-st.—Tea Dance Dly 3-5.30 Sat & Sun. Tea & Dinner Off shelter

GROSVENOR HOUSE.—GRO 6363 New Underground Restaurant. Dine and Dance in Safety Tea Dance Daily 4-6 Lipton's Band

HATCHETT'S, Picc.—Tel. REG 0217 Dancing in PERFECT SAFETY to Hatchett's Swingtet from 8.30 p.m PRIVATE SHELTER

HUNGARIA RESTAURANT, Picc.-cir. W.—WHI 4222 Gipsy Music & Dancing Open Sun Lch Din

LANSDOWNE RESTAURANT, Berkeley-square, W.1 —MAY 1657 New entrance in LANSDOWNE ROW Dancing to TIM CLAYTON & his Orchestra EXT. TO MORROW NIGHT till 2 a.m

KEMPINSKI'S TAVERN, Swallow-st.—Open at night Sing with George in one of London's safest places

MAY FAIR RESTAURANT in official air raid shelter Dncg to JACK JACKSON & HIS ORCH Cabaret MAGDA KUN, 11 p.m Extn. FRIDAY. May 7777

MEURICE (QUAGS) Bury st St. James's S.W.1 (Whi 7151)—Lunch, Dinner, Supper Reinforced Grill Room below ground level DANCING from 7 till Midnight VAN STRATEN ORCHESTRA

ODENINO'S, Piccadilly-circus.—Regent 4080 Dine & Dance to Roy Wallis's Orchestra safely under 10 Reinforced Concrete Floors

PICCADILLY HOTEL.—Reg 8000 Luncheon & Dinner in GRILL ROOM, 30ft. below ground level Dancing to Norman Cole & his Orchestra Tea dancing daily A.R.P Shelter

QUAGLINO'S.—Now MEURICE (See above.)

QUEEN'S BRASSERIE, Leicester-sq.—Lunch and Dine in comfort well below ground level Dancing to Java and his Orchestra

RESTAURANTS

L APERITIF GRILL, 102, Jermyn st., S.W.1.—Whi 1571 Lunch No music

AU JARDIN DES GOURMETS 5, Greek-st., W.1 — Ger 1816 Open lunch as usual. Closed eves. & Sun.

BOULESTIN, 25 Southampton-st., Covent-gdn.—Day & Night A.R.P shelter in restaurant.

LE COQ D'OR RESTAURANT, Stratton-street W.1 Mayfair 7807 8 Open for Luncheon as usual

LA COQUILLE Restaurant Francais, 79 St. Martin's-lane.—Oysters, fish shellfish, light wines Tem. 8768

GREAT FOSTERS, Egham —England's Leading Country Hotel Tele. Egh 444

HOLBORN.—Hol. 8671. Lunch 3/6. Dinner (Grill Room) 5/6, or a la Carte Sats excepted.

MAISON BASQUE, 11 Dover-st. W.1 Reg. 2652 OPEN FOR LUNCH AS USUAL

ROMANO'S (Tem. 2811.) OPEN FOR LUNCHEONS AS USUAL.

SCOTT'S Picc.-cir.—Still open for Luncheons Dinners, incl Suns Good Wine Good Food Good Company and A.R.P shelter Ger 7175

CLUBS

COSMO, 35, Wardour-st. Ger. 6417. Dancing to Morgan's Band, featuring Ray Millar & Barry Mills 12-1 3-11 sun. 7-10 Mbrshp. Apply Sec. A.R.P

THE EMBASSY CLUB opens daily for Luncheon Cocktails Dinner.

LIAISON CLUB.—Members, please note we are now open 12-2 & 4 p.m onwards Lunch, dinner, supper The brightest & most comfortable spot in Town

MURRAY'S.—Open as usual (Official Shelter) Lunch Supper Dancing 9, Beak-st. W.1

PARADISE CLUB, 189, Regent-st., W 1.—Reg 1514. Mbrs Blitz Party Dinner 2/9 Destephano's music

STARBOARD CLUB, 73 Grosvenor-st., is reopening to-day 1 noon-6 p.m Excellent lunch 3/-

CABARET 16 Beak-st. W.1.—Dancing from 9 p.m Cabaret at 1.30 a.m Invitation only

COCONUT GROVE.—Reg. 7675 (Guests only) TWO BANDS EDMUNDO ROS 10 p.m 5 a.m

HAVANA, 4, Denman-st., W.1 Dancing from 11 p.m COLOURED BAND (Guests only)

AMUSEMENTS, SPORTS, Etc

GREYHOUND RACING

* Licensed by the N.G.R.C

* **WEST HAM STADIUM**—Racing to-morrow at 1.30 Red Cross Stakes, 525 yds Tote

ICE-SKATING

SPORTSDROME Richmond —Re-opening Sat Next Daily 10-12.30 2.30-5, 6.30-9.30 except Mon & Tues morn Adm 2/-

TEACHERS OF DANCING

DE BRITT STUDIOS, 11 Panton-st. Haymarket S.W.1 WHI 3540 Strictly private lesson 5/6

GEM MOUFLET 11 Albemarle-st. PICCADILLY Reg 4629 INDIVIDUAL—Or friends share Fee

GWENETHE WALSHE, Palace Hotel Bldgs. Lancaster Gte Pad 8281/9578 Pvte. lsns dly. Tea dnce Sats

PHYLLIS'S, 469 OXFORD ST 3 Pvte lsns 10/6 Tea Dances Sats. Sunday Club Mbshp. May 7137

PRUNIER

72 St. James's St., London, S.W.1. Reg. 1373

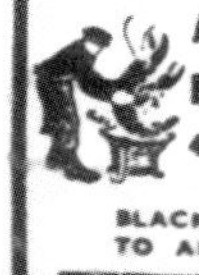

Air Raid Lunch 8/6

Black-out Dinner 10/6

4 courses including oysters or à la carte

BLACK-OUT TAXI SERVICE TO AND FROM PRUNIER'S

A PRUNIER MEAL AT HOME

A Prunier dish specially packed in an airtight tin — for use in your home. Write or ask for details and price list.

CROSSWORD

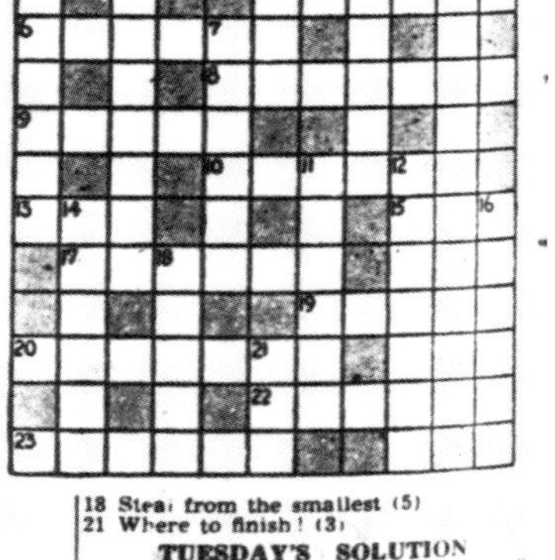

CLUES ACROSS

3 What an oppressive man! (6)
6 No, you won't find this office in the woods (6)
8 Playing a diamond?—no, a pigment (7)
9 May be added to that fixed charge (5)
10 Just a slave (6)
13 Woman in a white sheet (3)
15 Army without end (3)
17 The best way to lie if you're very tired (6)
19 A small bay (5)
20 It's smoked, and eaten (7)
22 What you may do if you don't follow suit (6)
23 Man of stone, perhaps (6)

CLUES DOWN

1 A superior woman (6)
2 Many of them came from Vienna (7)
3 A common enough article (3)
4 Enraged (5)
5 How to take your whisky if it's not strong enough? (6)
7 It provides a rest for baby (6)
11 He's a judge of cricket (6)
12 This vessel holds at least eight pints (7)
14 A very small place (6)
16 It's not quite a glove (6)
18 Steal from the smallest (5)
21 Where to finish! (3)

TUESDAY'S SOLUTION

ACROSS.—3, Surely 6, Acetic 8, Royalty. 9, Lather. 10, Ell 12, Whale. 15, Brief. 17, Eli 19, Licked 21, Arsenal 22, C-leave 23, Charge

DOWN.—1, F-allow 2, Central 3, Score. 4, Reaper 5, Little 7, Ire 11, Linkman 13, H-earth 14, Line-ar 16, Fodder 18, Place 20, Ill

DON'T MISS THE NEWS—

Have wireless in your A.R.P. Room or Shelter

FIX A PIX

Full volume without interference Fixed in a moment—press it, it sticks

2/- Double length 3/6

PIX LONDON S.W.4

SELF ADHESIVE STRIP AERIAL

NOVEMBER

27 Wednesday

Plymouth received a major attack at night and London was again only a secondary target. However, the London raid was heavier than for some nights – since the heavy bombing of 15th November and the subsequent switch away from London to provincial towns as the main targets for heavy raids.

28 Thursday

Another minor attack on London during a night in which Merseyside was to receive its longest single raid of the war.

29 Friday

During the autumn and winter of 1940 there were major attacks on London at the end of every month. In this end-of-the-month raid around 400 Londoners were killed or injured.

30 Saturday

Some minor raids during the day and after dark on London. Messerschmitt 109 fighter-bombers were still being used for daylight raids to beat London's air defences.

118. A London taxi almost buried by debris.

119. Business as usual! 'Musso's Lake' was the Mediterranean Sea over which the Axis Powers of Mussolini's Italy, Japan and Hitler's Germany claimed control as they had occupied all the countries, except neutral Spain, surrounding it.

CLOSING PRICES

EVENING STANDARD, December 3. 1940.

FINAL NIGHT EXTRA

Evening Standard

Amusements 8
Radio 8

BLACK-OUT 5.21 p.m. to 8.19 a.m.
MOON sets 9.39 p.m., rises 12.26 p.m.

No. 36,270   LONDON, TUESDAY, DECEMBER 3, 1940   ONE PENNY

Heavy Night Raid on Bristol: London Raid-free

RUSH HOUR DIVE-BOMBS ON LONDON TO-DAY

Going To New Homes

With their few belongings done up in bundles these women were going to new homes after the heavy bombing attacks on Southampton on successive nights. In the second raid the business centre was again the raiders chief target, but the suburbs also suffered heavily in the attack. [Another picture on PAGE SEVEN.]

19 BRITISH SHIPS LOST IN A WEEK

The Admiralty announce to-day that our mercantile losses for the week ended November 24-25 were 19 British ships, representing 75,560 tons, and three Allied ships of 12,415 tons, making a total of 22 ships with a tonnage of 87,975.

The Germans claimed to have sunk, during this week, 118,020 tons of merchant shipping.

Germany Claims 16 Ships in Convoy Sunk

The German news propaganda service made the following claims to-day:

"Two German U-boats yesterday attacked a British convoy on its way to England, and dispersed it.

"In spite of a strong defence put up by the escorting warships, 15 ships with a total tonnage of more than 110,000 tons, and the escorting auxiliary cruiser Caledonia (17,046 tons) were sunk.

"Two further ships of a total tonnage of 16,000 tons were also probably sunk.

"Another U-boat reported the sinking yesterday of two armed enemy merchant ships totalling 21,247 tons, including the modern British motorship Victor Ross (11,247 tons)."

*The Caledonia, after being renamed the Scotstoun and fitted as an armed merchant cruiser, was actually sunk by a U-boat in June. Loss was announced by the Admiralty on June 14.

"British Steamer Torpedoed"

The Mackay radio in New York reports having picked up messages from the British seamer W. Hendrik, stating that she had been torpedoed, 380 miles off the north coast of Eire, and from the seamer Alvonia, saying she had been attacked by an airplane 300 miles north-west of Ireland.—British United Press and Associated Press.

. The W. Hendrik, 4360 tons, is owned by the Euxine Shipping Co., Ltd., and registered at Newcastle.
There is no vessel named Alvonia in Lloyd's Register of Shipping.

More Sugar and Tea for Christmas Week
BACON: 12oz. A MONTH

Lord Woolton's Christmas box will be an allowance of 12oz. of sugar and 4oz. of tea in place of the existing rations of 8oz. of sugar and 2oz. of tea, for the one week beginning December 16.

Following on Lord Woolton's warning yesterday that from time to time there would be "even less" bacon, it was officially stated that the releases might be limited to the equivalent of 12 ounces per person in a period of four consecutive weeks—in other words, to give three weeks' rations in four weeks.

Apart from loadings for which arrangements had already been made, no cargoes of fresh or tinned fruit, except a limited quantity of oranges, would for the time being be brought to this country.

"There are going to be some oranges for marmalade," said an official. "The supplies will not be rationed."

The maximum price order of 2d. for a banana would be imposed on December 5. Other prices fixed were £30 per ton on a first hand sale and 1s. 6d. a dozen on a sale by wholesale.

FATS: NO CHANGE

The quantity of cereals to be imported for feeding animals must be reduced to make the best use of tonnage available for food supplies.

As the production of milk was regarded as of prime importance no further restriction would be placed on the import of oilcakes.

Those benefiting under the National Milk scheme for mothers and children were asked to obtain from local milk officers application forms for renewal of their permits for the quarter beginning January 1.

Asked about a German propaganda statement that there was to be a reduction in the fat ration the official said: "We do not expect, and have no reason to expect, that there will be any reduction in the existing box. of fats."

It was expected that next week a maximum price order would be issued in respect to apples both for cooking and dessert.

Proposal For Miss Susan Hall

ATHENS, Tuesday.

"Jerry," one of a group of R.A.F. men who returned to their squadron in Greece after being missing for three days, says he will never fly again without carrying the photograph of Miss Susan Hall, of Wargrave-road, Henley.

He is convinced that his bad luck on the flight was due to the fact that he forgot the photograph which his girl friend gave him before he left England.

"I carried it on scores of bombing flights in the Western Desert," he said, "and swore by it as my luck-bringer.

"When over the target on the last flight I slipped my hand in my inside pocket to have a look at Sue and found the photograph was missing. I knew I was for it."

Asked if there were any message for her, "Jerry" said:

"Yes. You can tell her I'm going to marry her after this job is over. She does not know it yet, but this goes as a proposal."

—British United Press.

Sons For Officer-Prisoners

Sons have been born to the wives of two British officers who are prisoners. One of the officers is Major W. F. Anderson, R.E. who was reported last July to be a prisoner He was awarded a bar to his M C His wife Kathleen, lives at Wrecclesham Grange, Farnham, Surrey

The other is Captain David H. Walker, of the Black Watch, who was stated on November 1 to be a prisoner of war. His son has been born in Montreal to Mrs Willa Walker.

Bomb Disposal Badge

It is understood that a special badge is to be given to members of the Forces who belong to bomb disposal squads. A Government announcement is likely soon.

Houses Wrecked: Series of Alerts

Bombs were dropped in two London districts in the first daylight Alert to-day when many people were on their way to work.

Enemy airplanes dived out of the clouds just after the warning sounded and dropped nine bombs in one district.

Two bombs fell in one street. One demolished seven houses; the other fell in the middle of the road.

A postman who was bicycling along the road said: "I heard the whistle of the first bomb, and fell flat on the ground.

"A few other men and I ran to one house and pulled out the old couple who were buried in the wreckage. They were badly hurt."

An hour later the postman was still picking up letters blown out of his sack into the road and gardens.

Blown Out of Bed

A woman named Mrs. Steel was blown out of bed in her night-clothes, and a motor-bicyclist was thrown off his machine by blast. He remounted and rode away.

Eight people were injured in another road.

Guns were firing in several districts soon after the warning sounded.

(Continued on Back Page. Col. Five)

British Bomb Two Ships Off Norwegian Coast

"Aircraft of the Coastal Command last night attacked shipping off the Norwegian coast," the Air Ministry announced this afternoon.

"One ship sustained a direct hit. A large explosion and a fire followed the bombing of the wharves at Feje Island.

"Yesterday another aircraft of the Coastal Command scored a direct hit on the stern of an enemy supply ship off the Norwegian coast.

"Aircraft of Bomber Command last night attacked the submarine base at Lorient.

"In these operations none of our aircraft was lost"

Fleet Street Mourns Lord Rothermere

A memorial service for Lord Rothermere, held to-day in St. Bride's, Fleet-street, was attended by representatives of the Prime Minister and of the Government departments.

The church was crowded. The service was conducted by the vicar, the Rev. Arthur Taylor. Twelve choirboys sang Tennyson's anthem, "Crossing the Bar," and there were two hymns, "Lead, Kindly Light," and "Abide With Me."

The vicar said that it could be stated of Lord Rothermere that he died in harness in the service of his country, and they could pay tribute to a life which appeared to have been a kind of crusade. His patriotism was always of a high order.

R.A.F. RAID NAPLES AND SICILY PORT

R.A.F. raids during the night on Naples and the port of Augusta, in Sicily, were admitted officially by Rome to-day.

The Greek High Command confirm that the Greek advance continues on all three fronts in Albania.

Evening Standard Correspondent
ATHENS, Tuesday.

The Italians are retreating faster to-day than they did after the fall of Koritza, according to reports from the front.

This is the latest communique of the Greek High Command,

The shaded area represents the approximate depth of the Greek advance into Albania.

who are noted for their restrained bulletins:

SOUTHERN SECTOR. — "In the Epirus front advancing Greek troops have the road from Santi Quaranta to Argyrokastro under fire.

CENTRAL SECTOR. — "In the Premeti sector our troops have occupied new positions.

"We have captured large numbers of prisoners, and four guns and various materials have also been taken.

NORTHERN SECTOR. — "In the Ostrovitse Mountains our troops have made successful attacks, dispersing enemy detachments. Officers and men have been taken prisoner.

"North of Pogradets (at the southern end of Lake Ochrida, Jugoslavia) the
(Continued on Back Page, Col. Four)

The Speeder-Up

A witness in the Divorce Court to-day described himself as a "time and motion study clerk."

Mr. Justice Henn Collins wondered what he meant.

"He is engaged in speeding up other people's activities," counsel explained.

Rain in Straits

Drizzling rain was falling in the Straits of Dover to-day and thick mist shrouded the calm sea There was a cold north-westerly wind.

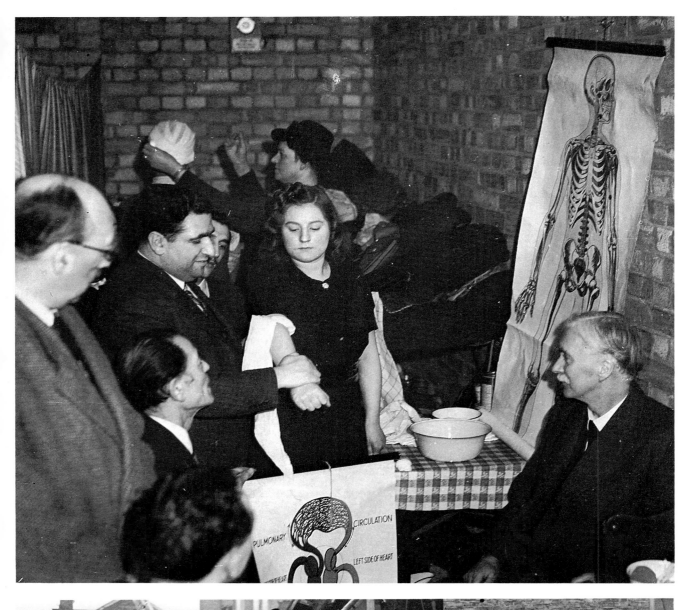

DEC

1 Sunday

As Southampton suffered its second major attack of the weekend, London received a minor attack between about 7.00 and 11.30 p.m. Casualties were few and damage was slight.

2 Monday

London had a quiet night and despite fog the *Luftwaffe* mounted a major attack on Bristol.

3 Tuesday

A minor night raid on London. By this period of the Blitz nearly all raids were carried out at night as the Germans had found that British defences were considerably weaker by night. However, the RAF were beginning to be supplied with a new plane, the Beaufighter, which carried improved radar equipment and heavier guns and was intended to be a better counter to night attacks.

4 Wednesday

London suffered slightly more severe raids than the previous night but they were far short of the scale of attacks the capital had seen in September, October and early November.

5 Thursday

Another minor attack on London.

120. An evening class in first aid in a London shelter at the beginning of December.

121. Nuns examining the wreckage of their convent hit during a recent night raid.

122

123

124

125

DECEMBER

6 Friday

Some bombs were dropped in the Home Counties but none in the London area.

7 Saturday

No bombing anywhere in Britain, probably due to extremely cold weather including ice and snow in Britain and on the Continent.

8 Sunday

The peace of the previous night was shattered when London was bombed by 413 aircraft from 6.00 p.m. on Sunday the 8th until 6.00 a.m. on Monday the 9th. It was the biggest raid on London since 15th October. Around 250 people died and more than 600 were seriously injured in a night that saw damage to the Houses of Parliament, Broadcasting House, the docks and a great deal of commercial and private property. Parachute mines were again in evidence.

9 Monday

No bombing attacks because of bad weather.

122. Bicycles in Grose's sports shop in New Bridge Street after a bomb had fallen.

123. New Bridge Street again – a rescue party at work after raids on night of 8th December.

124. The bomb which caused this damage to the Middle Temple Law Library fell on 8th December but the picture was not passed for publication until 20th December.

125. Salvaging books from the Middle Temple Library.

126. Salvaging furniture from a bombed home in Ilford.

127. Two women were buried for several hours when rubble and earth covered their Anderson Shelter. The rescue squads got them out.

128. Ilford again – several people were rescued alive from this rubble.

"CAN WE EVICT SHELTERERS?"

Marshals Ask for a Ruling

NEWS FROM UNDERGROUND

Evening Standard Reporter

Two hundred and forty shelter marshals are to meet the full Westminster Council at the City Hall on Thursday. They will ask the meeting to give an official definition of their status.

These marshals look after 100,000 shelterers in the Westminster area every night, but they are not quite sure of their duties.

"We know we have 'to maintain order,' but we feel there should be a definite ruling of how far our duties and our responsibilities extend," one of them told me.

"For instance, we want to know how we stand about evicting unruly and infectious shelterers."

These marshals are really shelter managers. Many of them are paid servants of the Council. They are responsible to the Council for the conduct of everyone using the shelters.

Every shelter in the Westminster area, with the exception of the Tubes, will have a representative at the meeting.

"CONTROVERSIAL"

An official of the council told me: "The meeting is purely a domestic one.

"There is no doubt many of the discussions will be controversial, but we hope the results will mean big improvements.

"Some of the matters to which shelterers raise objection may be brought before the meeting, and alterations may be made to make things easier for everybody.

"One matter that will be discussed is the subject of 'ticket only' admittance. Marshals have received very definite instructions that ticket holders only should be allowed to remain except those who are caught in the street while raiders are overhead.

"These casual users often protest when they are told they must not stay."

School Shelter Advice

The Board of Education, in a circular to be issued giving advice on school shelter accommodation, include details of the way in which time spent by children in shelters during raids can be spent usefully.

UNRULY

Turkeys at Christmas will be scarce and dear but this soldier and his wife found one to suit them to-day at a London market.

Dutch Troops' Christmas Party

Father Christmas arrives with his servants at the Christmas party held by Dutch troops in England.

CAMPAIGN AGAINST WEST END PESTS

Military Police Asked to Help

Evening Standard Reporter

The Public Morality Council to-day sent a request to the Provost Marshal's department in London asking for greater co-operation by the military police in a campaign to check the pestering of Service men in the West End by undesirable characters.

"Scores of undesirable women who left when the night bombing started have now returned to the West End," Mr. George Tomlinson, secretary of the Public Morality Council, said to me.

"The increase in daylight pestering is very serious, and is causing us much anxiety.

"We have been in communication with Sir Philip Game, the Commissioner of Metropolitan Police, and he has given instructions to the police to take action whenever possible.

"We are suggesting to the Provost Marshal that the military police should be instructed to exercise greater vigilance.

"Largely as the result of our efforts, most of the wretched little gambling and drinking dens to which soldiers were lured have now been shut."

Seven Tons of Food Eaten in the Tubes

The establishment of refreshment services at the 80 Tube stations, where upwards of 100,000 people take shelter nightly, was completed last night by London transport, acting as agents for the Ministry of Food.

The job had been finished in four weeks. It included arranging six railway depots for the receipt and despatch of food, fitting six special refreshment trains, installing 134 canteen points on the platforms, fitting 600 electric boilers and ovens, and half a mile of water mains, engaging, organising and training a new staff of 1000 employees.

The consumption of tea and cocoa now amounts to 12,500 gallons a night and the food distributed each night weighs seven tons.

A.F.S. Exchange

Arrangements have been made between Tottenham and Blackpool Corporations by which a score of members of the Tottenham A.F.S. will exchange duties with a score of the Blackpool A.F.S. at intervals.

Talking Turkey

Don't Polish Your Brass is the New Order to Troops

Brass on arms and equipment must now be left unpolished.

This instruction has been issued to the troops because shining brass makes them more conspicuous from the air.

The instruction does not apply to brass badges and buttons on Service dress used by troops for walking out.

Man With a Sack

A labourer carrying a sack was stopped by a detective-sergeant, who found that the sack contained scrap metal stolen from the hospital where the man was engaged on demolition work.

At a London police court to-day the labourer, Joseph Lionel Rust, 33, a married man with four children, pleaded guilty to looting and was sentenced to four months' imprisonment.

Carol Singing This Year as Usual: No Restrictions

Evening Standard Reporter

There will, I understand, be no restrictions this Christmas on carol singers or bands taking their traditional part in festivities.

The Ministry of Home Security are thus taking up the same attitude as they did last year.

It is, however, emphasised that all lighting regulations must be strictly observed, and there must be no ringing of bells or sounding of rattles, sirens, whistles or hooters.

In some areas special local restrictions are being imposed by chief constables.

P.-c. Kept 10s. a Schoolgirl Found

Sentence of a month's hard labour was passed at Bromley to-day on Special Constable Albert William Potter, who pleaded guilty to stealing a 10s. note which a schoolgirl, who found it in the street, handed to him. He kept the note.

Detective-inspector Vincent Green said Potter had been a special constable since 1926 and his conduct had hitherto been exemplary.

It was considered that this was an isolated lapse, but the Commissioner of Police wished the matter to be dealt with in open court.

And/Or

Mr. Justice Bennett announced to-day that he had relinquished, "as hopeless," his long campaign against the use of "and/or" in legal and commercial documents.

"I give up the battle and retire defeated," he said.

Mr Kenneth Swann, K.C.—Your observations on the subject may ultimately have effect.

Mr. Justice Bennett.—Not the slightest; although I still think it introduces an element of uncertainty as to what is meant.

Canadian Killed

Lance-corporal Matthew Thompson, of a British Columbia unit, died to-day as the result of a motor-bicycle collision late last night with Police-sergeant F. W. Clark, of Edenbridge, at Marlpit Hill, between Sevenoaks and Edenbridge.

Both men were riding motor-bicycles and the police sergeant's leg and hand were fractured.

'Evacuate or Go to School' Round-up

Evening Standard Reporter

School attendance officers in London were to-day continuing their house-to-house round-up of the 50,000 children who are not attending school and had not been evacuated.

It will be two weeks at least before their job is completed.

Already the flow back to the 365 schools, open from 10 a.m. to 3 p.m., has begun. But it is not rapid.

I understand that up to Saturday only 2000 children went back.

"Children must either be sent to school or evacuated. Parents who keep them at home in London are liable to be summoned," is the official warning given by the house-to-house visitors.

Longer Walk

"Thousands of children will have a longer walk than usual to school owing to the number of schools which are now rest centres and fire sub-stations," I was told.

Mr. Malcolm MacDonald, Minister of Health, is still considering whether the 81,000 schoolchildren who still remain in bombed London should be compulsorily evacuated to safer places.

He is taking into account the results of a questionnaire put some weeks ago by the Ministry to social workers in the worst-bombed districts.

Most of these experts are convinced that compulsion would be a mistake.

I spoke to Mrs. P. K. Young, an experienced social worker who is now in charge of the W.V.S organisation at Bethnal Green.

"There is a strong feeling against compulsion," she said. "In most cases of families who remain in this district, the parents definitely want their children with them and refuse to be parted. In some cases there is another consideration—they have had an unfortunate previous experience of evacuation."

Jewels for Maid

Mrs. Gertrude Mary Hepworth, of Ratton-road, Eastbourne, who left £6861 (net personalty £6740) bequeathed £100, her furs, clothes and jewels, and furniture, to the value of £50, to her maid, Mary Lamb, and the residuary estate to her for life.

DECEMBER

10 Tuesday

Continued poor weather suspended bombing operations by the *Luftwaffe*.

11 Wednesday

Slightly improved weather brought a major raid on Birmingham but only a few bombs fell on London.

12 Thursday

Another quiet night for London as Sheffield was selected for a major German attack.

13 Friday
14 Saturday

Poor weather conditions limited *Luftwaffe* operations and gave London two quiet nights – although, of course, the siren sounded Alerts as passing aircraft triggered the warning system.

129. Eton School sustained damage when stray bombs fell.

130. Eton boys removing their belongings from the damaged buildings.

BALLETS AND OPERAS

APOLLO.—Ger. 2663.— Daily at 2.15.
Boats 4 4.5. Seats 1.15 & 5.15.
ANGLO-POLISH BALLET
Under direction of MARIA HALAMA
and Z. KOMARSKI

ARTS.—Lift on .1. 2.15, 5.30. LUNCH BALLET
inc. Show Mbership 5/- with friends. Stalls 1.

THEATRES

COLISEUM.—Chasing Drum Mon. Dec. 23
TWICE DAILY 12 Noon & 4 p.m. Francis
Laidier's ALADDIN Book Now Tem. 3161.

COLISEUM HARROW—CHAR. 8363 7.30. 6.50.
Jean Forbes-Robertson in BERKELEY SQUARE.

GOLDERS GREEN.—Boxing Day & Bnis. 11.0 &
2.0 Daily at 2. ALADDIN Douglas Byng
Harry Welchman, Richard Bearne.

WINTER G'DN.—Nxt. week & Xy. 8 p.m. also Th. Sat.
11 a.m. WHERE THE RAINBOW ENDS

WYNDHAM'S.—Day 2.15, & Dec. 26th 11.30 a.m.
(Tem. 5028.)
A Mixture devised by Herbert Farjeon
DIVERSION
Edith Evans Dorothy Dickson
Walter Crisham Irene Manning
Joyce Grenfell The Aspidistras

CONTINUOUS REVUE

WINDMILL.—Proc Gr. 9th Yr. REVUE 11.27 Ed
(30th set.) Cont. 11.15 to 7.30 Sat to 9.15.

PICTURE THEATRES
(WEST END)

ASTORIA.—Charing .road. Continuous 11 to 7
JOAN CRAWFORD, FREDRIC MARCH in
THE GAY MRS TREXEL (A) 11.45, 2.25, 5.5

CARLTON.—(and cont.) G. Cooper
M. Brooke. De Mille's NORTH-WEST MOUNTED
POLICE, in Technicolor (A) Seats Bookable

EMPIRE. Leic sq. 11 a.m. William Powell
Myrna Loy, I LOVE YOU AGAIN (A) 2nd week

GAUMONT, HAYMARKET WHI 6655
U.K. PREMIERE of CHARLES CHAPLIN
THE GREAT DICTATOR (U)
Prog. comm. 10, 12.30, 3, 5.30. Usual prices
Matinee prices up to 11 a.m. Seats bookable

LONDON PAVILION.—From 10 a.m. Lana Turner,
John Shelton in WE WHO ARE YOUNG (A)

MARBLE ARCH PAVILION
U.K. PREMIERE of CHARLES CHAPLIN
THE GREAT DICTATOR (U)
Prog. comm. 10, 12.30, 3, 5.30. Usual prices
Mat. prices up to 11 a.m. also bkble. May 5112

METROPOLE.—nr 4675 THE GAY MRS.
TREXEL (A) WHEN THE DALTONS RODE (A)

MOULIN ROUGE (U) Windmill st. Ger 1655.
MOONLIGHT SONATA (U) Paderewski Three
BLIND ALLEY (A) Chester Morris 9d 1/2

NEW GALLERY.—Regent st. The Crazy Gang in
GASBAGS (U) 10.50, 1.0, 5.15. Box Off. Reg 8080

ODEON.—Leic sq. cont. from 10 a.m. ARGENTINE
NIGHTS Ritz Bros. & Andrew Sisters (U)

PLAZA.—Akim Tamiroff. TEXAS RANGERS RIDE
AGAIN (A) Geo Raft, C Lombard, Rumba (A)

PRINCE OF WALES.—WHI 8681-2
TOM TO-DAY U.K. PREMIERE
SPECIAL THEATRE PRESENTATION
CHARLES CHAPLIN
THE GREAT DICTATOR (U)
4 sep perfs Daily 10 a.m. 12.30, 3.10. 5.45
Box office Open All Res Seats
Box Office Open Sundays

REGAL Marble Arch.—Cont. 11.15 a.m. Gloria Jean
A Little Bit of Heaven (U) 12.55 4 & 7.5

RITZ Leic sq.—10 a.m. to 7 p.m. GONE WITH
THE WIND A. 4.5th WEST END WEEK

ROYAL West End.—Irene Dunne & Cary Grant in
THE AWFUL TRUTH A. The Spy in Black A

RESTAURANTS

A LA BROCHE REST.—2, Jermyn st., W.1.—
Dine in comfortable underground premises Mod
prices Amer. Bar. Chosen wines First class cuisine

AU JARDIN DES GOURMETS, 5, Greek st., W.1
—Ger 1815, open lunch as usual Closed evgs & Sun

L'APERITIF GRILL, 102, Jermyn st., S.W.1.—
Wm. 1577. Lunch. No dinner.

BOULESTIN, 25 Southampton-st., Covent-gdn
Day & Night. A.R.P shelter in restaurant.

LA COQUILLE, Restaurant Francaise, 79, St. Martin's
lane. Oysters, fish, shellfish, light wines. Tem. 8798

LE COQ D'OR RESTAURANT, Stratton-street, W.1
Mayfair 7807. Open for Luncheon as usual

HOLBORN.—Hol 8671. Lunch 3/6. Dinner (Grill
Room) 5/6 or a la carte. Sole excepted.

HUNGARIAN CSARDA, 77, Dean st.—Ger 1261
Open for Luncheons and Dinners as usual

MAISON BASQUE, 11 Dover st., W.1.—Reg 2652
OPEN FOR LUNCH AS USUAL

LE PERROQUET Belmore(st.), 33, Leicester sq.
WHI 2996. Open for Lunch and DINNER

PRUNIER, 72 St James's st, Reg 1373 Air-raid
Lunch 4/6 Black-out Dinner 10/6, both
courses including oysters or a la carte. Black out
taxi service to and from Prunier's

ROMANO'S
OPEN FOR LUNCHEONS AS USUAL

SCOTT'S, Picc. cir. Still open for Luncheons and
Dinners. Dine in comfort in the officially approved
air raid shelter. Taxi service. Ger. 7175.

CLUBS

COSMO.—DINE & Dance to Morgan's Band with Ray
Millar & Barry Mills 12-2 5-11 Sun 7 10 Mbership

THE EMBASSY CLUB opens daily for Luncheon
Cocktails Dinner

MURRAY'S.—Open as usual. Official Shelter
Lunch Supper, Dancing 9, deak-ot., W.1

CABARET, 16, Beak-st. W.1.—Dancing from
7 p.m. Cabaret at 11.30 a.m. Invitation only

COCOANUT GROVE.—Reg. 7675. (Guests only)
Harry Parry's Swingtette & Edmundo Ros

THE HAVANA, 4, Denman st., W.1.—Dancing
from 11 p.m. COLOURED BAND (Guests only)

PICTURE THEATRES
(WEST END)

WARNER, Leicester-square. Ger. 3423.
EDWARD G. ROBINSON
ANN SOTHERN, HUMPHREY BOGART in
BROTHER ORCHID (A)
with Donald Crisp, Ralph Bellamy, Allen Jenkins
Programmes commence 10.0, 11.40, 2.5, 4.55

PICTURE THEATRES
(SUBURBAN)

ELEPHANT & CASTLE TROCADERO.—OUR
TOWN (A) MILLIONAIRES IN PRISON (A)

KILBURN GAUMONT STATE.—BUCK BENNY
RIDES AGAIN (U) PHANTOM RAIDERS (A)

STEPNEY TROXY.—BUCK BENNY RIDES
AGAIN (U). QUEEN OF THE MOB (A)

SWISS COTTAGE ODEON.—BUCK BENNY RIDES
AGAIN (U). QUEEN OF THE MOB (A)

WATFORD GAUMONT.—Tommy Trinder, SAILORS
THREE (A). TURNABOUT (A)

WEST NORWOOD REGAL.—OUR TOWN (A)
MILLIONAIRES IN PRISON (A)

RESTAURANT ENTERTAINMENTS

GROSVENOR HOUSE.—GRO. 6363. New Under
ground Restaurant. Dine and Dance in safety

HATCHETT'S, Picc.—Tel. REG. 0217. Dancing &
Hatchett's Swingtet from 8.30 p.m. PRIVATE
AIR RAID SHELTER

HUNGARIA RESTAURANT, Picc cir. W.—WHI
4222. Gipsy Music & Dncg. Open Sun. Lch. Din.

KEMPINSKI'S TAVERN, Underground. Swallow st.
Reg. 1686. Lch., Din. Sing with George & D. co Music

LANSDOWNE RESTAURANT, Berkeley-square, W.1
MAY 1657. New entrance in LANSDOWNE
ROW Dancing to TIM LAYTON & his
Orchestra. 50 FEET UNDERGROUND

MAY FAIR HOTEL, May 8600. Luncheon &
Dinner in GRILL ROOM 10/6, below ground level.
Dancing to Norman Cole & his Orchestra. Tea
dancing daily. A.R.P shelter

QUAGLINO'S — Now MEURICE

QUEEN'S BRASSERIE, Leicester sq.—Lunch and
Dine in comfort well below ground level. Dancing
to Java and his Orchestra.

Another film boosts London

Darker London
By IAN COSTER

ALEX KORDA'S latest colour film, "The Thief of Bagdad," which was begun at Denham and finished in California, has been sent over, and it's going to the Odeon, December 23.

Three years ago Korda gave a banquet at the Savoy to mark first night of "The Drum," and Douglas Fairbanks senior, was there. Korda said he'd like to have the film rights of "The Thief" and star the Indian boy Sabu. Fairbanks looked across at Sabu in his red turban and said: " He's ideal. You can have the rights." So the film began.

ANOTHER film to turn our heads. Widgey Newman tells me that he and Butchers are showing a picture entitled "London's Got Grit" this week.

THEY'RE applying for special leave for Second Lieutenant John Mills to make that "Spitfire" film at Shepherd's Bush studios. Johnny turned down Hollywood offer to star in "Of Mice and Man" to get his gun, so they might give him time off.

LESLIE HOWARD has just signed contract to appear in "49th Parallel." So the rumour that he was not going to appear in that Canadian epic is blown out.

BRILLIANT performance being given nightly at the Players' Theatre by Bernard Miles. Chairman Sachs, introducing him, says "he positively reeks of the soil." He does. He comes on rolling a cartwheel and gives, with slow, earthy wit, the gossip of his Herts village.

In his commentary he explains why the mending of the village pump cost 3s. 4d.—"4d. for mending pump and 3s. for knowing how to mend it." There are no amateur performances at the Players, but Miles is faultless.

I have no comment to make on chairman's announcement that " our next chorus will be 'Oh, the Fairies,' led by Mr. Coster."

WAITER MICHAEL, of Claridge's Causerie, has written a song called "Haunting Me," and Carroll Gibbons is playing it. I understand it's not dedicated to any particular customer of the restaurant.

RATHER uninspired commentary—even though it's by Air Vice-marshal Sir Philip Joubert—to short film. "Fighter Pilot," released in London to-day. But the shots of Spitfires and Hurricanes at work are dramatic, exciting.

John Barrymore is maddened by his screen wife (Mary Beth Hughes) in "The Great Profile," coming shortly.

JOHN RIDLEY, in battledress, dancing at May Fair. And looking much fitter than he did when he was member of "That Certain Trio."

Former manager of the May Fair restaurant, tall, handsome Massara, now a private in the R.A.S.C. His successor, Brega, says light-heartedly, "He's keeping a place warm for me."

STARS, players and technicians working at Rock Studios, Elstree, used to take short cut to local pub by using side entrance and path. Now they have to go right round to the front. Because there's a notice which says: "This 12in strip of land is owned by Provincial Garden Cities, Ltd."

Strip runs alongside pub fence. But couldn't you step over it without trespassing? Legal friend says: "No, ancient Roman doctrine of nuisance applies, even to airplanes flying low over land."

NEW films starting to-day: "Atlantic Ferry" at Teddington, with Michael Redgrave and Valerie Hobson. And " Once a Crook" at Shepherd's Bush, with Gordon Harker and Sydney Howard.

Records for Christmas

Top of this month's list of gramophone records I place those made by the Prime Minister.

H.M.V. have recorded four of the greatest speeches of his life, those broadcast to the nation during this year, on May 19 ("In a Solemn Hour," H.M.V. C3198), June 18 ("This Was Their Finest Hour." H.M.V. C3199, C3200 and C3201), July 14 ("The War of the Unknown Warriors," H.M.V C3202 and C3203) and September 11 ("Every Man to His Post." H.M.V C3204).

No one who listens to these records can fail to be stirred almost as much again as on the occasion of Mr Churchill's broadcasts.

Records make an ideal Christmas present, and especially suitable for the season is John McCormack's recording of Mendelssohn's "Still Night, Holy Night" (H.M.V. DA 1755) and "O for the Wings of a Dove" made by the Albert Sandler Trio, with cello, piano, violin and organ accompaniment (Columbia DB 1958).

For those who want to dance, three "Swing Kings" have made recordings which should delight their fans, these are Harry James and orchestra playing "Feet Dragging Blues" (Parlophone R 2772), Count Basie and orchestra playing "Louisiana" (Parlophone R 2768), and Benny Goodman and orchestra playing "Cocoanut Grove" (Parlophone R 2767)

Other first class dance records are Carroll Gibbons and his Savoy Orpheans quickstep "The Ferryboat Serenade" (Columbia FB 2534) and Ambrose and his orchestra's recording of that old favourite "Star Dust" (Decca F 7641).

OF vocal records, Bing Crosby at his most melting singing "Can't Get Indiana Off My Mind" (Brunswick 03073-B), Dinah Shore is at her gayest singing "Maybe" (Rega: MR 3381), and "Hutch" is at his treacliest singing "There'll Come Another Day" (H.M.V. BD 887).

And for lovers of classical music there are two outstanding "plums"; Sir Thomas Beecham and the London Philharmonic Orchestra's recording of Mozart's Symphony No 38 in D major (Columbia LX 911, 912 and 913), and Hephzibah and Yehudi Menuhin's violin and piano duet of Schubert's Rondo in B minor, Op 70 (H.M.V. DB 3583 and 3584). P. W.

Standard quiz

1. To what famous man was Lord Lothian secretary during the last war? And what was his own name then?
2. What are the colours of the buses which have come to London from:
   a. West Riding. b. Bolton. c. Hull?
3. "The White Ensign can be flown only on naval craft or naval establishments." True? False?
4. PENGUINS are found in their natural state:
   On the shores of the American Great Lakes;
   In the Arctic and Outer Hebrides;
   Between the Equator and the South Pole;
   On Greenland and Baffin Land;
   In the North Polar regions?
5. What is a dragoman?
Key on PAGE ELEVEN

Film as Radio Play

HOME SERVICE
203.5 M. 296.2 M., 391.1 M., 449.1 M., 48.82 M.

6.0.—News and announcements. 6.30.—News in Norwegian.
6.45.—"David Copperfield": 5—Steerforth comes to Yarmouth. 7.15.—Music-makers' Half-hour; Dr. Thomas Wood. 7.40.—Taking Stock: Mr Harold Nicolson, M.P. and Colin Brooks. 8.0.—"Dandy Lion" in Dandy's Inferno.
8.15.—"The Lady of the Rose," a musical play, with Harry Welchman, Sylvia Marriott, Reginald Purdell, Eric Starling, Sylvia Welling, Dick Francis, Vivienne Chatterton, B.B.C. Chorus and augmented B.B.C. Revue Orchestra. 9.0.—News. 9.25.—"Think on These Things." 9.25.—Opening night of the "Great Dictator" 9.35.—B.B.C. Orchestra (Section C)
10.0.—"This Man is News": Play adapted from film of same name.
10.45.—News in Gaelic. 10.50.—Joe Loss and his Band. 11.40.—Pauline Juler (clarinet). Howard Ferguson (piano). 12.0.—News.

FORCES
373.1 M., 41.49 M.
5.30.—Ack-Ack, Beer-Beer. 6.0.—News in Dutch and French.
6.30.—Henry Hall's Guest Night. 7.15.—Variety, with Albert Sandler, Cyril Fletcher, Oliver Wakefield, Hal Moss and his Radio Band.
7.40.—Sandy Macpherson, theatre organ. 8.0.—Home Service. 9.0.—News in German.
9.20.—Radio Rhythm Club. 9.45.—Canadian News-letter. 10.0.—Records of armchair music. 10.30-11.0.—Jan Berenska and his Orchestra.

Barry K. Barnes and Valerie Hobson in the film "This Man is News." The radio version is being given to-night at 10 o'clock in the Home Service.

AMUSEMENTS, SPORTS, Etc.

GREYHOUND RACING
§ Licensed by the N.G.R.C.
§ DAGENHAM STADIUM.—To-morrow at 2 p.m.
Tote Adm 1/6, 3/-.
§ WALTHAMSTOW STADIUM.—TO-MORROW
at 2 p.m. Grand Special Meeting
NO MEETING SAT. DEC 21

ICE-SKATING
PURLEY.—Upl 1174. Re AR. 2.15 to 5.15 6hrs
2 TO DAY CECILIA COLLEDGE etc
SPORTS-DROME, Richmond.—Dy. 10-12.30, 2.30

TEACHERS OF DANCING
AMY GREENWOOD SCHOOL, 54, Bloomsbury st.
W.C. Pvte lessons. Sep. tuition. Mus. 0566.
DE BRITT STUDIOS.—Strictly private lessons. 3/6
11 Princes st. Hanover sq. H.1. May 3540
CEM MOUFLET, 11, Albemarle st., PICCADILLY
Reg 4629 INDIVIDUAL OR friends share free
GWENETHE WALSHE, Palace Hotel Bltrm. Lancaster
gate Pad 8281 or 9578. Pte lens. Tea dnc daily
PHYLLIS, 469 OXFORD ST.—3 Pvte Rooms 10/6
Tea Dances daily Sunday Club Mbership May 7157
VICTORY, 99, Regent st—Authentic tuition, 3/-
5/6. Qualified teachers T.D Sat. Reg 5015

GAUMONT IN THE HAYMARKET
Charles Chaplin
THE Great DICTATOR
PAULETTE GODDARD
Programmes 10.0 12.30
3.0 5.30
AND Marble Arch Pavilion

THE CRAZY GANG in Gasbags
Directed by MARCEL VARNEL
NERVO & KNOX · FLANAGAN & ALLEN
NAUGHTON & GOLD · MOORE MARRIOTT
TO-DAY at 10.50, 1.0, 5.15, 5.30
A GAINSBOROUGH PICTURE
NEW GALLERY

Lana TURNER · John SHELTON
WE WHO ARE YOUNG
With Gene Lockhart, Grant Mitchell
H. Armetta. An M-G-M Picture (A)
LONDON PAVILION
Continuous from 10 a.m.

Frankie DARRO "UP IN THE AIR" (A)
TO-DAY Continuous from 10 a.m.

CHARLES CHAPLIN in the GREAT DICTATOR
PRINCE OF WALES
10.0 12.30 3.0 5.30
CHARLES CHAPLIN in the GREAT DICTATOR
GAUMONT Haymarket

THEY CAN'T HAVE DINNER AT SCOTTS AFTER THE SHOW BUT YOU CAN
Scott's RESTAURANT
Lunch or Dine at Scotts afterwards
TOP OF THE HAYMARKET ONLY 100 YARDS FROM THE TWO CINEMAS
CABARET ON AT SCOTTS BAR
COCKTAILS AT SCOTTS BAR—DINNER IN THE RESTAURANT
Dine in comfort in the officially approved air-raid shelter
GOOD FOOD GOOD WINE TAXI SERVICE

DECEMBER

15 Sunday

A minor attack on London at night.

16 Monday

Continuing poor weather conditions meant again only a minor attack on London by the *Luftwaffe*, but the weather did not stop the RAF mounting a major attack on Mannheim in Germany.

The War Cabinet had been reticent to sanction the same sort of raid as Germany had directed against London, Coventry, Southampton, Bristol and other British cities – namely an attempt to destroy a whole area regardless of whether it contained military or war production targets.

But in the face of the destructive attacks on British civilian targets the decision was taken and on 16th December 134 RAF bombers flew to Mannheim.

17 Tuesday
18 Wednesday

No bombing operations anywhere over Britain due to poor weather.

19 Thursday

Slightly improved weather conditions brought another minor attack to London, aimed again at government offices and the City.

131. With a second wartime Christmas approaching, food rationing and shortages were becoming severe – although this picture of poultry on display in the City might suggest otherwise, but turkeys were 'off the ration'.

132. A Christmas concert given by ENSA in a public shelter decorated for the occasion.

(Copyright in All Countries.) ACH, HIMMEL ! VOT A SANTA CLAUS !

HEIL HEROD!

By MICHAEL FOOT

A CHRISTMAS such as King Herod might have planned will be celebrated to-morrow across the Continent of Europe.

Prague, Warsaw, Oslo. Copenhagen, Brussels, Bukarest, Amsterdam, Paris Eight dead cities. Eight hundred thousand other towns, in which children may laugh and play for a few brief hours while their mothers look on fearful, frightened by the stolen sounds of delight because they know how quickly these may change to tears.

How many Rachels will weep for their children and not be comforted because they are not! How many more will find Christmas painful through the contrast between its tradition of joy and their present misery.

Bitter memories made all the sharper by the season will find no recompense in the mockery of celebration. Two hundred million homes will wonder how long it may be before they enjoy the good things of this earth without trepidation for the security of their children.

Rome and Berlin will present a not much happier scene. Ten years ago and more to-day's young mothers of Italy were girls who sang the Giovinezza through the streets. Their brothers and husbands joined the Fascisti and took the Fascist vow. "Believe. Fight. Obey."

Now they are fighting and obeying across the sands of Libya or amid the snows of Albania. Back in Rome their wives await the news, believing no more, discovering in one swift hour of enlightenment that the prospects of their children mean much more to them than Mussolini's empire.

◆ ◆ ◆

THE same shadow, if not so thick, falls across Berlin. Some of her mothers marched through the streets ten years ago behind the Nazi bands and when they were married they were presented with a copy of "Mein Kampf."

Did they read it? Did they read how the bearing of sons to fight Germany's battles was the noblest task to which they could dedicate their lives?

This Christmas they will learn, perhaps for the first time, how sorely they were deceived. Their husbands are not coming home for Christmas. Upon their children's faces may be marked the pinch of under-nourishment. Perhaps they may ask themselves whether a life dedicated to their families might not have been better than a life dedicated to their Fuehrer.

Will they really watch the play about their chilly firesides, their eyes aglow at the thought that these sons will acquire the manhood which gives them passport to the battlefield, that these daughters will one day grow to womanhood, receive their copy of "Mein Kampf" and at last learn the same anguish which their mothers now suffer? If so, it will be a strange sort of Christmas.

I do not believe it. In all those eight dead cities, in Rome and Berlin besides, across a whole Continent, I believe mothers will have much the same thoughts. They will prize the more keenly because they cannot firmly grasp them all those simple enjoyments, which Christmas bestows, which the dictators taught their own people to despise and which they looted from their victim nations.

They will not know it, but if such are their thoughts they will be extolling the virtues of democracy with its brave assertion that the State was made for the individual.

Known laws, established liberties, the right of a people to form their own government, these together make something more than a system of society to be discussed and approved by political theorists. They protect friendship and laughter and the right to think your own thoughts and sing your own songs as surely as the Gestapo is designed to obliterate or circumscribe all these things in the interest of one gang.

However, democracy has discovered that these institutions are not sufficient of themselves to ensure their own survival. Some other guarantees were needed if these institutions were to be properly worked and enjoyed. In Britain over the past hundred years we have striven, fitfully often, to discover what those guarantees might be.

◆ ◆ ◆

WE made a beginning with the children.

A child, underfed from birth, driven to work at the age of ten, deprived of education would grow up to find our liberties a sham. Therefore we strove under the blessed slogan of equality of opportunity to repair these handicaps.

It was not always done generously. Sometimes it was not done at all. Yet the ideal was always there. The biggest social reforms of the last century prescribed special guarantees for the children.

In their name we defied the sacred laws of supply and demand and shackled the rights of private enterprise. After terrific struggle the State decreed that the bodies and souls of little children should not be broken in factory and mine.

In their name we invaded the private circle of the family and stood between the father and his son. The State decreed that no parent had the right to cheat his child of education.

In their name through modern days we have thrown overboard economic principles which lay at the root of our society. The State decreed that medicine, and in some cases even food, must be supplied according to need.

We paid homage to a precept more specific even than that the State was made for the individual. Above all the State was made for the child.

There were still children who went under-nourished and ill-clad through our streets, still children who were thrown without proper protection into the labour market. These were our failures. Yet despite them all the principle was enthroned.

Never did we so debase ourselves to accept the doctrine that children should be reared like cattle, their minds twisted and subdued, to feed a voracious war machine or an all-powerful State.

Children had rights of their own, which the State recognised as paramount.

To-day those rights have vanished in almost every city in Europe. They have been stolen by a gang which arrogates to itself the privilege of seizing young minds, bruising and moulding them, until young bodies shall be capable of serving their interest. The new King Herod makes a misery of the present and resolves to set his stamp on the future.

◆ ◆ ◆

LONDON is the last great capital of the West which has not succumbed to this fearful doctrine. How, then, does England treat her children this Christmas?

Everyone knows that war must reduce some of our social standards. But surely our proudest boast should be that the children least of all must suffer. We fight for the future. The future belongs to them, and even while we fight we must surely guard all those things which will enable them to enjoy it and shape it as they will.

I went to a London school to put this boast to the test. It reopened at the beginning of this month with 10 pupils. Now it has 70. Normally it has 350. Most of those 350 have been evacuated, but since this one reopened school caters for about five others closed the teachers reckon that 100 or more children in the district are roaming the streets as truants.

Of these 70 pupils 26 had been evacuated and had returned, some of them twice and more. Twelve had been bombed out of their homes, several more were sleeping in Tubes.

Most of these children have come to school again now after months of absence. Boys and girls of nine had forgotten reading and writing and they were the good ones who had come back. Outside there are many more, living their lives between the tubes, the shelters and the streets. They have forfeited in a year all the benefits which it took a century to construct. If they must live their childhood in such conditions they too must be counted as victims of the modern Herod.

◆ ◆ ◆

THAT is just one glimpse, perhaps an unfair one, of how England is treating her children in the midst of this war. Across our countryside in a thousand towns and villages, in London's boroughs teachers and local authorities are striving manfully against tremendous odds. Yet while such conditions remain in one London district we cannot claim that our duty has been done.

We shall not meet the challenge by patchwork. We shall only meet it when we understand that whatever other sacrifices are made, the State's obligation to the children remains.

In the days of the French Revolution the message of freedom was carried across the world under the title of the Rights of Man. I would like to see our Minister of Education announcing to the world as the first item in England's faith the Rights of Children.

No child in England shall suffer from Hitler's blockade. His ration is the first responsibility of the State. We build his body so that he may be strong to face the future.

No child in England shall find his claim to knowledge stripped from him by the blitzkrieg. We build his mind because we know that freedom can only be protected by those who can think for themselves.

Every child that we can we shall save from the bombers. His body, nerve and soul is counted too precious by us to be left to the indiscriminate ravages of cities under fire.

This young England we shall construct in the heat of battle as an example and inspiration to the dead cities of Europe.

It is the children that we are fighting for, and across those territories the children are beginning to fight for themselves. Behind the German soldiers who parade through Paris run urchins who wave their arms as if swimming, make a swishing noise with their mouths and shriek derisively. "Angleterre."

England is their hope. Let England proclaim their Charter.

The Captain Caught a Big Fish

By P. S. Le Poer Trench

"WE'VE had one fish," he said. He was a big, middle-aged man with grey hair and a wind-and-spray complexion. He wore the uniform of the Merchant Navy, with a captain's stripes and a medal ribbon from the last war. The other passengers had left the train and we were alone in the third-class compartment.

The captain reclined on the seat, his head propped on one hand as a man will do when he is accustomed to living under a low ceiling. You could have guessed his occupation from his attitude alone.

So long as there were other people in the carriage, he would not talk about his job, but now he could not resist his natural inclination to spin a yarn.

This man is in command of a 5000-ton oil tanker. His task is to carry across the ocean and deliver at British ports the fuel which forms the basis of modern warfare. He is as valuable as the pilot of a Spitfire. Because of his skill in navigation, the fruit of 35 years at sea, he could be replaced much less easily than the navigator of a Wellington bomber.

"WE were just off the Scottish coast," said the captain. He paused and inhaled cigarette smoke deeply. "It hit us for'ard." He pulled out his wallet and showed me a snapshot. There was a hole in the ship's side that you have driven a lorry through.

"Fuel oil went higher than the mast," he continued. "The fo'c'sle was smashed to smithereens. There were 15 men inside and, you wouldn't believe it, but one man had a finger broken and that was all.

"I pushed 'Sparks' through a hole in the wireless room and he sent out a distress. Then I ordered everyone into the boats. You see, we were expecting another one any minute."

"Did the U-boat surface?" I asked.

"No. We never saw a thing."

"I suppose you've got another ship now," I suggested, for the captain had told me that he was on week-end leave.

"No, the same one," he said, puffing his cigarette complacently. "This was in August. They patched her up in three months, and we've made another trip since then."

I asked him if he had managed to keep the tanker afloat by closing the bulkhead doors. He answered by drawing a diagram of a ship, which he divided into squares.

"This is the way a tanker is built," he explained. "These are all separate compartments with steel bulkheads between." He pointed to a spot near the bow. "These three went, but the other bulkheads held.

"After half an hour I took part of the crew back to the ship. The bow was awash and the stern was somewhere in the clouds. She was drawing 17 feet of water aft and 45 feet for'ard."

THE captain told me that two small vessels took the tanker in tow and brought her slowly into the nearest loch.

"Seagulls came riding on the waves right on to the deck," he recalled. "They were black with fuel oil. We had to wring their necks. There was nothing else you could do for the poor devils."

After lying in the loch for a while the tanker proceeded to the nearest port under her own steam.

The captain described this astonishing feat by saying merely: "I had to go pretty slow because I didn't know if the bulkheads would hold."

In port the cargo was transferred to another tanker to continue its journey, and the officers and crew received shipwreck leave.

The captain was on his way to visit his family in Shropshire. By now he is at sea again. Fish permitting he will bring back another cargo of oil to drive Britain's warships and tanks and lorries.

DECEMBER

20 Friday

Despite greatly improved weather conditions, especially after dark, London had a quiet night as Merseyside again suffered a major attack.

21 Saturday

Although Liverpool was the principal target again and London received only a minor raid, a bomb dropping on Victoria Station caused considerable damage.

22 Sunday

A minor attack on London on a night in which Manchester received its first major raid of the Blitz.

23 Monday

Manchester received another major follow-up attack and London another minor one targeted at the City and government offices.

24 Tuesday

Christmas Eve and the beginning of an unofficial truce in the *Luftwaffe*'s aerial bombing campaign.

133. *Looking into damaged Cloister Court with a camera. The picture shows where one of the high-explosive bombs fell. Daily Mail,* 24th December 1940. Damage caused to the Houses of Parliament on 8th December.

MEMBERS CLOAKROOM

Tried to Cut Way to Bombed Victims

FIRE GUIDED RAIDER

People were trapped during the night in an underground shelter in a large block of London flats. After two hours 11 were rescued alive.

People in an adjoining shelter heard the trapped people calling for help after the shelter had been wrecked by a heavy bomb.

700 ESCAPE IN BOMBED HOSPITAL

Debris Rained on Patients

Evening Standard Reporter

Seven hundred patients in a London hospital were shaken by the explosion of a huge bomb which fell in a road outside last night.

The whole building rocked, but though every ward in the hospital was damaged, not one patient was injured.

The out-patients' department caught the full blast and was completely wrecked. A doctor there was slightly hurt.

The nurses' quarters, which were empty, were severely damaged.

Glass and debris showered into the wards where patients were lying in beds.

Doctors and nurses worked all night clearing the wards and getting the patients ready for evacuation. They were being taken to other quarters to-day.

Still Calling

A recruiting office was damaged in London during the night, but a copy of the well-known recruiting poster of the last war, in which Kitchener points his finger, with the words "Your King and Country need you," was unharmed and left hanging on a wall.

A middle-aged invalid, Mrs. White, was believed to-day to be still buried under tons of debris. Her husband was killed and her daughter, who had a narrow escape, was taken to hospital suffering badly from shock.

A woman in the adjoining shelter said: "We could hear the people in the next shelter calling out, but although only a single wall divided us we were unable to do anything.

"Some of the men tried to hack their way through the wall, which was split with the force of the explosion. They were using pickaxes when wardens advised them against further work because of the danger of wholesale collapse of the shelter."

It is believed that the raider was guided by the glare of a gas main fire caused about 20 minutes before. A drapery establishment in this district was destroyed and a departmental store and a tailoring establishment were seriously damaged by fire.

Not far away a paper merchant's warehouse was completely destroyed, but houses on all four sides of the burning building were saved.

Bombed Wife Roamed Streets

A woman was found wandering the streets suffering from loss of memory and in a state of collapse to-day after wardens had been searching all night among the wreckage of her bombed London home.

She is Mrs. Leadwith, who, with her husband, was having supper when the bomb hit the house. Mr. Leadwith was found by wardens, but, as his wife was missing, they thought she was buried beneath the debris. Both are now in hospital.

Raiders Bombed Another London Church Last Night

Wreckage inside a church to-day after last night's attack on London. The steeple, too, was badly damaged.

Missed Bomb Death By Minutes, But His Wife Was Killed

Mr. and Mrs. F. Johnson, of a town in the London area, had promised to go to a bridge party last night. During a lull in the raid they decided to take a chance, and Mr. Johnson went to the garage at the bottom of the garden to get his car.

While he was starting his car a terrific explosion threw him to the ground. A bomb had demolished his house, killing his wife and maid.

Mr. Johnson was not hurt.

Trapped Girl Said, "Save Mother First"

A woman, who was sitting in the back room of one bombed London house last night with her 14-year-old daughter and an 18-year-old son, was killed.

The family had moved in only a week ago, the previous occupier having moved out of London after being bombed four times.

A rescue worker said to-day that the girl showed amazing fortitude. With her mother dead alongside her, she directed the defence workers. She was lying with her face near a fire which was still burning in the grate.

A neighbour who was one of the first to reach her said: "Her concern was for her mother. She kept saying: 'Mum is just behind me. Save her.'"

Bombed as They Said Prayers

When first-aid workers forced their way into a bombed house in a South Coast town last night, an old woman, Miss Constance Louisa Addison, was found lying dead over her cash-box.

Five houses had direct hits.

In one house two children were saying their prayers when the back wall was blown completely away.

Mr. E. Norgett, their father, although the ceiling fell on him, sustained only slight injuries.

He said: "If my children had not gone to a party they would have been in bed when the bomb fell, and would probably have been killed."

Saved the Baby and Husband

A London family were in a downstairs room when the upper part of the house was shattered by a bomb last night. The wife, Mrs. Rumble, lay on top of her baby on the floor.

Her husband was badly injured, but she moved some debris and pulled him clear. She also pulled her baby out.

Home Guards Patrol Street All Night

Two people were killed and a number injured, some seriously, when bombs fell in a London shopping street last night.

Houses were demolished and shop fronts blown out.

Home Guards patrolled the street until daybreak.

Synagogue Hit

A London synagogue was destroyed by a high explosive bomb last night.

Householders whose homes were bombed last night removing their belongings to-day.

WOMAN DOCTOR SAVED A DOG

Mr. and Mrs. Randall and their son were killed when their Anderson shelter was blown up in one London district last night.

Their dog was trapped in the house, and a woman doctor crawled into the wreckage to give the animal an injection before it was released.

Soon after daylight to-day a cat was found in London trapped in the wreckage of a dustbin which was almost flattened.

The bin had to be prised open with crowbars. The cat was released unhurt.

Bomb Hit Party

A bomb which fell in one London area last night demolished three houses and severely damaged a number of others.

Three people named Turner, a mother and two sons, are known to have been killed in one house.

A son Harold, aged 22, home on leave from the Army, and his brother, Stanley, 17, and probably some friends were among those believed dead. They were holding a party.

One family, living next door, were away for Christmas and returned to-day to find their home demolished.

His Own House

While a warden and his neighbours were dealing with 17 incendiaries in one London street last night a fire bomb fell on the warden's house.

The back rooms were destroyed before the flames could be extinguished.

BOMB KILLED FOUR SISTERS

In two London boroughs heavy calibre bombs caused widespread damage and a large number of casualties, including some fatal, during the night.

Six houses were destroyed in one borough near a hospital.

Four sisters were killed in one house. Their parents, Mr. and Mrs. Cane, had left the house a few minutes before and were unhurt.

Rescue squads released a man, Mr. Roth, after seven hours' work. His wife and daughter were killed.

A doctor crawled through a narrow tunnel with rescue squad men to give an injection to the trapped man.

In the other borough houses in three roads were badly damaged. At least eight people were killed and many injured.

Injured P.-c. Was All-Night Rescuer

When two heavy bombs fell last night on a London housing estate at least five people were killed. They were Mr. Nag, a teacher, and his mother, a Mr. Parr, and a young man of 20, Stanley Lakey. The body of another man has not yet been identified.

Mr. Parr's wife was rescued after being seven hours in the debris and was taken to hospital.

A policeman who had worked all night to pacify and help women victims was to-day taken to hospital with suspected fractured ribs.

Woman Swimming Champion Married

A bridal arch of divers greeted Leading-aircraftman Bounds and Miss V. Bassett-Lowke, the back stroke swimming champion, after their marriage at Northampton. A lucky spider was presented by Miss Joyce Harrowby, the sprint champion.

DECEMBER

25 Wednesday

Christmas Day and no German bombs fell anywhere in Britain. It was the second Christmas Day of the war and families sat down to whatever meat or poultry they could manage to find and afford, and to vegetables they had probably grown themselves; followed by a Christmas pudding made with precious eggs and fruit or substitute dried egg and grated carrot, parsnip or mashed potato. People exchanged Christmas presents, home-made from recycled materials, or treasured items of food such as a banana, an orange or a bar of chocolate. There were a few, limited, supplies of children's toys and games as not all factories had yet turned to war production.

26 Thursday

Another day of calm in the unofficial Christmas truce.

27 Friday

A major attack on London brought to an end the Christmas peace and left around 600 people dead or injured and a significant amount of damage.

28 Saturday

A quiet night in London.

134. Damage to Big Ben.

135. Cleaning away bomb debris at Savoy Hill.

136. A burning school fired by incendiary bombs in a raid just before Christmas.

CLOSING PRICES

EVENING STANDARD. December 30, 1940.

FINAL NIGHT EXTRA

Evening Standard

Amusements 8
Radio 10

No. 36,292   LONDON, MONDAY, DECEMBER 30, 1940   ONE PENNY

BLACK-OUT 5.27 p.m. to 8.38 a.m.
MOON sets 7.18 pm, rises 10.24 am.

7 Famous Churches Hit in Fiercest London Raid

"DELIBERATE ATTEMPT TO SET FIRE TO CITY"

The scene in St. Paul's Churchyard to-day as workers negotiated the fire debris and the pools of water left by the hoses.

Although the Eastern sky was still aglow with City fires when Londoners went to work to-day, it was soon clear that London's firemen had beaten the fiercest German fire raid of the war.

Some ruins were still smoking some hours later, but many famous buildings, churches, offices and homes had been saved.

THERE STOOD THE FIREMEN, SMOKE-GRIMED, EXHAUSTED, BUT KNOWING THAT WITH THE AID OF ROOF SPOTTERS, POLICE, WARDENS AND HUNDREDS OF CIVILIANS, THEY HAD TRIUMPHED IN THE GREATEST TEST LONDON'S FIRE-FIGHTING SERVICES HAVE KNOWN.

Four of these firemen died when a blazing wall collapsed, burying them. Many were injured.

BUILDINGS DYNAMITED

Scores of people had to be evacuated from their homes. Masked firemen dynamited buildings to stop the flames. Fire engine exhaust pipes were red hot with continued use.

THE BAD WEATHER CONDITIONS THAT DEVELOPED OVER THE CONTINENT PROBABLY CAUSED THE ATTACK TO BE CALLED OFF BEFORE MIDNIGHT.

R.A.F. fighters went up at one time to scatter the bombers. Machine-gun fire was heard.

ST. PAUL'S ENDANGERED

The Air Ministry and Ministry of Home Security announced at 8 a.m.:

"Last night the enemy dropped a large number of incendiary bombs on the City of London in a deliberate attempt to set fire to it.

"Damage was done to many famous buildings, including the Guildhall and several of the City churches.

"St. Paul's itself was endangered, but the neighbouring fires were extinguished in time. There was nowhere any attempt to single out targets of military importance.

"Fires were also caused in other parts of the London area, where damage was done to commercial buildings.

"London's fire services worked heroically and with success throughout the night. Casualties were few."

THE SEVEN CHURCHES

Famous City churches were among the buildings damaged. They were St. Bride's, Fleet-street, St. Lawrence, Jewry, St. Stephen's, Coleman-street, St. Vedast's, Foster-lane, St. Mary.

(Continued on BACK PAGE)

NAPLES & GERMANY BOMBED

Leaflets too, Says Italy

Naples was bombed last night, stated to-day's Italian High Command communiqué, quoted by Reuter.

Two waves of aircraft took part, it was stated, and dropped leaflets as well as bombs.

Buildings were damaged, and a number of casualties were caused.

An Air Ministry communiqué issued this afternoon stated:

"Very bad weather seriously restricted R.A.F. bombing operations last night.

"In spite of this, small forces of our aircraft attacked an objective in Germany, and invasion ports and air bases in enemy-occupied territory.

"Two of our aircraft are missing."

Would Eire be Left Free?

—ASKS ROOSEVELT

NEW YORK, Monday.

President Roosevelt made this reference to Eire in his speech last night:

"Analyse for yourselves the future of two other places even nearer to Germany.

"If the Nazis won could Ireland hold out? Would Irish freedom be permitted as an amazing pet exception in an unfree world?

"Or the Azore Islands?

"We think of Hawaii as an outpost of defence in the Pacific. Yet the Azores are closer to our shores than Hawaii."—Reuter.

Full report of speech—PAGE TWO.

"Not an Easy War"

ZURICH, Monday.

Signor Ansaldo, editor of Ciano's newspaper, the Telegrafo, in his latest Italian broadcast attacked people who thought the war would be an easy business, not realising the British Empire is "an old crocodile with a hard skin."—Reuter.

Swiss Saving Fuel

BERNE, Monday.

From January 2 railway station buffets and restaurants in Switzerland must not serve hot dishes after 9 p.m and must close at 11 p.m. "The object is to save fuel."—Reuter.

The ruined interior of St. Bride's Church, Fleet-street, to-day.

They Went to Work as Usual

AND THE CITY CARRIED ON

Evening Standard Reporter

City firemen were rolling up their hoses to-day. Scavengers were cleaning down the streets.

But the most heartening thing I saw during a tour of the City was the number of fire appliances back in their stations, spick and span, ready to tackle any new outbreak.

FIRE WATCHERS FOR ALL

Evening Standard Reporter

As a result of last night's fire raid on London, it is expected that small firms, and groups of firms occupying the same building, will be compelled to provide a fire watcher.

An important announcement on the subject will be made within 24 hours, I understand, by the Ministry of Home Security.

At present only firms employing 30 or more workers are compelled to provide fire-spotters.

Hundreds of fires which developed in last night's raid on the City could have been put out at the start if fire-watchers had been there to deal with them promptly.

Some ruling is expected, also, in regard to empty houses. Like empty offices, empty houses are a menace to London.

The City is very scarred. Some streets were impassable when I started my tour. But by mid-day many had been reopened again. The City was carrying on.

When workers arrived at London stations to-day they found they had to walk to the City. They did so cheerfully. Many of them were late. But they got there through streets lined with fire-hoses, past smouldering buildings and choking smoke.

I saw a number of young women, City clerks, stockbrokers, dodging the spray from hoses which were still operating.

STAFFS WAITING

Some banks were unable to open at the usual time because of fires near them. But their staffs were at the doors waiting to get busy.

It is remarkable how St. Paul's escaped. Crowds stood round the Cathedral to-day while others made their way past by climbing over heaps of masonry showered down into the churchyard by a high explosive bomb on a neighbouring building.

The grounds of the Cathedral were being used as a thoroughfare for pedestrians.

One fireman who had been on duty all night was standing, almost exhausted, against a heap of masonry playing his hose into a building. I asked him how long he

(Continued on Back Page, Col. Five)

DECEMBER

29 Sunday

The beginning of what became known as the 'Second Great Fire of London'. Sunday nights were often chosen for major raids and it has been suggested that it was because Civil Defences might be at a more relaxed and less alert level. Whatever the reason, the Civil Defence workers had their work cut out this night. Between 6.00 p.m. and 9.30 p.m. the *Luftwaffe*, attacking a favoured target of government offices and the City, dropped 127 tons of HE and more than 10,000 incendiary bombs, starting a series of massive fires which threatened to turn the City into one huge conflagration. Using 2300 pumps on a night when the river was at its lowest, 20,000 fire-fighters assisted by countless soldiers and civilians fought until dawn to control the blazing City.

30 Monday

As City workers turned up to their offices on the Monday they were met by scenes of devastation and among them the exhausted fire-fighters battling on to dampen down the smouldering fires. Fortunately bad weather suspended German bombing operations that night.

137. 'The War's Greatest Picture' – St Paul's stands unharmed in the midst of the burning City.

138. Fire-fighters battle to prevent the spread of the fire beneath St Paul's.

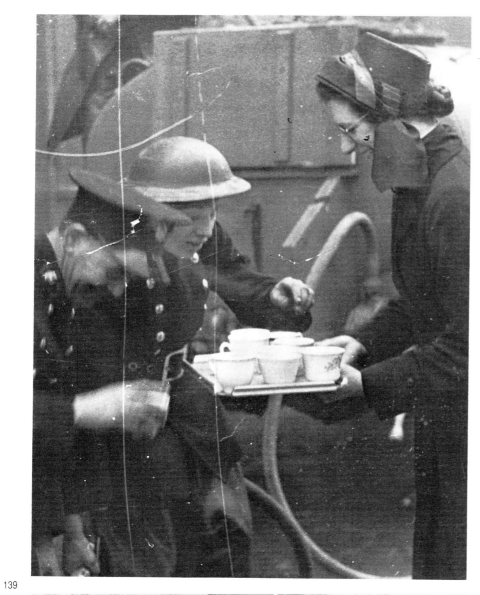

139

140

141

142

DECEMBER
31 Tuesday

Continuing severe weather again suspended all German attacks. However there was little time for New Year celebrations for Civil Defence workers in the City who got on with the major task of cleaning up.

139. A Salvation Army girl giving a welcome cup of tea to the fire-fighters.

140. A lone fireman among piles of debris damping down the embers of a fire.

141. Filling petrol cans for the water pumps.

142. Fire-fighters at work.

143 and 144. In Cannon Street workers walk to work past burnt out buildings and the fire tenders.

Broken Cup Football Rules may become permanent

Evening Standard Football Reporter

League football regulations have had to be stretched, some actually broken, to make professional football possible to-day. It is not improbable that certain broken rules will become peace-time permanencies.

When the game gets back to normal gaps will be repaired, and the whole machinery of the League overhauled and tightened up again. There is no reason why, if they have been beneficial, some of the war-time expedients cannot be adopted.

Official Soccer Spectacles

Bill Bowes, Yorkshire and England cricketer, has gained a Soccer distinction. He is the first wearer of spectacles to be registered by the Football Association as a referee since they recently changed their laws to allow men wearing glasses to take charge of matches.

Bowes passed the referees' examination with high marks.

Services Rugby Men With No One to Play

Scattered Services men still seem to be without the Rugby football they want to play in their brief leisure.

One Fleet Air Arm unit has the nucleus of a first-class team, but has no team against whom to play and no one to organise matches for them.

Players available include J. G. S Forrest, the Scotland and Cambridge three-quarter, E. H. Walshe, Irish Trials and Bedford centre, P. Sherrard, Cambridge stand-off half, J. R. E Evans, Harlequins stand-off half, N. Lester, Old Merchant Taylors forward, and H. G. Jones, Welsh Trials and Llanelly forward.

Ice Hockey Results

TORONTO, Saturday.

Canadian ice hockey matches played last night resulted :

Ontario Hockey Association.—Niagara Falls 6, Port Colbourne 0; Hamilton 2, Toronto Malboros 4; St. Catherine's 8, Oshawa G-men 2.

Big Five Junior League.—Oshawa Generals 9, Toronto Young Ranters 3.

Quebec Senior League.—Cornwall 6, Canadiens 3; Verdun 6, Concordia 3.

Cape Breton League.—Sydney 3, North Sydney 0.—Reuter.

Draw for London Senior Cup

Draw for the second round of the London Senior Cup competition, to be played on or before Saturday, February 15 (3.15), is:

Leyton v Tufnell Park.
Erith and Belvedere v. Wimbledon.
Finchley v Fords Sports.
Sutton United v Lyons Club.
Walthamstow Avenue (holders) v Briggs Sports.
Catford Wanderers v. Pinner.
Wealdstone v Metropolitan Police.
Barnet v Golders Green.

In Cup-tie football clubs in Scotland, as well as in England and Wales, agree that it is a good thing to minimise, as far as possible, the loss suffered by the many clubs whose interest goes with first-round defeat.

TWO GATES

As an experiment last year the Football League War Cup called for home and away games in the first three rounds Teams which did not survive the first round at least had a share in two " gates,"; those who were knocked out in the second round had a share in four.

The more conservative Scots played home and away games in only their first round; but they had a full programme of League matches.

The Cup competition begun this afternoon by the London clubs, against the pleasure of the Football League, takes the home and away principle further. Two groups, each of six clubs, are playing an American tournament, involving ten home and away matches for each club, to qualify two for the semi-finals.

FIRST ROUND ONLY

In other divisional cup competitions conditions are for home and away matches in the first round—there is only limited time to complete all matches. The League, however, are to carry the idea, if time permits, to include all rounds except the final

The system has satisfied the clubs. It remains to be seen whether the Football Association have been sufficiently impressed by this war-time method to make one of their rare alterations in F.A. Cup conditions.

Scotland Loses a Football Leader

Mr. W. C. P. Brown, who was associated with Heart of Midlothian F.C. for more than 40 years, has died at his home in Edinburgh. He was one of Scotland's leading football personalities, was twice chairman of the Hearts Club and was also a member of the Scottish F.A.

He took a leading part in the reconstruction of the Hearts ground at Tynecastle Park, and presented the club with a gymnasium.

Mr. Brown, who was one of Edinburgh's J.P.s, was one of the founders of the Ingliston Golf Club.

Arsenal Cup Man

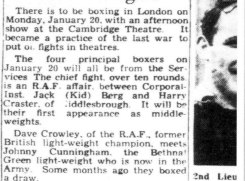

LESLIE JONES not one of Arsenal's regular Regional League team, returned for to-day's Cup-tie at Reading.

More Open Races for Leading Dogs

By R. S. Eckersley

There are indications of a considerable increase in the number of open races on greyhound tracks.

Many of these will be run in conjunction with the effort to raise money for war purposes, but a racing angle is that they will also provide many more events for top-class greyhounds than were possible last year.

Apparently the majority of the open races will be one event in a card, leaving seven other races at each meeting for the usual track dogs.

West Ham, for instance, announce a series of open stakes for the Red Cross during January and February, but these will be single races on specified dates.

Other promoters are likely to follow the same lines.

NEXT WEEK'S POOLS

All the return first round matches of the London Cup and other divisional cup competitions are included in the matches for next week's Unity Pool coupon. Matches marked with an asterisk (*) are included in the restricted list of 29 for Pool 4 (Four Aways). Penny Points Pool matches are marked "P." Twelve Results matches "R" and Easy Six matches "E."

Figures in parentheses in the Cupties are results of previous meetings this season in competition or friendly matches, the "h" indicating the home club. In the other matches the figures are results of meetings last season in Regional League matches, Cup-ties or friendlies. Where teams met more than once on the same ground the most recent result is given.

LONDON CUP—FIRST ROUND
Section A
Chelsea (h.6) v. Aldershot (0).
Crystal Palace (—) v. Brentford (—).
Q.P. Rangers (h.2) v. Fulham (5).
Section B
Arsenal (—) v. Reading (—).
Clapton Orient (6) v. Tottenham (h.7).
West Ham (h.5) v. Millwall (2).
MIDLANDS CUP—FIRST ROUND
Northampton (h 6) v. Mansfield (1) *
Notts Forest (3) v. Lincoln C. (h.2) * P.R.E

Stoke City (h.5) v. Leicester C. (3) *
Walsall (—) v. Luton Town (—) *
W. Bromwich (h.2) v. Notts C. (3) *
Bury (—) v. Blackpool (—) *
Everton (1) v. Liverpool (h.5) * P.R.
Man. Utd. (h.9) v. Blackburn (0) *
N. Brighton (h.6) v. Wrexham (2) *
Oldham Ath. (—) v. Bolton W. (—) * P.R.E
Rochdale (—) v. Manchester C. (—) *
Southport (—) v. Chester (—) * P.R.
YORKSHIRE CUP—FIRST ROUND
Bradford (0) v. York City (h.0) *
Huddersfield (h.1) v. Halifax (1) * P.
Leeds Utd. (h.1) v. Chesterfield (2) * P.R.E
Middlesbro (2) v. Bradford Cy (h.3) *
SOUTH REGIONAL LEAGUE
Bristol City (5) v. Cardiff City (2) *
NORTH REGIONAL LEAGUE
Crewe A (—) v. Preston N.E. (—) * P.R.
Doncaster (h.1) v. Sheffield W. (2) *
Grimsby (—) v. Newcastle (—) *
Rotherham (—) v. Barnsley (4) ... * P.R.
SCOTTISH LEAGUE
Albion Rovers (3) v. Morton (1) ... * P.R.
Celtic (4) v. Airdrie (2) ....
Dumbarton (1) v. Clyde (2) ..... * P.R.E
Hamilton (h.1) v. Rangers (0) .... * P.R.E
Hearts (—) v. Queen's Park (—) ....
Partick T. (—) v. Hibernian (—) * P.R.E
St. Mirren (—) v. Falkirk (—) .... P.R.
Third Lanark (1) v. Motherwell (1) * P

Unity Pool coupon, together with the full Form Guide, Olympian's Forecast and summary of experts' votes will be published in Tuesday's Special Edition of the Evening Standard.

Sidi Barrani the Racehorse

By J. H. Park

Lord Milford, racehorse owner, who is now breeding his own horses, has named a foal Sidi Barrani, after the Italian base captured by the British Army of the Nile.

Sidi Barrani is one of six filly foals. Another has been named Roman Justice and a third Brazen Molly.

Brazen Molly is a grand-daughter of Pretty Polly, one of the most famous mares in Turf history.

J. Jarvis, Newmarket trainer, bought Flamingo for Lord Milford as one of his first yearlings.

Flamingo went on to win among other races, the 1928 2000 Guineas He sired Flyon, Lord Milford's Ascot Gold Cup winner of 1939.

Theatre Boxing Matinees Again

There is to be boxing in London on Monday, January 20, with an afternoon show at the Cambridge Theatre. It became a practice of the last war to put on fights in theatres.

The four principal boxers on January 20 will all be from the Services The chief fight, over ten rounds, is an R.A.F. affair, between Corporal-Inst. Jack (Kid) Berg and Harry Craster, of Middlesbrough. It will be their first appearance as middleweights.

Dave Crowley, of the R.A.F., former British light-weight champion, meets Johnny Cunningham, the Bethnal Green light-weight who is now in the Army. Some months ago they boxed a draw.

Midland Cup Clubs Get More Time

The Midlands Cup committee have decided to make available three days for the completion of the first round of their tournament. These are to-day, January 11 and January 18

The second round will be played on January 25, and the final on a date to be arranged later.

It is possible that the final will take place either on Good Friday or Easter Monday.

SPORT SHORTS

Canadian in Line for World Fight

Dave Castilloux, **Canadian** lightweight **champion**, outpointed the Italian, Aldo Spoldi, in a ten rounds contest at Madison Square Garden, New York, last night, and probably earned himself a contest with the world champion, Lew Jenkins.—Reuter.

Only activities on the Old Rutlishian Rugby ground to-morrow will be women's matches, at **hockey and basket-ball**, against teams of Wrens Services Rugby men and others are however, invited to tea and dance

A B W Buchanan, the Scottish Trials and London Scottish Rugby forward, is **engaged** to Miss K. N Stiles, of Woking

R A Gerrard, the England Somerset and Bath **Rugby player**, who was a junior officer in the Territorials when war broke out, is now a major

Easter **cricket** classes for boys are to be held as usual at Lord's during the weeks April 7 to 12, April 14 to 19, and April 21 to 26. Applications should be made to the secretary of the M.C.C. at Lord's

Scottish Rugby is to have a second **inter-city match** this season. Edinburgh will visit Glasgow on March 8 Edinburgh won the first game.

1941
JAN

1 Wednesday

New Year's Day and the clear-up and inspection of damage continued. At night there was more poor weather but the *Luftwaffe* managed to mount some minor raids against the capital.

2 Thursday

Much clearer weather and Cardiff was the target for a major attack. London had a quiet night.

3 Friday

Some minor incidents in London on a bitterly cold night in which Civil Defence workers in Bristol had to contend with another major attack.

4 Saturday

A similar pattern to Thursday the 3rd, with Bristol receiving the now customary 'follow-up' raid and only a few bombs falling on London.

145. Refreshments for the fireman.

The Lord Mayor toured the City on New Year's Day to view the damage:
146. Amidst the rubble of the Aldermanbury.
147. In the ruined Guildhall.

148

149

150

JANUARY

5 Sunday

London had its heaviest raid since the 'Great Fire' of 29th December but on nowhere near the same scale – 28 people died and 124 were seriously injured.

6 Monday
7 Tuesday
8 Wednesday

There was some light activity during the day on all three days to take advantage of the only possible flying time during very poor weather but little damage was caused. Night-time operations by the *Luftwaffe* were ruled out by bad weather over both Britain and the Continent.

9 Thursday

Manchester was the principal German target but London also suffered a fairly heavy raid. Although the damage was not severe, it made more work for the squads of soldiers and civilians still clearing up from the 'Great Fire' eleven days before.

148. Blasting unsafe buildings in Newgate Street in the clear-up of the City.

149. Clearing debris around Tower Hill with the Tower of London in the background.

150. Salvaging papers from a ruined City office.

151. The Banqueting Hall of the Guildhall after the 'Great Fire'.

152. The Duke of Kent tours the City with the Lord Mayor of London on 6th January.

153. Carrying their books and ledgers office workers make enquiries as to the whereabouts of their new offices.

153

MAIN NAZI AIM—LONDON & THAMES

Three-hour Attack: Village Children Machine-gunned

London and Thames Estuary towns were the main targets for German bombers during the night.

The Air Ministry and Ministry of Home Security 7.30 a.m. communiqué to-day said:

"In an attack which began soon after dark last night and lasted for about three and a half hours, bombs were dropped in London and several places near the Thames Estuary.

"Many incendiary bombs were dropped and some damage was done by fire, but the fire brigade and other civil defence services very quickly had the situation in hand.

"Some people were killed and others injured, but reports so far received indicate that the casualties were not heavy.

"A few bombs were also dropped at isolated points in some other areas, but little damage and few casualties have been reported, though the casualties include a small number of people killed at a place in South-west England."

Up the Estuary

Those civilian fire watchers who were on duty in London defeated another attempt by the Germans to start hundreds of fires. They put out many incendiary and oil bombs.

Soon after the Alert the raiders flew in from several directions, principally through the Thames Estuary.

Anti-aircraft guns and fighters beat many off their targets, and the raid turned into an indiscriminate attack on houses and business premises.

Aided to some extent by low clouds some airplanes broke through the barrage and glided into the London area, dropping their bombs in groups and then scattering for home. Many bombs fell on marshland.

The Thames Estuary had the severest attack, but though many fires were started they were all under control within an hour. They gave no guidance in the high-explosive attack that followed.

Apart from London and the Thames Estuary several country districts were bombed. Two Welsh villages were machine-gunned, but there were no casualties. In one children had to run for their lives.

In London damage was mainly confined to houses.

Four men were killed and others injured in a large hostel for working-men when a heavy bomb fell at the back of the building.

Among the injured were members of the Pioneer Corps, who were billeted in the top floors.

The blast blew down houses in the street and people were trapped. Pioneers helped A.R.P. rescued squads to dig for them in the debris.

Five women and three children, taking refuge under tables and beds, were pinned by wreckage, but were dug out.

Private George Nogell was killed and three others injured, one critically, by a bomb in another district. They were passengers in a coach which was wrecked by blast.

A passer-by, a trolleybus driver, believed to be named Wicks, was also killed.

In another district a high-explosive fell near a trolleybus, which overturned. In this and other areas people were trapped in their wrecked homes.

Showers of fire bombs fell on one Thames Estuary town. They were quickly followed b. high explosives, one of which fell in the grounds of a hospital.

A ward was demolished. There were no casualties in the hospital, but a number of people were killed and injured in houses in the district.

Houses wrecked and casualties were reported from several other Estuary towns. In one a fire burned out in a laundry.

A number of towns in the West Country were also bombed. Incendiaries, an oil bomb and high explosives were dropped on one country town. People were killed and injured.

Bomb Through Ventilator Killed Nine

Mr. and Mrs. A. Wilkins owned a business in a London suburb, and in the basement of their shop was a public raid shelter.

They were the shelter marshals.

Mr. Wilkins helped mothers to put their babies to bed in the shelters and Mrs. Wilkins served coffee free every night.

They were both killed last night when a bomb hit the sandbag barricade and fell through a ventilator only 3ft. square into the basement.

Mrs. V. Carson and her two little girls, and Mrs. L. Townley and her three children died with them.

An A.R.P. worker said to-day: "The bomb fell fairly earl in the evening. Had it dropped later, more people would have been in the shelter and the death roll would have been heavier."

Buried, but Escaped

While Fireman Kemp was on duty in an East Anglian town last night his home was demolished by a bomb. His wife and two young children, sitting around the fire downstairs, were buried in the wreckage, but were released, suffering only from shock and bruises.

While Home Guards were putting out fire bombs in a Thames Estuary town last night, a high-explosive wrecked their post.

Bombed in London Shelter on Return From Country

All hope was abandoned to-day for people buried in a shelter under a block of offices in London which were hit by a high-explosive bomb on Saturday night.

Nine were rescued yesterday, but the majority, including sales-managers of the firm and people from a neighbouring block of tenements, were trapped under piles of concrete. The tenements were undamaged.

Among the people trapped were a young wife and her baby who, some months ago, were evacuated to the country. Last week her husband wrote: "You and baby can come home now. I have found a safe shelter."

On Saturday night he took them there for the first time.

One man employed by the firm has spent every night at the shelter since the heavy London raids began. On Saturday night he went to visit his mother in the East End. To-day he was one of the rescue workers.

After many hours' work the body of a man was recovered from inside a trap-door. His wife and two daughters were rescued yesterday. He lost his only son, his brother and brother-in-law in recent raids.

One of the firm's employees trapped in the shelter had two sons at Dunkirk. One was killed and the other was taken prisoner. His wife died a few weeks ago.

More Victims in Subway Brought Up

More bodies were brought out to-day from the ruins of the London subway which was hit in Saturday night's raid. The search for people is still going on amid tons of masonry.

A Royal Engineer penetrated the ruins by way of the emergency shaft to-day. The Engineers, Pioneers and demolition squads were at work early.

Thousands of Londoners during the rush hour saw the huge crater. Nothing recognisable remains of the subway apart from the general outline. Within was a tangle of boulders, slabs of roadway and wrecked steelwork.

Four 40ft. cranes were placed around the edge to-day, swinging tons of debris into lorries.

Oxy-acetylene burners were sent for to cut through a tangle of steel girders.

New York Wants to Move Chinatown

Evening Standard Correspondent
NEW YORK, Monday.

New York's famous Chinatown may be moved from Mott and Pell streets and rebuilt elsewhere.

The New York housing authority want to eliminate the firetraps which constitute old Chinatown, and establish a modern one on the lines of new housing developments.

Most Chinatown residents are opposed to moving on sentimental and business grounds. They say that tourists would not go elsewhere.

The Chinese Vice-Consul, Mr. N. S. Cheng, however, believes that a new Chinatown, including a modern Chinese theatre, would draw far more tourists than the old.

Canadian Athlete Killed in Air Crash

WINNIPEG, Monday.

R. S. Dixon, one of Canada's leading athletes, has been killed in an air crash.

Dixon, who was an officer in the Royal Canadian Air Force, won the Javelin Throw at the British Empire Games in London in 1934.—Reuter.

17 Trapped Shouted "Save the Others"

Seventeen women and children who were trapped in the basement of a London house damaged by a bomb last night shouted to wardens who went to their resue: "We're all right. Look after everybody else." Then they started singing "Tipperary" and shouting to the people in the road "Are we downhearted? No."

The wardens went to other houses to help trapped people. They found the body of a fire spotter named Hassett lying outside his home.

His own home had been demolished and rescue squads last night recovered the bodies of his daughter and her fiance, a private in the Pioneer Corps.

Wardens were to-day still searching for his wife and other daughter.

The bodies of a father, son and wife named Francis were recovered to-day.

"When we had summed up the situation generally, we returned to where the women and children were in the basement," the district warden, Mr. Arnold, told the Evening Standard.

"We got them out one by one. Most of them were unhurt. I have never seen such a display of courage."

They Were Killed Reading the Bible

Two London Salvation Army women, Adjutant Edna Mortimer, 32, and Lieutenant Gertrude Cocksedge, 24, went out every night during air raids selling The War Cry, and serving tea to A.R.P. workers.

Last night, after being out as usual, they returned to their local headquarters because of the severity of the raid.

They were sitting alone by the fire reading the Bible when a bomb fell on the house and both were killed.

Six Gipsies in Shelter Killed

Several heavy bombs fell during the night in a gipsy encampment in the south-east of England.

One came down at the entrance of a brick and concrete shelter recently built and blew the shelter to bits. Six people inside were killed.

"We do not know really how many people there were in the shelter," a man said to-day. "Few of the gipsies in the encampment know each other, and, as they are always on the move, it is difficult to keep check on them."

U.S.A. Liner Aground

WEST PALM BEACH (Florida), Monday.

The United States liner Manhattan, bound for San Francisco with 200 passengers and a crew of 500, has gone aground nine miles north of Lake Worth inlet, Florida.

Apparently she is in no immediate danger.—British United Press.

His Glorious Week

A man accused at Leeds to-day of stealing £45, said: "Yes, I admit I got it. I spent it on whisky. I have had one glorious week."

Mr. Horace Marshall (stipendiary magistrate).—"Impossible. He would be dead."

A detective explained that others helped to drink the whisky.

Cakes from Petain

Hundreds of France's traditional Epiphany "galettes des rois" (flat pastry cakes) were distributed to poor children in various towns of unoccupied France yesterday.

They were given by Marshal Petain.—Reuter.

R.A.F. STRIKE FROM SICILY TO NORWAY

(Continued from PAGE ONE)

announced. It follows the R.A.F. daylight bombing raid on Friday and was the fourth day in succession that the R.A.F. have struck in daylight.

Brest Once Again

Then this afternoon the Air Ministry announced: "Targets in France, Germany and Italy were the objectives of the R.A.F. last night.

"The docks at Brest were attacked with incendiary bombs and high-explosives.

"A number of heavy bombs burst along the water front, and fires broke out. A warehouse was set ablaze and a larger fire started in the Port Militaire.

"Le Havre and L'Orient were also attacked, and high-explosive bombs were seen to burst in the docks at both these enemy-occupied harbours.

"Airfields including those at Varnes, Chartres, Evreux and Morlaix were raided and good results were observed.

"At Varnes and Chartres airfield buildings were set alight and at Evreux a number of hostile aircraft on the ground were fired.

"From these operations over France none of our aircraft is missing.

"A further communiqué on operations over Germany and Italy is being issued."

Damage Admitted

The Italians, however, have already admitted the raids on Italy. The Rome communiqué to-day said that the R.A.F. bombed Tunis, Venice and Catalania (Sicily).

"Damage was caused and there were casualties at Turin and Venice," it was admitted.

The Royal Arsenal and the Fiat Works are at Turin, which was bombed by the R.A.F. on Saturday night.

Giving details of the Hurricanes' daylight attack yesterday, the Air Ministry news service said that the R.A.F. fighters swept low over the Belgian and French coasts.

The first patrol was led by a squadron-leader with the D.S.O. and D.F.C., who came down to sea level and twice attacked an E-boat 800 yards off shore. Hurricanes swept the decks with bullets and then attacked a drifter.

Me. 109's Engaged

Another patrol attacked a second E-boat from astern from sea level. The boat made for shore. The patrol continued across the coast and machine-gunned troops in beach trenches. Two other small ships were machine-gunned.

The third patrol attacked a large two-masted schooner and a number of small ships. Heavy and accurate anti-aircraft fire was encountered and Me. 109s sent up to intercept were engaged.

Two of our pilots are missing.

One pilot thought he had been hit, for he looked into his mirror and saw what seemed to be damage to his elevator tip. When he landed he found that a bird was entangled in his aerial.

The German news agency said to-day that the R.A.F. attempted to penetrate into the coastal region of Northern France yesterday.

It was stated that British bomber aircraft undertook a raid on the Mole of Zeebrugge yesterday for the second day in succession.

Sunshine In Straits

Brilliant sunshine returned to the Straits of Dover to-day. The sky was clear and the sea was smooth. An icy north-easterly wind was blowing.

EVENING STANDARD & ST. JAMES'S GAZETTE (with which is incorporated THE STANDARD).—Printed and Published by the EVENING STANDARD CO., LTD., 47, Shoe-lane, London, E.C.4.—MONDAY, JANUARY 13, 1941.

STOP PRESS NEWS

Telephone Number: Central 3000
See also PAGE ELEVEN

BIG R.A.F. RAIDS

(See Back Page)

During raid on Lorient, R.A.F. battered dry and wet docks with heavy bombs, says Air Ministry News Service. One pilot saw salvo explode in crimson sheet of flame among buildings on river bank.

At end of attack, store-houses and other buildings near Port Militaire and power station were burning fiercely.

At Brest, heavy bomb burst near power station. Big fires were seen in the docks.

While on patrol along coast or Norway another aircraft of Coastal Command bombed supply ship, hitting stern, then silenced its deck gun with machine-gun fire. Ship was left shrouded in smoke.

Blenheims of Coastal Command, also off Norway, attacked and hit a second large German supply ship.

British Talks With Turkey Beginning

British sources in Ankara say the military talks between Britain and Turkey were being opened to-day. Important effect was possible on war developments in Mediterranean, Middle East and Europe.

R.A.F. BOMB OIL REFINERIES

(See Page One)

Officially stated aircraft of Bomber Command were over Germany, Belgium and Italy last night, making oil targets their main objectives.

Small force was sent to Regensburg (Germany) and another to Porto Marghera, near Venice; both towns have important oil refineries. At Regensburg several fires were caused and at Ostend large explosion followed by fire was observed.

At Porto Marghera target was set on fire by incendiaries dropped by first of attacking aircraft. Hour later, when last arrived, whole target was still alight.

Anti-aircraft defences were first silenced by machine-gun fire from few hundred feet. Then heavy bomb was released from a very low level and blew up one of the large refinery buildings.

More bombs set oil storage tanks on fire. Second large building nearby hit by two bombs and seen to collapse and fall in pieces.

Sheds nd workshops were machine-gunned rom almost ground level. Targets left blazing. From these operations one of our aircraft is missing.

C.-in-C. RESIGNS

(See Page One)

The official Italian news agency said Soddu's ill-health would "force him to pass several months in treatment and rest."

FIREWATCHER ACCUSED OF ARSON

George Edward Young, aged 20, Westbury-lane, Bristol, remanded in custody at Bristol to-day accused of setting fire to B.B.C. offices at Bristol. Stated that Young was engaged as fire watcher at premises.

OFFICE TEA TO GO ON

The Ministry of Food have extended for a further period arrangements which enable groups of industrial, business and clerical workers to obtain

JANUARY

10 Friday

A quiet night in London while Portsmouth received a major attack.

11 Saturday

A major attack on London. Between 6.30 and 9.30 p.m., 144 tons of HE and nearly 600 incendiary bombs were dropped. There was a significant amount of damage but the worst incident was at Bank Tube Station where the booking hall received a direct hit. More than 110 shelterers and travellers were killed.

12 Sunday

A 'follow-up raid' on London. It had become part of the *Luftwaffe* strategy to follow a major raid one night with another within the next 48 hours. This was an attempt to cause maximum disruption and deal a blow to morale, for the already stretched Civil Defence workers would see their day's clearing up undermined.

13 Monday

A quiet night in London.

154. Looking across the City from St Paul's at the gutted buildings.

Evening Standard

Amusements 8
Radio 8

BLACK-OUT 5.50 pm to 8.30 am.
MOON rises 9.32 pm, sets 10.42 am.

No. 36,307   LONDON, THURSDAY, JANUARY 16, 1941   ONE PENNY

R.A.F. LEAVE HUGE FIRES IN GERMAN NAVY BASE

Wilhelmshaven Once Again

"THE NAVAL BASE AT WILHELMS-HAVEN WAS THE MAIN OBJECTIVE IN LAST NIGHT'S OPERATIONS BY THE BOMBER COMMAND," THE AIR MINISTRY ANNOUNCED THIS AFTERNOON.

"The attacks, which continued throughout the night, caused extensive fires in the target areas.

"The docks at Emden, Bremerhaven, Rotterdam, and Flushing were also bombed, as well as airfields and other targets in North-West Germany and Holland.

"The harbour at Brest was

again attacked by a force of Coastal Command aircraft.

"From all these operations, one of our airplanes is missing."

The Italian communique to-day admitted that last night British airplanes bombed Catania. Material damage was small, it was said, but there were some dead and wounded.

Catania is the base for the German Stuka dive-bombers that attacked the Fleet in the Mediterranean last Friday.

Out of Action

Wilhelmshaven, the Heligoland Bay base, was having its fortieth raid of the war last night.

In this, the third raid in a week, targets of vital military and naval importance were subjected to the "heaviest attack ever."

It is believed that the base was so severely hammered that it will be a considerable time before it will be able to resume its normal work.

The German news agency said to-day: "The R.A.F. attempted an attack on a north German port, despite the mass A.A barrage.

"According to news so far received, no military damage was done."

Airplane With Ten "Down in Atlantic"

An Italian transatlantic airplane bound for Europe from Brazil with ten passengers on board, is believed to have been forced down in the Atlantic.

Herr Alexander Safarowsky, of the German Foreign Office, is one of the passengers.

The airplane informed the airfield on Fernando Noronha, the island off the Brazilian coast, yesterday morning that she was returning there because one of her engines had failed.

So far, however, she has not appeared, though the airfield was kept lighted all night.—British United Press

First-Class Dog

A black Labrador dog is awaiting a claimant at Alton police station. It has no collar and was found at Alton station in a first-class compartment of a train from Waterloo.

NIGHT FIGHTERS GOT 2 NAZI RAIDERS

Moonlit Dogfights Over London

R.A.F. night fighters destroyed two German bombers raiding Britain last night, it was announced to-day.

BOTH CRASHED ON THE OUTSKIRTS OF LONDON IN BRIGHT MOONLIGHT.

One, a Dornier 17, was chased. There was a rattle of machine-gun fire and the raider burst into flames.

IT SCREAMED OVER THE ROOFS AND FELL IN A WOOD. THERE ITS BOMBS EXPLODED.

A warden found two of the crew burned to death.

The raider was followed down by night fighters, who circled over it for some time.

The other enemy bomber, after being attacked by fighters, exploded in the air, wreckage falling over a wide area.

Three in Five Nights

Only five days ago it was officially disclosed that our patrols destroyed one of the two Portsmouth raiders that were shot down.

In the moonlit sky over London last night the fighters swept up to harry bombers trying another fire-raising attack which started much later than previous similar raids.

Anti-aircraft guns ceased fire the rattle of machine-guns could be heard as the airplanes zoomed and dived in battle.

The fighting did not last long.

Midlands, Too

The Air Ministry and Ministry of Home Security communiqué at 7.50 a.m. to-day said:

"During last night enemy aircraft crossed the East Coast and dropped bombs, mainly high explosive, on several coast towns and in the Midlands.

"Bombs were also dropped in the London area, including a consider-
(Continued on Back Page, Col. Four)

Trains to Stop For Three Days

All passenger train traffic in Hungary is to be suspended from midnight, with the exception of international and workmen's trains, it is officially announced in Budapest, according to a message to the Stefani news agency quoted by Reuter.

The suspension will probably last three days.

This decision, the announcement says, is taken by the management of the Hungarian railways because of the bad weather and interruption of communications in neighbouring countries.

Uniform for P.O. Girl Messengers

Post Office girl messengers are to be given a uniform similar to that supplied in 1915.

It will consist of a coat, skirt, felt hat, sou'wester, waterproof cape, shoes and gaiters.

The only differences in the outfit, compared with those of 1915, is that shoes will be supplied instead of boots, coat shoulder straps will be dispensed with, and the piping on the cuffs and pockets will be modified.

Hundred

Mrs. Eliza Maishman, of Roxborough-road, Harrow celebrated her 100th birthday to-day.

Nazi Airman Surrenders To a Woman

Mrs. Hopkins, living in a cottage on the outskirts of London, heard banging on the door during the night.

Someone was crying "German, German."

Mrs. Hopkins opened the door—and there leaned a wounded German airman of 22, the ribbon of the Iron Cross on his breast. He could speak no English

She took him in, placed him on a couch, and called the police who took him to hospital.

The German had baled out from an airplane which one of our night fighters destroyed. His parachute has not been found.

John Mills Married To-day

Second-lieutenant John Mills, R.E.—the John Mills of stage and screen fame—was married to-day to Miss Hayley Belle at Caxton Hall register office.

MANY TRAPPED IN HOSTEL DEBRIS

More than 200 men, including Pioneers, were to-day working in the hope of extricating survivors in the wreckage of a men's hostel in London, demolished last night by a heavy bomb.

The Minister of Transport, Colonel J. T. C. Moore-Brabazon, visited the scene in daylight.

There were a number of casualties, but many people were rescued, though gravely injured.

The hostel was full to capacity when the bomb fell.

The rescue squads heard some of the trapped men tapping for help.

Drills were used to bore passages through to them. Headlamps of motorcars were played on the debris during the night to help the rescuers.

A tunnel was cut through the debris and a mirror, placed at the entrance to it, reflected the light around the tunnelling rescuers.

Quickly on the spot were the young women drivers of the Mechanised Transport Corps and of the American Ambulance service.

His Cup of Tea

One of the trapped men, Tom Dowbekin, a Lancashire engineer said to-day: "I was awakened by a blinding flash and found myself lying face down on an iron girder on the second floor. Dust was choking me, I could smell gas, and I was in the middle of a tangle of electric wires, gas pipes and broken lattices.

"A heavy beam pinned down one of my legs.

"I heard movements outside and someone shouted, 'Anyone in there?' It was a rescue worker.

"I shouted back and tapped on the girder They reached me, and the first
(Continued on Back Page, Col. Three)

Nazis Shoot Belgian for Aiding Britons

News has been received in London from reliable sources that a well-known Belgian industrialist of Ghent has been shot by the Germans for aiding British fugitives, says Reuter.

Two of his friends were sentenced to deportation in Germany.

A woman well-known in Brussels society has been sentenced to two years' imprisonment for pro-British activities.

Convicts Give Pay to Spitfire Fund

Under a scheme recently introduced, some convicts at Lewes Prison are able to earn pocket money up to 1s. a week.

The men have contributed part of their earnings to the local Spitfire Fund.

"Happy" is Dead

Miss Marion Field, wardrobe mistress at Drury-lane Theatre, who was known to hundreds of stars and thousands of chorus girls as "Happy Fanny," was killed in a recent air raid on London.

She was in charge of the costume department of E.N.S.A.

War-sick Children Must Leave London

The Minister of Health, Malcolm Macdonald, has made an order applying to the Greater London evacuation areas the defence regulation, made recently, which provides for the compulsory evacuation of children in certain circumstances.

The regulation provides that local authorities may order the medical examination of any child under 14 years of age who, there is reason to suppose, "is suffering in mind or body as a result of hostile attacks, or is in such a state of health as to be likely so to suffer if he or she remains in that area."

Areas Affected

The areas to which the regulation now applies are:

City of London, Metropolitan Boroughs of Battersea, Bermondsey, Bethnal Green, Camberwell, Chelsea, Deptford, Finsbury, Fulham, Greenwich, Hackney, Hammersmith.

Hampstead, Holborn, Islington, Kensington, Lambeth, Lewisham, Paddington, Poplar, St. Marylebone, St. Pancras, Shoreditch, Southwark, Stepney, Stoke Newington, Wandsworth, Westminster and Woolwich.

County boroughs of Croydon, East Ham and West Ham.

Boroughs of Acton, Barking, Brentford and Chiswick, Chingford, Ealing, Edmonton, Erith, Hornsey, Ilford, Leyton, Mitcham, Tottenham, Walthamstow, Wanstead and Woodford, Willesden and Wood Green and urban district of Penge.

Parts of Areas

Evacuable parts of the following areas:

Boroughs of Barnes, Beckenham, Bexley, Dagenham, Dartford, Gravesend and Wimbledon, and urban districts of Crayford, Enfield, Hornchurch, Merton and Morden, Northfleet, Swanscombe, Thurrock and Waltham Holy Cross.

It is not proposed at present to apply the regulation to any other areas.

Technical Hitch

Rome radio appeared to have had great difficulty to-day in broadcasting the High Command communiqué.

Usually the communiqué is broadcast in Italian, and immediately afterwards in German, French, Spanish, Portuguese and English.

To-day, after a delay of 20 minutes, an announcer started reading the communiqué in English, but he stopped several times, and each time a voice could be heard saying in English, "That's all right. Go on. Go on."

A babel of voices in Italian was heard in the background.

The announcer, however, did not carry on in English. After a further delay, the communiqué was read in Italian.

Citrine Invited

Sir Walter Citrine, general secretary of the T.U.C., who has been touring the United States, is being asked to visit Australia says the Commonwealth Department of Information.—Reuter.

JANUARY

14 Tuesday

Severe weather conditions over Britain and the Continent prevented any night flying by the *Luftwaffe*.

15 Wednesday

Improved weather conditions brought widespread, although not severe, bombing throughout the London area.

16 Thursday

Only a few incidents of bombing were reported in the London area.

155. City workers salvaging books from their wrecked offices.

156. To overcome difficulties with telephone and telegraph communications, still not properly restored since the 'Great Fire' of 29th December, the Post Office instituted a "street telegram service". Messengers advertising their function paraded the streets ready to receive and dispatch telegrams.

157

158

JANUARY

17 Friday

As on the previous night there were only two or three reports of bombs falling in London.

18 Saturday

No bombing as *Luftwaffe* planes were grounded by bad weather.

19 Sunday

London was attacked at night by about 55 German aircraft which dropped bombs in areas adjacent to the Thames but damage was not significant. Photographs for publication were by now subject to the '28-day rule'. This meant that pictures of bomb damage to an area or building could not be published until 28 days after they were taken, but if they were struck again within the 28-day period the first set of photographs could be published. This was to prevent the Germans from linking pictures with a specific raid and so gaining knowledge about the accuracy of their bombing.

20 Monday

Bad weather prevented any bombing attacks by German aircraft.

157. Rescue workers at the scene of the direct hit on Bank Tube Station on 11th January.

158. A scene after the explosion of a time bomb on the outskirts of London.

159. Damage to the BBC caused by a bomb that fell in the first week in January.

160. *BBC Hotel was Bombed: The Union Jack still flies across the entrance to the Langham Hotel only a short distance from the BBC Headquarters in Broadcasting House – which was bombed during a recent raid. Daily Mail*, 15th January 1941. The 28-day rule meant that the paper had to use a picture from a December raid to illustrate the story of January's attack.

SILK STOCKINGS SOON BUT AT DOUBLE PRICE

"Fairly Plentiful"

Evening Standard Reporter

Silk stockings, stocks of which are now low in the shops because manufacture was forbidden in November, are expected by the trade to be fairly—but only fairly—plentiful in a few weeks.

That is because there are a few million stockings lying undyed in the warehouses of manufacturers. If they are kept there too long they may rot.

HOME GUARDS TO HAVE OWN M.O.s

An honorary medical officer may soon be attached to every Home Guard battalion in the country.

A voluntary scheme for medical inspection of volunteers has been operating at Salford, for two months.

Dr. E. Wynne-Jones, writing about it in the British Medical Journal to-day, states that the men have as full an examination as circumstances permit, but they are not told what their physical condition is.

"Instead," says Dr. Wynne-Jones, "I make a report to the C.O., and men are then placed on duties which they can easily perform.

"In this way the voluntary nature of the Home Guard is kept up, and so far as is humanly possible, no man is called on to do work of which he is incapable.

"The Director-general, Home Guard, (Lieut.-general T R. Eastwood) said that he would try to make an honorary M.O. an integral part of every Home Guard battalion in the country after he had heard and seen what we have done."

Fire-watcher, 13

John Adams, of Palmers Green N., is only 13. but he is one of the keenest volunteers in a local fire watching "squad" He has been given a "group" of about 20 houses to look after.

Professor Must Wait for His Medal

Because of the war, Professor Stodola, a Swiss of Czech birth, could not come to London to receive the James Watt International Medal—the highest award in the world of mechanical engineering.

Instead, the medal was handed over to the Swiss Minister in London, Mr Walter Thurnheer.

Professor Stodola, who is over 80, will have to content himself with a silver gilt stamping of the medal until the war ends, for war-time restrictions on the export of bullion have made it impossible for the Institution of Mechanical Engineers to send him a gold one.

Counsel Aid Poor

A woman who brought a divorce suit as a "poor person" in the Divorce Court to-day was told by Mr. Justice Hodson that the solicitors and counsel who had acted for her had earned her gratitude.

"I think it is very notable in these times when counsel and solicitors have difficulties in carrying on their own business that they are able to give assistance to poor litigants in the way they are doing," said the judge.

Accordingly the Board of Trade is taking stock to find how many there are before deciding what to do with them. Returns should be completed soon.

The Government would like to export them, particularly to the United States. Britain wants the dollars. Those which cannot be exported because there is not sufficient overseas demands will be released for the home trade.

U.S.A. Has Enough

A London hosiery manufacturer told me that the United States have probably nearly as many silk stockings as they need, because they have lost so much of their export to Europe.

"The best market now," he said, "is probably the Dominions, especially South Africa. It should leave a reasonably large surplus for home sales.

'But the stockings on sale here will be expensive. The qualities which could be bought at 6s. 11d. a pair in November are likely to cost nearer 15s.

Stopping Spending

"There is the purchase tax to allow for, and there is an expectation in the trade that the Government may put an additional tax on silk stockings to stop women from spending too much on them.

"Still, the women will buy them if they are to be had.

"Beige and other neutral colours will be almost the only tones available. There will definitely be no 'showy' colours."

There will still be artificial silk stockings. "They will go up in price too," he said. "The 4s. 11d. quality may reach 7s. 11d. or even a higher price."

Judge Tells Actress: "This Case Must Come to an End"

When Mrs. Ada Virginia Prentice, five-times married American film actress, opened the eighth day of her divorce appeal in Edinburgh to-day, Lord Aitchison (Lord Justice Clerk) told her:

"This case must come to an end. I am not going to tolerate this any longer. If you are out to waste the time of the court we will not tolerate it. I must ask you finally to proceed with the case. There is a length to our patience. Is it your purpose to spin this case out as long as you can?"

Mrs. Prentice replied: "I am sick and tired of it."

Mrs. Prentice is appealing against the decree of divorce granted Thomas Prentice, chartered accountant, of Cliveden gardens, Glasgow, on the ground of her adultery with a French language teacher, Guy Cotte.

She claimed to-day that full recognition had not been given to the evidence of witnesses called on her behalf.

More Sunday Cinemas

Beccles, Suffolk, Town Council have decided to apply for an order permitting cinemas to open there on Sundays.

He Thought Daughter Was in Bomb Debris

The father of six children urged, through his solicitor at West London police court to-day, that he stole while his mind was temporarily unbalanced by days of anxiety when he believed that his 16-year-old daughter's body lay buried in the ruins of a bombed air-raid shelter.

Sir Gervais Rentoul, the magistrate, accepted the plea

The father, John Thomas Nolan, 48, a postman, of Braybrooke road, Hammersmith, was bound over and placed on probation for twelve months on a charge of stealing a postal packet containing £2 10s.

Mr. H. Pierron, defending, said

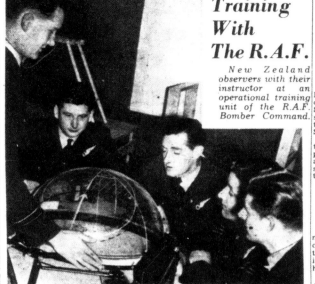

Training With The R.A.F.

New Zealand observers with their instructor at an operational training unit of the R.A.F. Bomber Command.

Big Holiday Cuts for Civil Servants

Evening Standard Reporter

Big reductions in the annual leave of Civil Servants have been made by the Government.

Under arrangements agreed by the Civil Service Clerical Association the new scheme provides that Civil Servants who normally get 28 days' annual leave will now get 21 days; those who formerly got 48 days are reduced to 24.

The new arrangements will come into effect in May.

Civil Servants of all grades will not be allowed to take more than 12 days holiday at a stretch from May to September. They will have to take the rest of their holidays in long weekends or separate days during winter

Days off will be granted in place of Bank Holidays if they are worked, provided they are not cancelled by the Government

Civil Servants will continue to get their normal rest-days

Mr W J Brown, general secretary of the Civil Service Clerical Association, told me :

"All Civil Servants realise that they have got to sacrifice some leisure They are doing so willingly It may be necessary, of course, to make even further cuts."

Norwegian Province and Town Fined

Punishments imposed by the German authorities on towns in the West of Norway indicate the opposition which the invader is meeting in these areas, states a Stockholm despatch to the A.F.I. (Independent French Agency)

The province of Vestopland, near Bergen, was recently sentenced to pay a fine of 100,000 kroner (about £5000 at pre-war rates), while a fine of 60,000 kroner (about £3000 at pre-war rates) has been imposed on Trondhjem.—Reuter.

Silver Bugle For Mayor

The Mayor of Deptford, Councillor C G Blanchard, who commands a company of the Home Guard, has been presented by a former quartermaster of the Royal Scots Fusiliers with a silver bugle carried at the battle of Loos.

PAPERS STOLEN BY AUSTRIAN

"**I**t is unfortunate that when you are enjoying the hospitality of your enemies you should be convicted of this offence, said Mr. McKenna, the magistrate, at Bowstreet to-day.

He imposed a fine of £3 on Joseph Franz Bachmann, aged 75, an Austrian consulting engineer and chemist, of St. George's-road, Southwark, S.E., for stealing a number of patent specifications from the Patent Office, Southampton Buildings, W.C.

Mr. W. S. Bourne, prosecuting, said the documents had been missed over a period of ye rs. They were irreplaceable, and their loss might have serious consequences to the public, as they were used largely in civil actions.

After Bachmann's former address had been bombed the police found documents which made it appear that he might be engaged in "certain activities." But these suspicions had proved to be groundless.

Bachmann said he took the documents while making searches for clients and fully intended to return them. His German clients were all interned or had left the country, and his business had suffered.

'Little Harry' Saved 5 Trapped People

HIS WIFE WAS KILLED

Mr. H. Harrington, of Grove-road, Walthamstow, a local rescue worker, saved the lives of five people trapped in a bombed building in Stoke Newington during a recent raid.

He was unable to save his own wife—the sixth and last person in the building. She was dead when extricated.

Mr. Harrington was off duty at the time, and worked in wreckage liable to collapse at any moment.

The Mayor of Stoke Newington (Councillor J. Newman Butler) has drawn the attention of the A.R.P. controller of Walthamstow to Mr. Harrington's heroism.

Mr. Harry Harrington, known as "Little Harry" to his colleagues, is the smallest member of his squad, being only just over five feet in height. His son of ten is evacuated to Wales.

Not Going to School

Tottenham Education Committee are to enforce school attendance among children who still remain in Tottenham, and are to take legal action against the parents who keep children from school. About 83 per cent. of the children in the district are attending school regularly.

---

that day after day Nolan haunted the bombed shelter searching for his daughter.

When it was established that she could not have been there on the night the shelter was hit. Nolan toured the London hospitals until the police found the girl living elsewhere and quite well

Since the death of his wife eight years ago Nolan had been both father and mother to his family.

He had been a postman for thirteen years, and had never been in trouble before.

Sir Gervais nodded his head in agreement when a probation officer said that he, too, believed that the worry about his daughter had affected Nolan's brain.

JANUARY

21 Tuesday
22 Wednesday
23 Thursday
24 Friday

Continuing poor weather severely limited *Luftwaffe* operations. Even though planes were scrambled none attacked the capital.

By day the clearing-up operations continued. It was an almost never-ending task in some areas which were hit time and again. In the early days of the Blitz it had become obvious that there were not enough men for the demolition squads and troops had to be called in to assist with the job of shoring up buildings, removing debris, salvaging personal belongings and building materials that could be reused, and knocking down unsafe masonry. For the soldiers engaged on such work it may have been hard labour but for many it was preferable to the boredom of being confined to barracks and the endless round of drill and training which was the lot of a high percentage of the British Army. For while the seaman and the airman at this period of the war were almost constantly on active service, the soldier, since the retreat from France at Dunkirk some eight months earlier, had few opportunities to be involved in fighting.

161. Royal Engineers pulling down dangerous City buildings after the 'Great Fire'.

162

163

Low cloud and severe wintry weather grounded *Luftwaffe* aircraft apart from a few sorties to attack coastal shipping during the day and, in one case, a minor raid on Cornwall.

162. After the 'Great Fire' the City attempted to carry on as usual. By the end of January most offices had been relocated and scenes like this one of workers collecting their wages in the street disappeared.

163. Royal Engineers laying a charge ready for demolishing a dangerous wall.

164. Manpower, in this case the Royal Engineers, was the principal tool of the demolition squad.

165

166

167

28 Tuesday
Very slight damage was caused when a few bombs were dropped during the day. Night operations were grounded by bad weather.

29 Wednesday
Another heavy attack on London at the end of the month despite continuing poor weather.

165. Fire damage at St Bride's Church caused in the 'Great Fire'.

166. During a daylight raid policemen, neighbours and passers-by quickly rushed to help save belongings from homes threatened by fire.

167. A home-made shelter. Many people did not shelter in officially approved shelters, preferring instead not to leave their homes. They built their own protection, although seldom as sophisticated as this!

168. The largest bomb crater in London, caused by the bomb which scored a direct hit on the Tube Station at Bank. The picture was not passed for publication.

CLOSING PRICES

EVENING STANDARD, January 30 1941.

FINAL NIGHT EXTRA

Evening Standard

Amusements 8
Radio 8

BLACK-OUT. 6.15 pm to 8.11 am.
MOON sets 9.28 pm., rises 10.11 am.

No. 36,319   LONDON, THURSDAY, JANUARY 30, 1941   ONE PENNY

BEVIN: 'ALL POSSIBLE WOMEN IN INDUSTRY'

Millions More Men in Training Soon

Mr. Bevin, Minister of Labour, told the House of Commons to-day that he intended to secure the co-operation of the construction departments so that in industry generally women should be employed on work suitable for them to the utmost extent, thus releasing men for work that necessitated the employment of males.

Evening Standard Reporter

Plans for the training of many hundreds of thousands more men are now being made by the Services.

They are preparing for the big speed-up in the intake of men for the Forces expected this spring, when the plan starts for building up the biggest Army, Navy and Air Force this country has ever known.

During the last war the United Kingdom mobilised nearly 5,000,000 men. It is expected that this figure will be greatly exceeded by next September, after only two years at war.

4,000,000 NOW

Mr. Churchill has told the House of Commons that, counting the Home Guard, we had a total of about 4,000,000 armed and uniformed men.

The men to be called up under the proclamation signed yesterday, together with half of the 1903 class, who are liable under the old proclamation, will probably yield another 2,000,000 men, apart from those who will be removed from the Schedule of Reserved Occupations.

During the winter the call-up of men has been deliberately slowed down so that the outdoor training camps could be cleared ready to take the recruits this year.

Many more training camps have (Continued on Back Page, Col. Five)

Channel Guns Firing To-day

German long-range guns mounted on the French coast, which were in action last night, again opened fire across the Straits of Dover shortly before daybreak to-day.

There was only a brief burst of shelling. No casualties or damage were reported.

Then in daylight the Germans resumed firing and sent over shells at irregular intervals for two hours. A single gun appeared to be in action.

Saved Her Baby as Bedroom Blazed

Mrs. C. L. Cambridge, a young London mother, rescued her two-year-old daughter after the top of her house had caught alight through an incendiary bomb last night.

"The back bedroom was alight," she said. "My little girl was sleeping in the front bedroom. I rushed upstairs, seized her, and took her next door. She was sleeping through it all."

A fire squad saved the house. Dozens of incendiaries were showered over the district, but no serious blaze occurred. One penetrated the roof of a bathroom burst waterpipes and flooded the house.

West End Night Club Raided and Closed

BAG O' NAILS WAS RESORT OF SERVICES

Evening Standard Reporter

In the early hours of to-day Scotland Yard men served an order under the Defence Regulations to close down the Bag o' Nails, Kingly-street, W., one of the best-known night clubs in London.

The order was signed by Sir Philip Game, Commissioner of the Metropolitan Police.

The club was raided late last Saturday night by Scotland Yard men who had a warrant issued under the Licensing Act. Names and addresses of 39 persons were then taken.

Ran It Eleven Years

The proprietress and manageress of the Bag o' Nails is Miss Milly Hoey.

Miss Hoey, who is Dublin born, has been for 18 years in the night club business. She has conducted the Bag o' Nails for eleven years.

The Bag o' Nails has been during this period one of the most frequented clubs in the town by officers of all arms.

Pretty girls from the Bag o' Nails have married into some of the most famous families of England. Others have found fame in films and on the stage.

Known World Over

The club was known the world over, and so was Milly Hoey, who received hundreds of letters a month from club members, including prisoners of war in Germany.

Before the war it was said: "If you blew a bugle in Milly's you would have the guests standing to attention."

NO GRAND NATIONAL

Mr. Morrison, the Home Secretary, told the House of Commons to-day that he had asked the Stewards of the National Hunt Club not to proceed with their proposal to hold a substitute Grand National at Cheltenham.

He said he had come to the conclusion that the fxture was undesirable.

This is the first time the Grand National, or a substitute race, has not been run since it was instituted 104 years ago. During the last war there were substitute races in 1916, 1917 and 1918 at Gatwick.

Showman Bostock Left £58,000

Mr. Edward Henry Bostock, of Glasgow, the showman, menagerie and theatre proprietor, who died in September, aged 81, left personal estate in Britain valued at £58,257.

Straits: Dense Fog

Dense fog blotted out the Straits of Dover to-day, allowing 50 yards' visibility. An easterly wind was blowing.

"Early in February"

Observers in Vichy, says the New York Times correspondent, expect an attack on Britain early in February.—Reuter.

London Bombs To-day: Night Fire Raid

WATCHERS BEAT INCENDIARIES

Houses in three streets were damaged and women and children were trapped in debris during one of London's four daylight Alerts to-day.

There were fatal casualties.

This followed a night fire-bomb attack which was again defeated by civilians.

There were many stories of heroism—and of tragedy. They are told in PAGE TWELVE.

A SINGLE RAIDER DROPPED THE DAYLIGHT BOMBS THAT CAUSED THE CASUALTIES.

One bomb fell in a street, another near a tram track, and a third near the gates of an industrial building.

Several passengers were in a trolleybus when one bomb fell, but although the windows in the bus were shattered and the driving cabin and sides damaged, the passengers escaped injury.

Both the second and third Alerts were caused by single raiders, but the first came when a small force of bombers approached from the East.

None reached the London area. They were turned off by anti-aircraft fire over the Thames Estuary and made their way back across the coast.

With its engines misfiring, a single raider made off towards the coast after having been subjected to a terrific

(Continued on Back Page, Col. One)

Officer's Bride

Miss Edith Ommaney was the bride of Lieutenant E. G. L. Temple, London Rifle Brigade, at Holy Trinity, Sloane-street, S.W.

War Minister to be Asked About Lipstick

Captain L. F. Plugge, (Con. Rochester and Chatham) is to ask Captain Margesson, the War Minister, "whether, in view of the assistance given by the State to the Red Cross organisation, he will state the policy with regard to the use of lipstick by women serving in that organisation."

Captain Plugge is also to ask Sir Archibald Sinclair, Air Minister, and Mr A. V. Alexander, First Lord of the Admiralty, the policy of their departments with regard to the use of lipstick by women attached to the Royal Air Force and Naval Services respectively.

Mrs. C. D Fellowes, assistant commandant of a Suffolk Red Cross hospital, resigned following criticism of her lipstick by Brig-general Sir Archibald Home, Suffolk county director of the British Red Cross.

Interned Curate Back

The Rev. K. Kurt F Schwabacher, a curate at St. Marks Church, Plumstead, S.E., who was interned some months ago, has now returned to the Parish. Part of Mr Schabacher's internment was spent in Canada. His father is a prominent industrialist at Aussig, Czechoslovakia.

Wilhelmshaven Bombed

Targets in the Heligoland Bay naval base at Wilhelmshaven were bombed by the R.A.F. last night.

This was learned officially in London this afternoon.

It was the thirty-ninth raid on Wilhelmshaven, which, before the R.A.F. started bombing it, was one of the finest naval bases in Europe.

"Groups of British airplanes penetrated into North-western Germany this morning and dropped bombs at several points," stated the official German news agency to-day. "Several people were killed and injured in a harbour town."

To-day's Italian communiqué admitted a "British air raid on certain Italian air bases."

Hitler's Speech

The speech Hitler was making late this afternoon was to be "extemporary," according to Nazi officials quoted by the Berlin correspondent of the British United Press, and was to take "60 to 80 minutes to deliver."

Dutch Submarine Lost

It was officially stated in London to-day that a Netherlands submarine engaged in Allied war operations had been lost The next of kin have been informed

This is the second submarine the Dutch forces have lost since their navy joined the British. The loss of the first was announced on December 9

'NO FIRE WATCHER AT CITY OFFICES'

Twelve Firms Summoned

Twelve City firms with offices in Stone House, Bishopsgate, hit by an incendiary bomb on the night of October 21, were summoned at the Guildhall to-day for failing to have a fire watcher on duty. They were:

Messrs. Jacobs and Partners, Ltd.

The Ougree Steel Trading Company.

Messrs. Kalis, Son and Company, Ltd

Turner, Brightman, Ltd.

R. G. Lane, Ltd.

Hogg, Robinson and Capel-Cure, Ltd

National Association of United Kingdom Oil and Seed Brokers, Ltd.

Nitrate Corporation of Chile, Ltd.

Upsons, Ltd.

A. Lewis and Co. (Westminster), Ltd.

Guy Pearce and Co., Ltd.

Westminster Bank.

Could Not Get In

An information was laid by Inspector Edward Beasley, of the City Police, saying that an incendiary bomb fell on the roof of Stone House. Police tried to get in, but could not gain admission. It was subsequently learnt that the resident housekeeper had spent the night in a public air-raid shelter.

The next morning Sergeant Willison and other officers examined the building.

Did Not Spread

It was found that a hole had been burnt in the roof, and the floor boards and the matting covering them were smouldering. The rubble brought down by the bomb had prevented a fire which had started on the sixth floor from spreading.

The inspector added that he was told that although about 150 persons were employed in this building, no arrangements had been made to appoint fire-watchers.

Willkie Plays Darts

Mr Wendell Willkie to-day went to London's quaint old Shepherd Market, in the heart of Mayfair, walked into a public house, ordered a pint of beer, and played a game of darts with a builder's labourer.

Barred for Life From Keeping a Dog

Found guilty of ill-treating their dog. Mr and Mrs. L. H. Dowsett, of Slutt Green, Great Wakering, Essex, were fined £1 each, and barred for life from keeping a dog, by the Southend magistrates to-day.

Evidence was given that the dog was so thin that it had to be shot

Mrs Dowsett said she did not realise the dog was in such a bad condition. She had given it all the food she could spare.

Pawn Shop Hunt for Binoculars

Pawnbrokers holding binoculars in North-eastern England are to be asked to get the owners' permission to sell them to the Ministry of Supply.

It has been found that in some of the larger North-eastern centres many racing people pawn their binoculars at the end of the flat season redeeming them when the sport is resumed.

JANUARY

30 Thursday
31 Friday

On both days, taking advantage of slightly better weather during the day, the *Luftwaffe* sent single aircraft to bomb London at fairly frequent intervals. Deteriorating weather at night grounded all bombing operations.

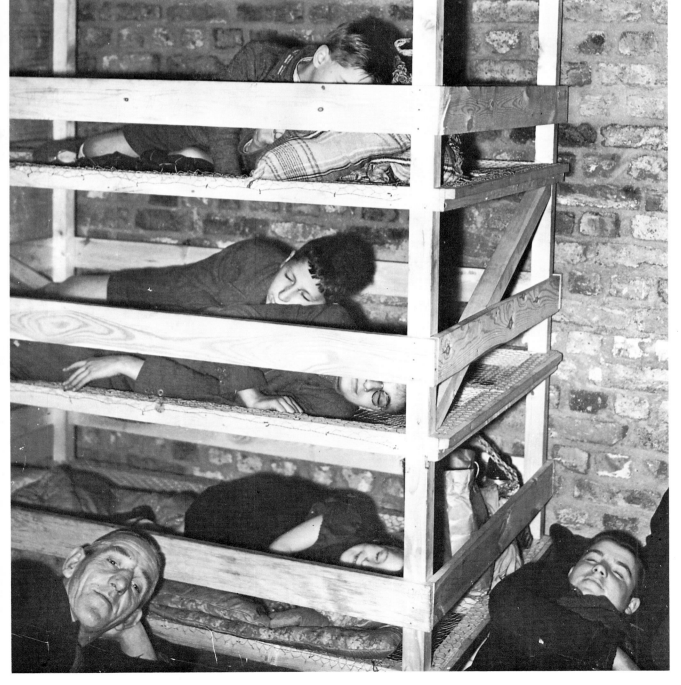

169 and 170. Shelter comforts! The less pleasant aspects of shelter life – cramp and damp! Public shelters were originally intended to be used for a couple of hours at a time during the day. When the Blitz came they mostly proved uncomfortable for a whole night's occupation and the government sanctioned a massive upgrading of the standard of shelters which was well underway by the end of January. More bunks, like these chicken-coop bunks pictured here, were installed, at first only for children; canteens run by the WVS, Salvation Army, local authorities or private firms like Marks & Spencer provided food; and shelter social life became more organised with games, evening classes and entertainment.

CLOSING PRICES

FINAL NIGHT EXTRA

EVENING STANDARD, February 3, 1941

Evening Standard

| Amusements | 8 |
| Radio | 8 |

BLACK-OUT 6.23 pm to 8.5 am
MOON rose 11.22 am, sets 1.40 am

No. 36,322   LONDON, MONDAY, FEBRUARY 3, 1941   ONE PENNY

'NO ALERT' BOMBS ON 5 PLACES IN LONDON

Raiders Resume Hit-and-Run Plan

Daylight raiders, operating singly or in pairs, dropped bombs at five places in the London area to-day. They had apparently resumed the hit-and-run tactics of last week.

THERE WERE ALSO REPORTS OF ENEMY AIR ACTIVITY FROM EAST ANGLIA, THE SOUTH-EAST COAST, THE NORTH-EAST COAST, AND SCOTLAND.

In the London area anti-aircraft guns opened fire, but the Alert was not sounded.

A number of houses were damaged and a small number of persons were injured but they were mostly minor casualties. The 18-month-old son of Mr. and Mrs. T. Robson was seriously injured.

At the South-East Coast town, a raider dived out of low clouds, released a stick of bombs and scored a direct hit on a Methodist church, which was wrecked.

Several other buildings were badly damaged.

Believed Hit

It was feared that a woman and boy were killed. Other civilians were taken to hospital for treatment.

The raider was believed to have been hit by A.A. fire before it made off, chased by a Spitfire.

Two raiders were heard over another part of the South-East coast.

A raider which appeared to be in difficulties over a Home Counties town dropped five bombs. They all fell in open ground.

Bombs were dropped at two points in East Anglia.

13th Quiet Night

An Air Ministry and Ministry of Home Security communiqué issued at 7.30 a.m. stated : "There is nothing to report."

It was London's thirteenth quiet night out of fourteen, and the second successive raid-free for the whole of Britain.

Fleet Air Arm Raid Sardinia

The Admiralty issued the following communique to-day:

"On the morning of Sunday, February 2, naval Swordfish aircraft carried out a successful attack on one of the main sources of power supply in Sardinia.

"One of our aircraft is missing from this operation. The next of kin are being informed as soon as possible.

"DAM HIT"

The Italian High Command communique to-day admitted the raid. It said :

"Enemy airplanes came from the west and dropped bombs and two aerial torpedoes on the dam of the River Tirso.

"One of the airplanes was forced down and the crew were taken prisoner."

Woman Dies as Spy in Germany

BERLIN, Monday.

Ruth Schubert, 20, of Hildesheim, who was accused of espionage, was executed to-day. She was the first woman to be executed this year.

Karl Schapper, 62, convicted of high treason, was executed at the same time.

Three men were executed in Germany as spies in January.—Associated Press.

18, a Mile Fine

A motorist, who admitted exceeding the speed limit by travelling at 44 m.p.h., was at Old-street to-day fined 44s.

The magistrate, Mr. Frank Powell, said: "Forty-four miles per hour in City-road just before dark is a disgraceful speed."

They Dance the Tuscana

ATHENS, Monday.

The Athens newspaper Estia states:

"Authoritative information from Northern Europe states that a new dance is coming into vogue in many European capitals.

"It is called the Tuscana, or Tuscany wolf dance, and has been dedicated to the brave Italian nation. It is an easy dance to learn —one step forward and three steps backward."

The "Wolves of Tuscany" was the name given to an Italian division of reinforcements recently routed in Albania.—Reuter.

Gaol to Luxury Hotel

Roy Jardine Angus, 50, engineer, was at Bow-street to-day sentenced to three months' imprisonment for obtaining credit for £11 17s by false pretences at the Green Park Hotel, Mayfair.

It was stated that he went to stay at the hotel on the day he was released from prison after serving five years' penal servitude for fraud.

DARLAN IS TALKING WITH ABETZ

ADMIRAL DARLAN, NAVY MINISTER IN THE VICHY CABINET, ARRIVED IN PARIS TO-DAY TO START HIS CONVERSATIONS WITH ABETZ, HITLER'S "AMBASSADOR" THERE.

It was announced in Vichy, says British United Press, that he was expected to return by special train to-night.

The object of the talks has not been revealed, but it is understood that he has been sent by Pétain to find an acceptable way for Franco-German collaboration.

Whether the pro-German Laval will return to the Cabinet, from which Pétain dismissed him in December, is likely to be settled by the Paris talks

"If My Wife Remarries—

COMPLIMENT TO ME"

Mr. Eustace Sharpley Meddings, of Beechwood, Kent-road, Harrogate, who died on November 16 last, left £19,030 4s 9d gross, with net personalty £18,366 2s. 4d. (estate duty £1589 13s. 6d.).

He stated:

"I desire to express my gratitude to my wife, who has always been the source of my greatest happiness in life and the hope that she will remarry if she so desire with the assurance that I should consider her doing as a compliment to myself; but it is my earnest wish that she should continue to exhibit the same wisdom and business ability that she has always displayed in my life-time and retain her capital in her own hands."

Mr. Noel Coward

Mr. Noel Coward left Auckland, New Zealand, for the United States to-day in the Pan-American Clipper.

Germans girls at an A.T.S. recruiting station in London to-day.

"I WOULD USE A RIFLE": German Girl

Another willing to bomb

Evening Standard Reporter

Adela, Ilse, Elloi and Antoni, four German girls, were among the first to enlist in the A.T.S. to-day.

It is only recently that the authorities have allowed alien women to join.

The girls were smiling and eager ; you would not have thought they had a care in the world. Yet at least one of them had been living for months on £1 per week, all had been bombed here and all had been driven out of Germany before the war.

Three of them have relatives in Germany, yet they were taking the risk of joining one of the women's services, knowing that there was a chance that their move might become known in Germany That is why their surnames are not published.

Brothers in Pioneers

Two have brothers in the Auxiliary Military Pioneer Corps.

"Hundreds more have applied," said a high A.T.S. officer to me, "and we are very busy interviewing them. They are keen to serve in practically any capacity, so long as they are doing Hitler as much harm as they can."

Adela is a German university girl who rose to be a director of the firm in Germany for which she had been working as a private secretary That was five years ago.

"Then Hitler drove me out," she said. "I came here with practically no money, and have been working as a clerk

"Last June I wrote to the Army asking if it was not possible for alien women to join the A.T.S I was overjoyed when, on December 27, they wrote saying that it had been decided to allow some of us to join.

"Would Use Rifle"

"I don't know what the A.T.S. will want me to do; but if they put a rifle in my hand I would certainly use it if I saw a German."

Ilse is 19 Her mother and brother are still in Germany. She came over before the war to improve her English, and became a nurse in a British hospital. But she had to leave when the war began because the area around it was declared prohibited.

"Ever since," she said, "I have been *(Continued on Back Page, Col. Five)*

Adela

Fire Watcher Must Stick to His Post

Whether a fire watcher must be on duty even when no Alert was in progress was a question described by Sir Gervais Rentoul, the West London magistrate, to-day as a matter of considerable public importance.

"I think this is a matter on which employers are seeking some guidance on exactly what are their obligations," he added.

Before the court was Edward Whyley, of Sedgeford-road, Shepherd's Bush, the first fire-watcher to be summoned for "being a person who had undertaken to act as a fire watcher did fail to be present on the premises at all times during the period for which he had undertaken to act as a fire watcher."

He pleaded guilty.

His employer, Colville Ernest Hobden, of Leysfield-road, Shepherds Bush, pleaded not guilty to "failing to secure that a person who had undertaken to act as a fire watcher was at all times present on the premises."

The summonses were adjourned for a week.

Paris 'Phone Breakdown

Several telephone exchanges in Paris have been out of action since last night, according to German authorities in the city, while the work of a number of others is dislocated. In addition, the interruption of electric power lines has cut off the power and light supply of certain telephone exchanges.—Reuter.

"It's a Symbol"

"It's a symbol," said Mr. Wendell Willkie to-day when, during his tour of Liverpool, he saw that construction of Liverpool Cathedral was continuing. "I guess that is stimulating."

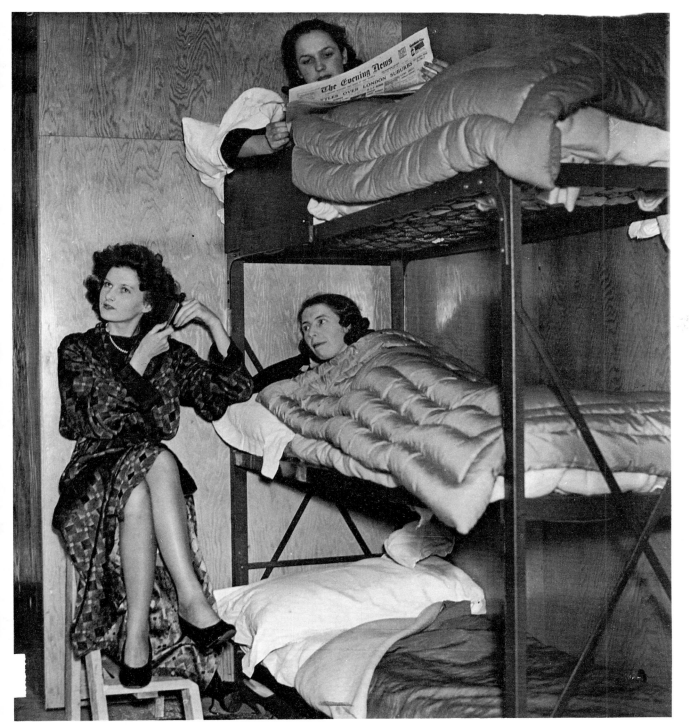

FEB

1 Saturday

2 Sunday

A quiet weekend in London as poor weather limited *Luftwaffe* operations.

3 Monday

Both during the day and at night a few bombs were dropped by single aircraft flying over the capital.

4 Tuesday

Improved visibility in better weather brought more German bombers to London but as the main attack of the night centred on Derby, London did not suffer badly.

171. Bunks in a shelter – in this case the shelter at the Berkeley Hotel. They look rather more comfortable than the chicken-coop bunks on page 121.

172. An indoor domestic shelter given government approval.

173

174

FEBRUARY

5 Wednesday

Although Chatham was the principal German target, poor visibility meant that targeting was difficult. London inevitably received some of the bombs intended for Chatham. The *Luftwaffe* generally targeted their bombs visually but they did have navigational aids to help when visibility was poor. The first was dead reckoning, used by all airforces. It involved calculating the aircraft's position by taking into account height, flying time, wind strength, etc., but was not terribly accurate.

The Germans also had a series of radio beacons all along the European coast facing Britain by which they could fix their position – direction finding. However, British defences could monitor these frequencies and possibly intercept the aircraft. As a counter to this, the *Luftwaffe* set up a series of more sophisticated and precise radio beam systems working on VHF frequencies. These systems were *Knickebein*, the least accurate of the systems and available to all *Luftwaffe* pilots; the *X Verfahren* or X system, and the *Y Verfahren* or Ypsillon – both of which were limited to only small groups of specially trained pilots.

6 Thursday
7 Friday

Two quiet nights in London and the rest of the country as weather limited *Luftwaffe* operations to a few aircraft flying by day.

173. Shelterers asleep in their bunks while passengers wait for the last train of the night at Holborn Tube Station.

174. The largest bomb crater in London at Bank Tube Station – now spanned by a temporary road bridge. This picture shows the first traffic crossing after it was opened by the Lord Mayor. The *Daily Mail* received permission to publish the picture with the following proviso in heavy blue letters on the back: 'Must not be used unless entire background is painted out. Only roadway of bridge to be shown.'

175. Some of the more unusual scenes to be viewed in a city under threat of aerial attack – this is the strange effect of ventilators for shelters under this South London street.

TWELVE DAYS IN THE INFERNO

The Saturday Book Page

— By —

HORACE THOROGOOD

WHEN, in years to come, we want to recall this war, not in its historical details, but as it affected us as individuals, J. L. Hodson's diary, "**Through the Dark Night**" (Gollancz, 12s. 6d.), will do it for us. This is a book to keep on the shelves; we shall often want to pull it down, and read again, and think again.

It ends at October 20 last year and we are not yet "through the dark night." But by that date we had already gone through formidable experiences of which Mr Hodson had seen more than most of us. He had been war correspondent in France with the B.E.F. and R.A.F., at sea with the Navy, a reporter in the war industry areas and a Londoner during last autumn's heavy air raids.

He was Mr Everybody in Everybody's War.

One of the things it will remind us of, should reminder be needed, is the dramatic change that came over our attitude to the war when Hitler smashed through the Low Countries.

Up to that time the diary is largely a record of amusing incidents. The war was the "phoney" war. The popular song (God forgive us!) was about hanging out the washing on the Siegfried Line. Maginot was a name to conjure with.

Afterwards, no more of that!

Mr. Hodson makes us live, then and there, in the exciting, agitated days that ended at Dunkirk. He was on leave in England when the German drive began, and returning to France on May 20 was rolled back to Boulogne with the retreating Army. He was back in England on the 22nd. So he saw none of the fighting. But his record of those twelve days and nights among the bombs and the refugees and the collapse of armies reproduces the strain, the stretched nerves, of the war-tortured land: a record of debacle.

It passes on to the Britain that arose, right-minded, from the shock, and since that is the Britain of to-day, we can enjoy Mr. Hodson's stories of the earlier phase. Here are some:

Flustered sentry: "Halt! Who am I? Advance and be circumscribed."

Meditation by Yorkshire private, overheard during trench-digging: "Company officer, 'e seems to think I'm McAlpine's mechanical excavator. I'st soon ha' dug o'er every bit o' France my brother didn't dig last time."

General Gamelin's alleged reply to invitation to Mme. Gamelin to be chairman of a nursing association: "My wife finds herself so occupied that I am writing on her behalf."

Soldier's letter to Pensions Committee: "My wife has had no clothes for a year and has been regularly visited by the clergy." *Another*: "The teeth on top are all right, but the ones in my bottom hurt terribly."

R.A.F. slang: North Sea or Atlantic Ocean, "the drink." Gun turret, "the dust-bin." The C.O., "the Station-master." Job badly done, "a black"; well done, "a brown." To dislike something is to take "a poor view." To be reprimanded, to "tear off a strip." Crashing the under-carriage, "hitting the deck."

The man who brought us out

MR. HODSON got back from Boulogne in time to read Mr. Churchill's famous speech to Parliament on the capitulation of King Leopold ("Meanwhile, the House should prepare itself for hard and heavy tidings.") It is included in Mr. Randolph Churchill's collection of his father's speeches since May 1938, "**Into Battle**" (Cassell, 8s. 6d.).

How magnificently they read! And now, reading them, we must thank our stars that in Churchill we have a great orator as well as a great statesman.

There is many a passage in those speeches which, when we heard it first, we knew were destined never to be forgotten.

"*I have nothing to offer but blood, toil, tears and sweat.*"

"*Never was so much owed by so many to so few.*"

"*We shall fight on the beaches, we shall fight on the landing grounds, we shall fight in the fields and in the streets, we shall fight in the hills; we shall never surrender.*"

The thrill with which we listened to the masterful voice comes again from the printed words.

Picture of life in a convent

KATE O'BRIEN'S "**The Land of Spices**" (Heinemann, 8s. 6d.) is a novel of rare beauty.

Most of the action passes in an Irish convent school, between the arrival there of the youngest pupil, six-year-old Anna Murphy, and her leaving ten years later. At the back, as it were, of Anna's story, Miss O'Brien builds up a portrait of a very noble woman, the Mother Superior, the book's dominant character.

She is an Englishwoman, brought up in Brussels, admired and respected by the Irish nuns and Irish schoolgirls in her charge, but not loved—she is too English. They think her "cold," and they resent her refusal to permit Irish nationalist ideals to intrude in the convent's educational policy.

There had been one great tragedy in her life—the discovery of an intolerable sin in her beloved father. It was the shock of that which drove her to enter the Order of Ste. Famille. As teaching nun in Turin, Vienna and Cracow before her appointment to Ireland, she had won the affection and trust of the Mother General, who, dying at the end of the book, nominates her as her successor.

Anna, too, has her tragedies—a drunken father, an unhappy home, finally the death by drowning of the young brother on whom she had heaped all her earthly affection.

A spiritual affinity grows up between the young girl and the Reverend Mother, who have both seen the solitary passion of their lives brutally destroyed—and that is Miss O'Brien's subject, developed with a tender wisdom and an exquisite literary art. It is, at the same time, a charming picture of convent life with its different types of nuns, its very "human" bunch of Irish schoolgirls, and its problems of discipline.

Is this the greatest golf hole in the world? Henry Longhurst asks in "It Was Good While it Lasted" (Dent, 15s.). Describing the fifth at Pine Valley, near Philadelphia, he writes: "Green and tee are on a level, 225 yards apart, but between the two lies a vast depression, with a lake full of turtles and other unlikely creatures. The green itself, long and narrow, slopes sheer away on the right, and a ball that misses the green bobbles merrily down until stopped by a tree trunk. On the left a gravel pit gnaws its way into the green."

Crime novel by a woman

THE lighter literature of the week includes a volume of 13 short stories of China by Pearl Buck, "**To-day and Forever**" (Macmillan, 8s. 6d.), and a crime novel, "**Death and Mary Dazill,**" by Mary Fitt (Joseph, 7s. 6d.). The former, beginning with a missionary idyll of the peaceful China of early this century, traces the increasing contact of the Chinese with the terrifying new age, up to Japan's war.

Miss Buck idealises the Chinese. Are they all really such dears? But the stories are good to pass the time with.

Miss Fitt's novel has a higher literary quality than most crime novels. Her Mary Dazill, whose advent as governess companion in the family at Chetwode Lodge occasioned such upset, and led to two mysterious deaths and a third which was never detected for the murder that it was, is a clever psychological study.

None of the characters is the sort of puppet that usually fills the cast of a murder story, and perhaps that is why the tale seems to me to lack conviction. Miss Fitt has rigged up a fantastic plot which one could swallow from a puppet cast but which becomes unacceptable when played by "real" people.

Churchill Speaks To-morrow

Week-end Radio

TO-DAY

HOME SERVICE

203.5 M., 391.1 M., 449.1 M., 49.38 M.

1.30.—Joe Loss and his Orchestra. **2.15.**—Royal Philharmonic Concert. **3.15.**—Dudley Beaven, theatre organ. **3.45.**—Talk about our export trade.

4.0.—B.B.C. Military Band. **4.30.**—Prize Puzzle Corner, No. 3. **5.0.**—News and talk in Welsh. **5.20.**—Children's pantomime.

6.0.—News and announcements. **6.30.**—News in Norwegian. **6.40.**—News about books, pictures, science and films.

7.0.—In Town To-night.

7.30.—The Yellow Streak, story by Somerset Maugham, adapted as play.

8.0.—Music Hall: Major and Minor (Fred Yule and Alec McGill), Billy Matchett, Bertha Willmott, Naughton and Gold, Florence Desmond and Robb Wilton, B.B.C. Variety Orchestra. **9.0.**—News. **9.20.**—American Commentary: Raymond Gram Swing.

9.35.—Good Old Timers—Marie Lloyd: with Clarice Mayne, Bransby Williams, Marie Lloyd junior, Alice Lloyd, Rosie Lloyd, Daisy Wood, Jean Webster Brough, Fred Yule, Meg Dion Titheradge, Ian Sadler, Naomi Jacob, B.B.C. Chorus and B.B.C. Revue Orchestra. **10.15.**—Prayers.

10.30.—B.B.C. Orchestra (Section B). **11.10.**—Jack Payne with his Orchestra. **12.0.**—News.

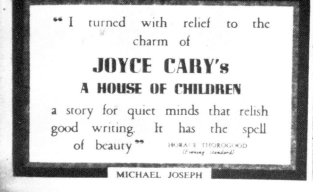

CONSTANCE CUMMINGS—Forces, 3.30 p.m. to-morrow.

FORCES

373.1 M., 41.49 M.

1.30.—Home Service. **2.15.—"Stranded!"** A light-hearted thriller. **2.30.**—The story of Judy Garland; illustrated.

3.0.—Joseph Lewis and his Orchestra. **3.30.**—Gossip Column: An indiscreet revue. **4.0.**—International Football: England v. Scotland (commentary). **4.45.**—Records. **5.0.**—Melo-Melodies, with George Melachrino and James Moody. **5.15.**—News in German. **5.30.—Speak to Me of Love**—Ireland. Love story with music.

6.0.—News in Dutch and French.

6.30.—ENSA Half-hour, with Laurence Olivier, Vivien Leigh, Morton Fraser, and Arthur Salisbury and his Savoy Hotel Orchestra.

7.0.—Home Service. **7.30.**—Fredic Bayco, theatre organ. **8.0.**—Home Service. **9.0.**—News in German.

9.20.—Scots Concert: Ella McConnell (contralto), Ian Smith (tenor), Arthur Hedges (piccolo), and strings of B.B.C. Scottish Orchestra. **9.35.**—Home Service. **10.15-11.0.**—Joe Loss and his Orchestra.

SUNDAY

HOME SERVICE

7.0.—News. **7.15** (app.)—Bernard Crook Quintet. **8.0.**—Christopher Stone records. **8.30.**—Horace Finch, theatre organ. **9.0.**—News. **9.15.**—Records. **9.30.**—Service. **10.15.**—John McKenna (tenor).

10.30.—Alfred Van Dam and his State Orchestra. **11.0.**—In Town To-night (recording). **11.30.**—Clifford Curzon, piano. **12.0.**—Donald Thorne, theatre organ.

12.15 p.m.—B.B.C. Military Band—listeners' requests. **12.45.**—Everyman's Music: Sir Walford Davies. **1.0.**—News. **1.15.**—B.B.C. Salon Orchestra. **1.45.**—We Go Seeking Cities: 2—Brighton (records). **2.15.**—In Your Garden: C. H. Middleton.

2.30.—B.B.C. Orchestra (Section B). **3.30.**—Orchestre Intime.

4.0.—B.B.C. Theatre Orchestra. **4.45.**—Everyman's Book 15—Is there a way out? **5.0.**—News and talk in Welsh. **5.15.**—Children: Part 4 of The Story of David, a play.

6.0.—News, followed by records. **6.30.**—News in Norwegian. **6.40.**—Talk by George Blake (recorded).

6.50.—Red Dog: Play adapted from Rudyard Kipling's Jungle Story. **7.30.**—Greetings between parents in this country and their children in Canada and U.S.A.

8.0.—Christian Endeavour Diamond Jubilee Service: Address by Rev. Geoffrey King. **8.40.**—Week's Good Cause. **8.45.**—National Anthems.

9.0.—The Prime Minister. News. Postscript by J. B. Priestley. **9.30.**—Brahms Trios—6.

10.5.—A Play is Born: Based on "How a Play is Produced," by Karel Capek.

10.35.—Epilogue. **10.43.**—Mary Jarred, contralto. **11.5.**—Joseph Seal, theatre organ. **11.25.**—Kenilworth Octet. **12.0.**—News.

FORCES

6.30 a.m.—Cheerful records. **7.0.**—News. **7.15-8.0.**—Records.

10.20.—News from India. **10.30.**—For Indian Forces. **11.0.**—Service. **11.15.**—Anniversaries recalled by Christopher Stone. **11.30.—Irish Rhythms Orchestra.** **12.0.**—Donald Thorne, theatre organ. **12.15 p.m.**—News in French.

12.30 p.m.—Variety; with Jack Warner, Joan Winters, Adelaide Hall, Johnny Lockwood, Debroy Somers and his Band, Bryan Michie. **1.0.**—News in Dutch. **1.15.**—Music-Hall (recording).

2.15.—Sunday Matinee, featuring Evelyn Dove, Scott and Whaley, Ken Johnson and his West Indian Dance Orchestra. **2.50.**—The World and its Works: Rev. Anthony Otter. **3.0.**—Oscar Grasso and his Band.

3.30.—Variety: with Gabrielle Brune, John Clements and Judith Furse, Jack and Eddie Eden, Dorothy Dickson, Walter Crisham, Ronald Frankau, Constance Cummings, Reg Pursglove and his Band.

4.30.—Evelyn Laye entertains at a naval dockyard. **5.0.**—Close-up (interviews). **5.15.**—News in German. **5.30.**—Ice-hockey from Canada. **6.0.**—News in Dutch and French.

6.30.—Hi, Gang, with Bebe Daniels, Vic Oliver, Ben Lyon, Jay Wilbur and his Orchestra, Greene Sisters, and Sam Browne. **7.10.**—Weekly News-Letter. **7.30.**—Community hymn-singing.

8.0.—The Happidrome; with Murray and Mooney, Rupert Hazell and Elsie Day, Lily Morris, Sidney Burchall, Tommy Handley, Renara, Harry Korris. **9.0.**—News in German.

9.20.—Tango Time; Harry Engleman's Quintet. **10.0.**—Epilogue. **10.8-11.0.**—Jack Payne with his Orchestra.

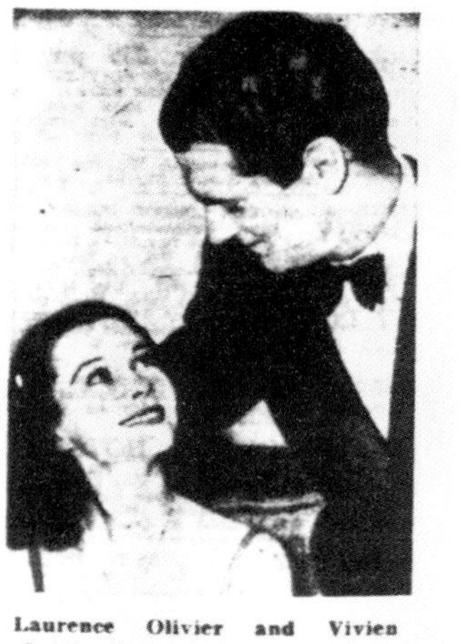

Laurence Olivier and Vivien Leigh—Forces, 6.30 p.m. to-day.

Standard quiz

1. Who is the new United States Ambassador to London? Is he a *Republican*? a *Democrat*?

2. GOOD KING HENRY is the name of a:

French monarch, Fleet-street inn, poem by Tennyson, battleship, vegetable?

3. What is the port of Athens? And of Jerusalem?

4. "He that hath wife and children hath given hostages to fortune."

Quotation is from *Shakespeare, the Bible, Milton, Bacon, Keats, Lamb?*

5. GUTTA-PERCHA is:

A mineral, made from the sap of trees, a kind of clay, a root product, part of a whale?

Key on Page Twelve

FEBRUARY

8 Saturday
9 Sunday

Low cloud, drizzle and mist all severely restricted German bombing operations. Most activity was centred on attacks to coastal shipping.

10 Monday
11 Tuesday

Continuing poor visibility but some minor raids were mounted at night, Monday seeing the largest of the attacks. Bombs were widespread throughout the whole of the South East but nowhere was damage significant.

176. Some hospitals had evacuated to the Home Counties, usually to the premises of Mental Institutions, at the beginning of the war. More hospitals or numbers of wards from hospitals were evacuated a year later at the beginning of the Blitz – but some hospitals remained open or partially open and staffed throughout the whole war, even after they had been damaged in air raids. The picture shows two nurses viewing the damage to their hospital in a recent daylight raid.

177. Even after five months of air attack Londoners had not given in to Hitler's attempts to terrorise them into surrendering. In fact all the bombing, on both sides, only seems to have strengthened civilians' resolve to win.

Mrs. Miles Traces 2000 People 'Missing' in War

91,000 NAMES IN HER FILES

Evening Standard Reporter

In a small office in Bayley-street, W.C., to-day, I saw Mrs. Sonja Miles, whose war-time work has made her known to thousands of people all over the country and in the Dominions as London's No. 1 woman detective.

Mrs. Miles is in charge of the Homeless Bureau of the London Council of Social Service.

Her job is to find people and reunite them with their relatives after they have been "lost" through wartime conditions.

She has been at work only a few months, but in her file are the names and addresses and full details of more than 91,000 people who have either been bombed from their homes or evacuated.

She knows the new homes of all these people so that when she receives an inquiry from the other side of the world from a son who cannot get in touch with his mother, or a soldier whose family have "disappeared" she can locate them almost immediately.

Mrs. Miles deals with about 200 inquiries a week and she told me to-day that she is able to satisfy the requests of about 50 per cent. of her correspondents.

The bureau covers London, Middlesex, Sussex, Kent, Essex, Suffolk, Norfolk, Cambridge, Huntingdonshire, Bedfordshire and Hertfordshire.

Local authorities in all these areas give Mrs. Miles details of all the people who have been evacuated from their districts.

When Mrs. Miles took over the Homeless Bureau she had two young girls working for her. Now she has a staff of ten.

They have already satisfied the inquiries of more than 2000 worried relatives.

SHEER WASTE

Some of the thousands of tyres needlessly scrapped every week. If they had been removed in time many of them could have been Tyresoled and given new tyre mileage. Tyresole your smooth but sound tyres.

Save for yourself and the Nation by having tyres
TYRESOLED

Every make and size of tyre can be Tyresoled and given guaranteed new tyre mileage over again at half cost. The Purchase Tax is not payable on the Tyresoling of your own tyres. Tyresoles also available from stock in most of the popular sizes (these carry Purchase Tax). *Ask your garage or local Tyresoles factory for prices.*

TYRESOLES
New Tyre Mileage at Half cost

TYRESOLES LTD   WEMBLEY
'Phone Wembley 3808 (6 lines)
13 FACTORIES throughout the Country.

Tea for Three

One cup of tea and three to share it—a picture at a London station.

Babies Go Away

Very young children leaving London to-day under the L.C.C. evacuation scheme.

The Girl With a Superiority Complex

SHE PUZZLES THE MAGISTRATES

Frances Beatrice Harris, a pretty, 17-year-old shop assistant, of High-street, Orpington, Kent, pleaded guilty at Bromley to-day to obtaining £36 from the Post Office Savings Bank by forging her employer's name in his bank book.

Mrs. Leatherdale, probation officer, said the girl suffered from a superiority complex.

The girl's father said she was more interested in boys than in her work, and added: "She wants supervision She ran away from a high school to which she had been awarded a scholarship"

"When she was 14 I was told, on authority, that she had the brain of a girl of 18."

It was stated that the girl withdrew the money—£3 at a time—at various post offices in London, and told a detective: "I did it because I wanted to visit my boy friend at Plymouth."

The chairman, Mr. H. Forbes White, said to her: "We are dismayed and puzzled about you."

The girl was remanded on bail, and an order was made for her to repay the money.

Man, 72, Accused of Looting Umbrella

Frederick Arthur Chandler, aged 72, was charged at a South Coast police court to-day with looting. He was alleged to have stolen an umbrella from a bomb-damaged house.

He was remanded in custody.

Jutland Veteran Says 'No Women At My Funeral'

Surgeon-captain Francis Bolster, R.N. (retired), who will be buried at Biggleswade, Beds, to-morrow, asked before his death that there should be no women at his funeral, no mourning, no public bodies represented, and no flowers.

He is to be carried in a farm wagon.

In the last war he was in H.M.S. Warrior, which was sunk at the Battle of Jutland.

Bus Service Changes Next Week

London Transport announce the following changes in bus services, to be made next Wednesday:

Buses for the short journeys on **Route 90**, between Kew Gardens and Hanworth, will be diverted at Hanworth to Feltham.

Route 7 (Liverpool-street — Acton Vale), which now runs via St Quintin avenue, Wormwood Scrubs, will run instead via St Mark's-road and Barlby-road. Journeys which at present end at Wormwood Scrubs will be extended to the King's Arms, Acton Vale, and some journeys which now end at Acton Vale will be extended via Acton and Acton Town Station, to Kew.

Route 70 (Hampstead—Kew Green) will be curtailed at Gunnersbury Park.

Buses on **Route 18** (Wembley-Harrow Weald) will be diverted at Wealdstone via Locket-road, Belmont Station Weston-drive and Wemborough-road to Edgware Station.

The service on **Route 113**, between Edgware Station and Canons Park, which ran only at busy weekday hours, will be withdrawn, but this service will continue to operate between Oxford-circus and Edgware Station.

Took Lorry to Get Fish and Chips

Driver H. G. Rogers, of the Tyneside battalion, Royal Engineers, pleaded guilty at a court-martial to-day to conduct to the prejudice of good order and military discipline by using a War Department vehicle for his own purpose and to a second charge of being absent without leave.

He said he took the section lorry to get some fish and chips. Afterwards he heard the lorry had been smashed up and damage amounting to £200 had been done.

He had nothing to do with the smashing up of the vehicle, but as the evidence strongly pointed to him he became frightened and ran away.

Bitter Blow

For the first time for several weeks there were oranges on sale at Woolwich Market to-day.

Shoppers gathered quickly on hearing the news, but there was very little sale, because they were marmalade oranges. Most housewives did not want them, because they had not enough sugar to make marmalade.

LANDLORD NEED NOT REPAIR BOMBED HOME

To a tenant who had left his home which had been damaged by blast, Judge Earengey said this at Clerkenwell county court to-day:

"Tenants come before me and complain about damage done by the enemy. They seem to think that it is the landlord's obligation to put the premises in condition.

"Perhaps the main provision of the Landlord and Tenant (War Damage) Act is that even if there is a covenant to repair, it shall not be enforceable. Tenants do not seem to know that."

The tenant said that he had left his home and the landlords had not repaired it.

An order for the payment of the rent was made.

"Led Astray by a Canadian Soldier"

When Cyril Hugh Dowding, 36, a contractor, of Ravensbourne-road, Bromley, was charged at Bromley to-day with receiving ten petrol tins, two pounds of tea and other articles belonging to the Canadian Government, he said he was led astray by the persuasive tongue of the Canadian soldier from whom he bought the goods.

Dowding, who is due to be called up, was fined £20 and ordered to pay three times the value of the stolen goods—£10.

Daughter for War Prisoner's Wife

A picture at Esher, Surrey, of Mrs. A. C. Davidson-Houston and her baby daughter, who is soon to be christened Sarah. Captain Davidson-Houston is a prisoner of war.

Until They Come Home

Fleet and Aldershot have opened funds for their prisoners of war. The money will be kept for them until they come home.

FEBRUARY

12 Wednesday

A quiet night in London.

13 Thursday

Despite no real let-up in the poor weather conditions a few minor raids were aimed at London. During the night a massive 2500 kg bomb fell on a street of terraced houses in Hendon – just before the Alert had been sounded. It was not the first time one of these huge bombs had been dropped in London or Britain but here in Hendon the devastation that one single heavy bomb could cause was clear to see.

14 Friday

A much heavier attack on London than in the last several days even though the weather was still poor. Again a 2500 kg bomb was dropped, this time on Harrow.

15 Saturday

A few incidents of bombs dropping in the London area were reported but the weather remained difficult for flying.

178 and 179. The scene after a single massive bomb had fallen on Hendon on 13th February. Rescue workers and ARP officials searching the wreckage for anything of value after 84 houses were totally destroyed and nearly twice as many made uninhabitable. Around 75 people were killed, 150 seriously injured and 600 people made homeless.

FEBRUARY

16 Sunday

Poor weather continued to restrict *Luftwaffe* operations and London had a quiet night.

17 Monday

In the largest attack on London for about two weeks the German bombers had to rely on radio aids to help target their bombs as the weather conditions and visibility had only marginally improved. In most cases the night's bombing caused little damage but a direct hit on a shelter under a railway arch at London Bridge Station killed about 90 people and showed the inadequacy of the protection given by some of the unofficial sheltering places.

18 Tuesday

All the *Luftwaffe*'s night bombing operations were grounded by severe weather.

19 Wednesday

A minor attack lasting only about one hour was targeted on the docks but bombs dropped in many districts adjacent to the river. The worst incident of the night was when a bomb fell on St Stephen's Hospital in the Fulham Road.

20 Thursday

A few stray bombers attacked London during an attack on the Naval docks at Chatham.

180. As Civil Defence workers were salvaging furniture from this bombed house German aircraft flew overhead. Neighbours looked up, fearful of more bombing, but the Civil Defence workers, used to working under such conditions, did not even spare a glance.

181. Rescue men worked all night and into the day to free a woman trapped under this pile of masonry.

182. Part of the wrecked wards of St Stephen's Hospital where several male patients were killed.

183. Informing the public that all female patients were safe – but 19 male patients were dead.

Wife Pleads In Vain For Divorce

"SHE CAUSED THE FIRST MISCHIEF"

Mr. Justice Hodson in the Divorce Court to-day refused the petition of Mrs. Dorothy Mary Goodhew, of Hedge End, Kingston Hill, Surrey, for divorce.

Her petition alleged the adultery of her husband, Donald Frederick Goodhew, with Mrs. Joan Mercer.

Mrs. Goodhew asked that the discretion of the court be exercised in her favour in respect of her adultery with the husband of Joan Mercer.

Mr. and Mrs. Goodhew were married on May 27, 1937, and there are no children.

Holiday in France

Mr. Justice Hodson, giving judgment, referred to a holiday which the two couples spent in France in June 1939, during which misconduct took place between Mrs. Goodhew and Mr. Mercer and for part of the time with the knowledge of Mrs. Goodhew, the other two persons slept together.

Mrs. Goodhew broke with Mr. Mercer after her return from France and had since had nothing to do with him. She tried without success to make her husband break with Mrs. Mercer.

"Mrs. Goodhew was so reckless in relation to her husband's association with Mrs Mercer that I am unable to say that I am satisfied that she had not, in any manner, been accessory to or connived at the adultery of her husband," said Mr. Justice Hodson

Reconciliation Possible

"She took no effective steps so long as her infatuation for Mercer lasted to stop her husband's association with Mrs. Mercer, and she was compelled to admit that she was careless whether or not her husband was at the same time committing adultery

"Mrs. Goodhew was the person who caused the first mischief in the married life

"I have no reason to doubt that she has worked hard for reconciliation and I ought not, therefore, to hold reconciliation to be impossible."

Greeks Honour Bishop

The Rt. Rev. Harold Jocelyn Buxton, Bishop of Gibraltar, has been presented with the freedom of Candia, Crete.—Reuter

---

British Machine-Gunners in Action

British machine - gunners in action during the attack on Derna, whose fall preceded the capture of Benghazi.

The main body of Italian forces had retreated and the town was defended by about 1000 mines, barbed wire and many machine-gun nests. There was no heavy artillery. Picture received to-day.

Married Her Stepfather, Now Gets Decree

A woman who went through a marriage ceremony with her stepfather was granted a nullity decree nisi by Mr. Justice Hodson in the Divorce Court to-day on the ground that the marriage was within the prohibited degrees.

She is Mrs. Sylvia Hannah Scott (otherwise Hunt), of Tolworth Park-road, Tolworth, and she married Mr. Edgar William Scott on October 7, 1939.

In April, 1919, Mr. Scott married the petitioner's mother, who died in August, 1939.

The case for Mrs. Scott, whose husband did not defend the suit was that after her mother's death Scott asked her to marry him, and said he had been informed by a solicitor that it was legal to do so. She left Scott when she learned that the marriage was not legal.

NIGHT BOMBS ON HOME COUNTIES

Stick Across a Village

"**E**nemy activity last night was not heavy and soon ceased.

"Bombs fell in a town on the North-East Coast and at a number of scattered points near the East Coast and in the London area."

This was stated in the Air Ministry and Ministry of Home Security communiqué at 7.30 a.m. to-day. It added:

"Little damage was done, and there were few casualties.

Scattered attacks were carried out in many parts of the country by single raiders.

London had two alerts, but only a few districts were bombed.

A number of people were injured when 14 bombs were dropped in one area.

Three fell near trench shelters, but they were empty. Another high-explosive fell near a public house damaged in a previous raid.

Church Damaged

In another London area a stick of bombs was dropped across a residential area. They damaged a church, vicarage, a school and houses No one was seriously injured. Five bombs fell in the grounds of a nursing home.

A Home Counties village suffered heavily when a stick of high explosives were dropped right across it. More than 20 houses were damaged. Though people had to be evacuated, there were only two seriously injured.

Five high-explosives were dropped in another Home Counties district They damaged bungalows, and there were slight casualties.

Eighteen houses were damaged in a village in the same county People were evacuated here, too

Farm buildings in another Home Counties district were damaged

The most severe attack of the night was made on a North-East Coast town where hundreds of incendiaries and many high-explosives were dropped

Four people were killed and many injured. In a neighbouring village fires were started, but were quickly put out by firewatchers and the fire service.

Several high explosives were dropped on another north-east coast town People were trapped in demolished houses, and four were killed The town was showered with incendiary bombs

It's an Old English Custom

When a builder was charged at Highgate to-day with stealing a hand truck belonging to another builder, he said: "I admit I took the truck, but I didn't steal it. It is a way we have in the trade to take one another's tools, and when we have finished with them, we take them back."

The magistrate, who said he knew this to be the practice, dismissed the case

Soldier in Cupboard Allegation

A woman was alleged at Cromer to-day to have concealed an absentee soldier in a cupboard.

The woman, Miss Muriel Ethel Sarah Steward, of Church-street, Sheringham, was committed for trial on a charge of assisting an absentee without leave to conceal himself at Sheringham

More Piggeries Plan

Paddington Council's pig-keeping has proved a financial success, and the Emergency Committee report that a larger scheme for setting up additional piggeries at Mill Hill and others at Paddington Recreation Ground is to be proceeded with.

Raid On Hospital Hastened His Death

Dr. J. C. Clothier stated at an inquest to-day that the death of Joseph Frank Seyer, 78, of Ebury-street, Pimlico, who was taken to hospital following a fall, was accelerated by enemy action.

The day after Seyer was admitted with a fractured arm the hospital was bombed. Seyer died the day after the raid.

Verdict, accidental death.

Killed a Few Yards From His Wife

William Davis, a stretcher-party member, was on guard outside his post in a London area last night when he heard the whistle of a bomb.

He dived into the door of an off licence premises. The bomb exploded near, killing Davis and injuring eight other people

Mrs. Davis was in the post at the time, as a party was being held there The party ceased when the warning went, but Mrs. Davis was waiting for the All Clear to go before she went home.

Her husband's fellow workers went out to tend the wounded 'and found Davis dead They returned and told his wife

Bomb Kills Lady Moore and Daughter

Lady Moore, widow of Major-general Sir John Moore, her youngest daughter, Mrs Patricia Parley, and Lady Moore's housekeeper, Mrs Rebecca Henry, were killed recently when a bomb demolished the house in which they were staying in London.

Sir John Moore who was director of the Army Veterinary Service in the last war, and its colonel-commandant from 1932 to 1934, died a year ago, aged 75

Mrs. Parley was an ambulance driver

"Merrie England" Survives the Raid

More than 20,000 band parts belonging to a philharmonic orchestra were destroyed last night when an incendiary bomb set fire to a hall in the London area.

About the only piece of music to survive was a copy of Edward German's "Merrie England."

An album containing the national anthems of Germany and Italy and the overture from Faust was destroyed.

Needle in Lung

A verdict of death by misadventure was recorded at Hammersmith inquest to-day on Albert Victor Redknap, 36, of Harwood-road, Fulham, who died at St Luke's Hospital, Chelsea, after an injection in the chest for tuberculosis. The injection needle had penetrated a lung because of his abnormal condition

He Found 10s. Note

William George Bailey, 37, a window cleaner, of Middleton-road, Dalston, was at Hendon to-day fined £5 for stealing by finding a 10s. note. He was stated to have had £31 10s in his wallet when the theft was discovered

---

She Lost Her Son in the Glorious

GIVES MONEY FOR FLEET AIR ARM

Sending £2 to the Ministry of Aircraft Production towards the purchase of an aircraft in the Fleet Air Arm, Mrs. J. W. Cook, of Bosham, Chichester, stated that the gift was "in memory of my son who went down in the Glorious."

The aircraft-carrier Glorious was sunk at Narvik last year

Other gifts acknowledged to-day with gratitude by the Minister, Lord Beaverbrook, were.

The Boys' Club, St Wymondley Hitchin, Hertfordshire, £2 Stanley Robert and William Tandy (two crippled boys of the Children's Hospital Sevenoaks, from the sale of home-made airplanes and rescue boats) £4 5s 6d. Mrs. Lees-Milne, Evesham (twelfth contribution of £100 on behalf of Vale of Evesham Spitfire fund) £100 People of Antigua (£1660 in all), £500 County of Gloucester A.R.P. Scheme Area 2 Authority, £3420.

Marquess's Heir In Car Crash

Lord Edward Fitzmaurice, brother of the Marquess of Lansdowne and Mr. John Wallace, son of the late Captain Euan Wallace, both of Balliol College, Oxford, and two other people, who were injured when the car in which they were driving was involved in a crash with a lorry on the Witney-Burford road, during the blackout on Saturday, were to-day stated to be as comfortable as could be expected.

Lord Edward, who is 19 and the heir to the marquessate, is suffering from concussion and laceration of the face Mr. Wallace has shock and minor injuries.

They, along with Mr J P Maze, of University College, who has concussion, and his sister, Miss Pauline Maze, with concussion and lacerations, are in Radcliffe Infirmary

---

FEBRUARY

21 Friday

As Swansea received its third night of heavy bombing London was in receipt of only a minor attack which caused no significant damage.

22 Saturday

A quiet night in the capital.

23 Sunday

Some bombs fell in the London area at night, probably more by accident than design as *Luftwaffe* pilots unable to spot their specified targets outside London dropped their loads before heading home. This was not an unusual occurrence as London's size and the distinctive bend in the Thames made it an easier target to spot, especially if visibility was patchy.

24 Monday

Another quiet night in London but not without the siren sounding the Alert as the few aircraft that did fly from Continental Europe crossed over London's air space and set off the warning systems. In some ways there was more danger in these infrequent attacks as the population could be lulled into thinking that it was just another false alert and not take to their shelters when a real attack was approaching.

25 Tuesday

Although some bombs dropped in South East England, London had a quiet night.

184. The demolition squad at work.

FEBRUARY

26 Wednesday

A more severe battering than the capital had had for several nights in a typical end-of-the-month attack. Damage and casualties, too, were much greater than for a week or more.

27 Thursday

Poor weather conditions grounded all *Luftwaffe* night bombing operations. Daylight activity was restricted to attacks on coastal shipping. *Luftwaffe* attacks on shipping were a constant feature of their operations – either in the form of direct bombing of ships or in the dropping of mines in the waters around Britain. On February 6th Hitler had issued a directive emphasising the need to attack British merchant shipping, ports and harbours in an attempt to break the supply of food and other goods from the USA and the Colonies

28 Friday

Only three aircraft were over Britain at night and they dropped only a very few bombs on London.

185. Salvaging furniture and belongings, including toys, from a bombed out house.

186. A picture passed for first publication in the evening papers of Wednesday 26th February shows salvaged books in the Guildhall Library cleared of the initial debris caused by the 'Great Fire' of 29th December.

Woman Who Walked Into Sandbags Was "Negligent"

JUDGE WARNS PUBLIC

Mr. Justice Cassels, in the King's Bench Division to-day, dismissed the damages claim of a woman injured by sandbags, and warned the public that under war conditions they must exercise proper care.

Mrs. Elsie Margaret Jelly, of Woodford-avenue, Ilford, walked into the sandbag baffle wall of a public shelter and injured her eye.

She alleged negligence by the Borough Council in not lighting or whitewashing the sandbags.

They had been placed there only a few hours before the accident.

Mrs. Jelly, said the judge, was herself negligent. She had just emerged from lighted premises where for two hours she had been having her hair attended to.

She should have walked slowly or stood still until her eyes had become accustomed to the darkness.

Stepped Off Platform While Reading

Walking along a platform at Catford Bridge Station while he was reading, Arthur Henry Edward Ellis, 38, a clerk in the Gas Light and Coke Company, fell on the line and was killed by an electric train.

At the inquest at Lewisham to-day a verdict of accidental death was recorded.

GERMAN AIR CAPTIVES

This German airman arrived in London with a new batch of captives.

Bombed-Out from Any Area May Now Go to Ireland

The Governments of Northern Ireland and Eire have agreed that the facilities for evacuation to these countries should now be extended to mothers with children, in no matter what area they live, if they have been rendered homeless by bombing.

The schemes for assisting private evacuation to Eire and Northern Ireland, which have been in operation for more than two months, provide that mothers with children of school age or under, living in evacuation areas, who have made their own arrangements with friends or relatives in Northern Ireland or Eire will be given a free travel voucher.

The householder with whom they stay will receive a weekly lodging allowance of 5s. for each mother, 5s. for each school child of 14 or over, and 3s. for each child under 14.

This assistance will now be available to mothers and children who have lost their homes and wish to go to friends or relatives in Eire or Northern Ireland.

"Is there any chance of my getting a copy of the picture?" asked this officer, who spoke perfect English.

Major Beatty's Wife is Suing For Divorce

A petition for divorce brought by the Hon. Victoria Alexandrina Sibell Beatty against Major William Vandeleur Beatty, whom she married in 1925, is in the defended list for hearing in the Divorce Court this term. She is a daughter of Lord Southampton.

Major Beatty, the trainer, is brother of the late Admiral of the Fleet and uncle of the present Earl Beatty.

Formerly in the 19th (Queen Alexandra's Own) Royal Hussars, he served through the last war, and, attached to the 10th Mounted Infantry in the South African campaign, was mentioned in despatches.

Some years ago he lost his left leg through an accident while steeplechasing, but in a few weeks he was riding again and won the Bedford Stakes at Newmarket.

3 DYING SOLDIERS: SURVIVOR TELLS

Reference to a breach of the regulations was made at the resumed inquest to-day on three soldiers who were found dying in a military detention barracks.

The inquest was on Private Frank Girvan, 28, of Burnside, Cupar, Fife; Private Glen Roy Williams, 24, of Quarella-road, Bridgend, Glamorgan; and Private Harold Smith, 19, of Mauldeth-road West, Withington.

A fourth soldier, Gunner Ronald Charles Finch, of Gerrard-street, Hafod, Swansea, was found ill, but later recovered.

It had been stated that the four men were placed in a cell overnight, and the next morning when they were found to be overcome, a "queer smell" was noticed in the room. A gas jet which lit the room during the night was still burning.

Captain R. S. Stephens, R.A.M.C., said that when admitted to hospital the men were treated for carbon monoxide poisoning. There was no doubt about the diagnosis.

The coroner said a sergeant had told him he would take personal responsibility for leaving on the light. He asked if this was a breach of the regulations.

Lieutenant Faulkner replied that it was, but to his way of thinking it was desirable, otherwise the work of supervising new arrivals could not be done properly.

Gunner Finch, the survivor, said: "We were told by one of the sergeants not to touch the light, as it would go out itself.

"I remember waking during the night, feeling very sick. I got to my feet, found I could not stand, and just fell back on the bed. The next thing I remember was waking a day or two afterwards in hospital."

Splints Made Bridal Arch

Nurses and first-aid workers held splints aloft to form a bridal arch for Aircraftman William Woolhouse and Nurse Ella Utteridge, at Rayleigh, Essex.

Tennis Star Is Night Fighter

Flight-lieut. C. E. Malfroy, the New Zealand Davis Cup lawn tennis player and old Cambridge Blue, is with the night patrol fighters now after a spell as instructor.

In France he fought with a crack fighter squadron, and one day in May shared their success in bagging seven Heinkels and Dorniers "before breakfast."

Now he goes out "after supper."

3 Nazis Bale Out When British Pilot Gets 21st Victory

The Dornier bomber destroyed off the East Coast in daylight yesterday was shot down in single combat by a fighter pilot, who already had twenty confirmed victories to his credit.

The pilot, a Hurricane squadron leader, was on patrol over Norfolk when he sighted the enemy raider some 4000 feet above him.

He chased it out to sea, caught it about 75 miles from the coast, and silenced the bomber's rear gunner with his first burst of fire. His second and third bursts, delivered at close range, set the raider on fire in two places.

As the Dornier glided down towards the sea, with smoke pouring from it, three of the crew of five were seen to bale out.

Following his victim down, the squadron leader again came under fire, bullets striking his windscreen and mirror.

Closing in, he gave the raider a final burst and the Dornier crashed into the sea, sinking immediately.

Only one man was seen to come to the surface.

Boy "Borrowed" His Employer's Van

A 16-year-old boy admitted at East London Juvenile Court that he took his employer's motor-van away without consent, and that he drove it without a licence.

It was stated that the youth took the van to move furniture from his grandmother's house to his mother's house. He intended returning it. He had never driven before.

The youth was disqualified from obtaining a licence for twelve months, and fined 11s.

Bombed Out, Then Fined for Black-Out

Mr. Percy Arthur Clement, secretary of a firm which it was stated had moved to Kent after being bombed out in the City, was fined £10 at Bromley to-day for a black-out offence.

"A firm that comes into the country from London after being bombed out there should of all people be the most careful," said the magistrate, Sir Waldron Smithers, M.P.

Threat to Name the "Black Spots"

Councillor H. A. Rutt, chairman of Finchley Civil Defence Committee, is threatening to name "black spots" in the district where residents are slow in volunteering for fire-watching duties.

Streets which have not completed their fire-watching schemes by the end of this month will be mentioned at the next meeting of the council.

MAR

1 Saturday

Some minor damage in London when a few bombs fell at night.

2 Sunday

A quiet night in London.

3 Monday

Better weather conditions, especially over the Continent, than had been present for several days allowed more *Luftwaffe* aircraft to attack Britain but London only received a few bombs on a night in which Cardiff was the principal target.

4 Tuesday

The *Luftwaffe* attacked the dock area of London but the raid was minor. Cardiff suffered a second night of heavy bombing.

5 Wednesday

After dark, mist and fog grounded all *Luftwaffe* bombing missions.

6 Thursday

During the day some bombs fell on London but there were no reports of bombs after dark.

7 Friday

No attacks on London either by day or by night.

187. An artist sketching St Paul's while cleaning-up operations continue below the dome.

GORDON BECKLES

SAYS HE IS

Fed up with all this talk about food

LORD WOOLTON gets a vast amount of attention paid to his declarations on food.

The last hullabaloo was about the "eating out" order which starts to-day. We were going to be asked to tighten our belts. Millions of hours of talk were wasted in discussing the grim prospect.

Then the Evening Standard goes and asks West End restaurants what it will mean. The universal answer is "almost nothing."

Am I wrong—but don't we pay too much attention to food? Dangerously too much attention? At any rate, we talk a devil of a lot too much about it. Gandhi did not fast with more publicity than we propose to reduce our over-eating.

Now Napoleon, if he had cared less about his plump little tummy, might have ended up quite well. As it was he never allowed even the disaster of 1812 to lessen his attentions to the table.

A year later, on a critical evening of the three-day Battle of Leipzig, he devoted himself to the pleasures of the table; next morning a "curious lassitude" assailed him.

The truth was that he was forced to retire from the battlefield by a violent attack of colic. And he lost the battle and with it his empire.

To-day you might think at times that we are being asked to starve just a bit. And if we were—what of it?

Hollywood beauties do a gruelling 12-hour day on a diet of tomato juice, biscuits and lettuce, reinforced with a little coffee.

The fact is that, between the vitamins, we are the victims of a lot of illusions.

TAKE the idea that we are a nation of terrific meat eaters, that our renown is based on beef, that without the sirloin we will wither.

This dates from the eighteenth century when Henry Fielding wrote a jingo lyric called "The Roast Beef of Old England," in which it was alleged that roast beef "ennobled our hearts and enriched our blood." It added, too, that we would never have beaten the Armada without our ration of roast beef.

This song started a notion as false as that which credits the 'Nineties with being Naughty.

The ordinary man and woman in Elizabethan days, and immediately before the fifteenth and fourteenth centuries, lived mostly on fish, usually herring, with barley bread, beer and peas or beans.

Fresh meat was available only during certain months, and during the long winter and the spring into the warm weather it was a case of salted meat or game. The side of beef roasting on the spit in the baron's kitchen, or in the open air of the market place—was a symbol both of wealth and festivity. It was not a commonplace.

Until the eighteenth century English cattle were scraggy animals, on a par with tropical chickens. When you read of the heroes of those days eating half a sheep, please understand that a medieval sheep was the size of a modern lamb. The science of breeding the barrel-sided monsters of to-day was unknown. One simple reason was that because roots like the turnip were still unknown fodder was scarce, and the beasts had to be slaughtered before winter set in. The diet of those stout archers of Crecy and Agincourt was not so vastly different from that of Mr. George Bernard Shaw, except for certain carnivorous orgies when the opportunity arose.

The Virgin Queen's almost invariable breakfast (quite a meal in those days) was salt beef, bread and strong ale—just how strong one can guess.

NOR did the passing of a couple of centuries change England's diet

LORD WOOLTON
His "main dish" plan for restaurant feeding came into force to-day.

very much. Mr. Pepys' constant references to large meals referred only to the privileged classes, and the prices he quotes emphasises this fact.

In 1800 we were not in such a difficult position as we are to-day. There was a food shortage. The Government were gravely concerned. Manifestos were issued. Appeals to the ruling classes were made in stirring terms. But it was not a balanced diet, or lack of this or that vitamin, that worried them; it was all about BREAD!

With bread you lived; without it you starved.

Very few Englishmen at the time when we were repelling the last would-be invader ate wheaten bread. Even in prosperous times seven out of ten ate barley, rye or oatcake. Others ate blencorn, which was made of the coarsest meals. The white wheat of Heston was for the upper classes.

And even of bread the Englishman ate sparingly, about one-third that of the Frenchman. In the latter half of the eighteenth century the average consumption was estimated at six ounces a day, equivalent to three modern rolls.

Beer, plenty of mixed vegetables, game, bread and more beer (you drank it almost from the cradle) was the staple diet. Nelson managed to rule the seas with crews who lived on hard tack and rancid pork; but he carried it too far. Scurvy was almost as great an enemy as the French fleet. There was no method of keeping greenstuff aboard.

How did the men of centuries ago display such energy when they never knew that sugar is the great energy-giver? Most of the sugar used to have to come all the way round from Venice and was not for the common people. Somehow our ancestors seem not to have lacked vigour or enterprise.

NOW I make the suggestion that we should eat what is given us and shut up talking so much about it. There is no such thing as a standard diet, because there is no such thing as a standard man.

The finest physical specimen I ever knew was an Italian. He and his family—they are a hard-working race of road-builders and labourers all over the world, really admirable colonists in spite of Mussolini—were brought up on a diet of what looked like mummified fish (usually English herring, rejected at home), bread and red wine, flavoured with occasional lemons and garlic. I don't think my Italian would have known an A vitamin from a B if he had seen one.

It is true that William Pitt ("Roll up the map of Europe, it will not be wanted these ten years") died with the immortal words upon his lips: "I think I could eat one of Bellamy's pies," but it would have been a sounder precept if the legend were correct that his last words were: "My country! How I love my country!"

There was indeed ten years to come before his map of Europe would be wanted. Years often of hunger.

We may not have to wait so long in our battle against a bigger bully than Napoleon, but it seems just a trifle early yet to have both food on the brain as well as in the belly.

ROLL UP THE RED CARPET. THAT'S THE LAST (Copyright in All Countries.)

MARCH

8 Saturday

Despite some frost and fog London received its first major (i.e. more than 100 tons of HE) attack for almost two months. A significant amount of damage was caused to the railway system but the night's bombing was marked by two incidents which were widely reported.

One was a bomb which fell on the North Lodge at Buckingham Palace, killing a policeman; the other was when the Café de Paris in Coventry Street received a direct hit, killing 34 and injuring around 80 people. The Café de Paris was a fashionable London restaurant with live entertainment, frequented by officers and women from the wealthier classes, and was believed to be one of the safest restaurants in London as it was underground. This made the tragedy all the more poignant.

Looting at the scene of the incident was a problem, as it was at every bomb tragedy. Often 'looting' was simply a matter of picking up a cup or saucepan apparently abandoned among a pile of debris, but at the Café de Paris the looting was of an altogether more distasteful sort as some people systematically worked their way through the dead and injured removing anything of value. As a story guaranteed to damage public morale and the belief of 'all pulling together' in the face of adversity, the looting was of course not reported in the press.

9 Sunday

In a heavy follow-up attack on London the Germans dropped nearly 100 tons more of HE, mainly in North East districts. There was significant damage with the usual, temporary, interruptions to services – rail, road, water, electricity, gas and telephone.

10 Monday

Although Portsmouth received the heaviest raid anywhere in the British Isles since the beginning of the year, London had a quiet night.

THREE BOMB CRATERS

188 and 189. Buckingham Palace was hit again by bombers on 8th March.

MARCH

11 Tuesday

Birmingham was the target for a major attack but the *Luftwaffe* did drop some bombs in the London area.

12 Wednesday

Merseyside received a massive attack of around 300 tons of HE dropped by German aircraft. London received only some stray bombs, jettisoned by returning aircraft.

13 Thursday
14 Friday

Two quiet nights in London but Glasgow was hit by a total of more than 500 tons of HE in two major attacks on the city and dock areas on successive nights. With just over 500 people killed, the raid illustrated the average ratio of deaths to tonnage of bombs dropped fairly neatly – ten times less than the ratio calculated from the air attack casualties from the First World War and much less than the fifty deaths for one ton of HE estimated as the worst scenario after the bombing casualties in the Spanish Civil War.

15 Saturday

London's turn for a major attack in what amounted to a new aerial bombing offensive by Germany. January and February, while by no means devoid of major attacks, saw much less *Luftwaffe* activity than the first two weeks in March, no doubt due to the weather conditions.

190. *Palace Escaped: Buckingham Palace has been bombed again, but the palace itself escaped. The Daily Mail picture below gives an idea of the damage done in this deliberate attack. Daily Mail,* 13th March 1941.

191 and 192. Wreckage and reminders of the earlier revels at the Café de Paris, struck by a bomb on the night of 8th March. At first the press could only refer to it as a 'London Restaurant' – it was several days before the Café de Paris could be named openly.

HEAVIEST LONDON RAID OF YEAR

Four Public Shelters Hit: One Raider Shot Down

One raider was shot down by anti-aircraft guns and fell in flames in the London area during the fierce attack last night. Two others were so badly damaged that they probably did not reach their bases.

The Alert sounded earlier than usual. From that moment waves of raiders poured in from all directions.

Three Lives

Ginger the cat must be getting used to being bombed from home. He is seen to-day after being bombed out for the third time.

Woman Attacked By Her Collie Dog

Miss K. Burgess, aged 53, of Braintree, Essex, was toasting bread in her bungalow when her five-year-old collie sheep dog suddenly attacked her.

Her hands and arms were badly mauled and one finger was broken.

Neighbours put her to bed. During the night the dog crept into the room, jumped on the bed, and slept there. To-day he was destroyed.

The dog, known as "Teddy Bear," had previously been docile and affectionate, Miss Burgess said to-day.

"A Slight Case of Murder"

One London street suffered badly in last night's raid.

To-day outside one house was a chalked notice—"Just a slight case of murder."

Another notice ran: "The bloke who did this can't fight."

Attacking in groups, the bombers rained down high explosives and fire bombs for several hours almost without a lull.

Berlin says the main aim was the harbours and docks.

Thousands of incendiaries showered down. Fire watchers worked for hours putting out the bombs as they fell.

Kicked Off Roofs

Men kicked them off roofs and out of buildings to save premises they were guarding. Others fought to keep the flames spreading to A.R.P. control headquarters in one district.

There was a continuous barrage which shook houses as if bombs were being dropped.

Searchlights were in operation for the first time for many nights. Above the drone of the raiders which tried to dodge their beams could be heard the diving of our night fighters.

Yellow parachute flares — "like golden beads on strings"—were first dropped in a number of parts. Then came the fire bomb showers and later high explosives.

In one district after another the technique was repeated.

An Air Ministry and Ministry of Home Security communiqué issued early to-day said:

"Last night enemy activity was almost entirely confined to London, which was somewhat heavily raided, the attack being violent at first but dying away soon after midnight.

"Preliminary reports do not suggest very heavy casualties but considerable damage was done by fire and by high explosive bombs, both to private houses and to other buildings.

"At some points public services have been temporarily affected, but the damage was not extensive.

"The situation was always well in hand and in particular the fires were either extinguished or under control before daybreak.

"Outside London there is little to report. A certain number of bombs fell at various points on both sides of the Thames Estuary and on the South Coast, but both casualties and damage were small.

"One enemy bomber was shot down by anti-aircraft fire."

Police Station : 8 Die

When a police station in London received a direct hit last night at least eight people, including a police inspector, two sergeants and two canteen workers were killed.

Rescue workers are still searching to-day for people under the debris.

"Come On, Boys!"

Buried all night under debris of her demolished home, a London woman was calling out to rescue workers to-day: "Come on, boys. I'm getting cold."

NURSES WALK ON BOMBED HOME

These nurses walked to-day over the wreckage of what used to be their home. It was attached to a London hospital, one of the five bombed last night.

Many People Buried Under Their Homes

Families lost their homes in last night's London raids, and in many areas people were trapped in wreckage. Rescue squads had their busiest night of the year, working until dawn to-day.

In one district a rescue squad extricating people from demolished houses were themselves trapped when another high-explosives dropped near.

Four public shelters were hit, but there were no casualties. Three were empty; the other was hit by fire bombs and was burnt out. The shelterers got to safety before the fire got control.

Residents in a large block of flats took sheets from their beds and brought towels to make bandages for the injured when four high-explosive bombs were dropped on the building and in the grounds.

Some Were Refugees

More than 400 people, some of them refugees, were in the flats. Six were killed.

Firemen were injured when fighting several big fires. Guided by the glare raiders circled overhead and dropped high explosives close to where the firemen were working.

An assembly hall was destroyed when 30 incendiaries fell on the roof and the fire watchers were unable to deal with them. The flames spread and set fire to a number of houses in the neighbourhood.

In one street several families were buried beneath their wrecked homes. Thirty people were extricated by rescue squads searching with torches throughout the night, but it was feared to-day that several were still buried.

Casualties in suburban areas were to-day feared to be heavy, because since the lull in the raids people have abandoned the shelters for their homes.

In many districts people were trapped under wrecked houses while garden shelters were intact.

Famous Inn Bombed

A famous London inn was severely damaged by a heavy bomb early in the raid. Customers were injured, most by flying glass.

A large house adjoining was demolished and rescue squads were still searching to-day for people believed to be trapped beneath the debris.

A large party of soldiers left the public-house a few minutes before the bomb fell. They returned to help in rescue work.

One member of the staff at the inn, though severely cut, refused to leave until she had made certain that the gas was turned off.

Five Nuns Injured

A heavy bomb which hit a convent school in the Home Counties last night injured five nuns, three seriously.

The girl pupils were in the school shelter. None was hurt.

Another heavy bomb fell near a building used by ex-Servicemen disabled in the last war.

Five Trapped Nurses Saved —By Nurses

One hundred patients were rescued from a blazing London hospital during the night.

Three bombs hit the hospital and 50 patients were injured, one dying from shock.

The bombs demolished the chapel, the nurses' home and one wing of the hospital.

Only five nurses were in the home at the time, and they were buried under debris. Other nurses assisted rescue workers to release the girls, who were removed to another hospital with serious injuries.

Fire broke out, and nurses, many with cuts to their faces and hands, carried the patients out.

Fire bombs set light to the second hospital, destroying one wing. Nurses and two doctors, helping to rescue patients, were among those injured.

One person was killed and several injured. All the patients were evacuated.

There were several casualties at the third hospital.

There were 1200 patients at the fourth hospital, but there were only a few minor casualties. Eight wards were wrecked and 12 more put out of action.

At the fifth hospital there were no casualties.

VICTORY IN THE SKIES

The Channel coast .... Greece .... Libya .... Germany .... wherever there is fighting to be done and the offensive to be taken, the R.A.F. is on the spot.

Thousands of new machines are leaving the factories of Britain, the Empire and the U.S.A. Thousands of aircrews are training throughout the Empire.

But there's still room for you, for in the months to come the R.A.F. is going to hit the enemy harder and more often.

And, if you volunteer at once for Flying Duties in the R.A.F. you'll be qualified in time to play your part in the decisive air actions of the future.

Lose no time! VOLUNTEER TO-DAY!

If you are between 17½ and 32, go to the R.A.F. Section of the nearest Combined Recruiting Centre (address from any Employment Exchange) and say you wish to volunteer for Flying Duties. Reserved men can now volunteer. ● Men aged 17½–31 who are suitable for flying duties but require tuition to pass the educational test will be coached in their spare time, free of cost. If you cannot call, post this coupon for fuller information.

FLY with the RAF

To Air Ministry Information Bureau, Kingsway, London, W.C.2. Please send me details of Flying Service in the R.A.F.

NAME

ADDRESS

V/20/3

MARCH

16 Sunday

17 Monday

Two quiet nights in London. On Sunday Bristol was the target for the German bombers which were grounded by poor weather on the Monday.

18 Tuesday

Several bombs were dropped in the London area, probably as an alternative target for inexperienced pilots who failed to pinpoint Southampton, their designated target.

19 Wednesday

A massive attack on London. Some 470 tons of HE were dropped between roughly 8.00 p.m. and midnight. Several parachute mines were also dropped.

The attack centred on the docks and the East End and many fires were started – 3 conflagrations, 10 major, 53 serious and more than 1,800 small. Public utilities and transport were all severely disrupted. In the dock area many warehouses and their precious contents were destroyed and many public and private buildings were either destroyed or damaged. The death toll at 631 was the highest for any single night of the Blitz to date.

20 Thursday

A follow-up raid on the capital was only minor and did little damage.

193. A man salvaging clothes from his bombed out home. It was vital for people to salvage whatever they could from their wrecked houses. The shops were virtually devoid of all household goods and clothes so anything left in the house because it was slightly damaged or dirty could not be replaced even if there was the money to do so. Clothes rationing was to be introduced on 1st June 1941.

MARCH

21 Friday
22 Saturday
23 Sunday
24 Monday

Four days of calm in London. Plymouth was the target for the German bombers on the Friday night while on the Saturday, Sunday and Monday poor weather conditions grounded all *Luftwaffe* night bombing operations.

194. *Another Nazi picked out a Surrey Convent School . . . shattered woodwork lay around as nuns checked damage.   Daily Mail,* 21st March 1941.

195. *. . . . Convent schoolgirls collected books hurled from ruined classrooms. Footnote: Berlin says the main aim was the harbours and docks. Daily Mail,* 21st March 1941.

196. Damage at one of six London hospitals hit in the major raid on Wednesday 19th March. Here nurses are salvaging bedding.

Night Out in Wartime London

By P. S.

Le POER TRENCH

AT a quarter past five this morning I finished my whisky and soda, stubbed out the last cigarette and went to the cloak room to get my hat and coat. The band were swinging "The Duce" and several couples were still on the dance floor.

I had been moving around the West End since dinner time yesterday. Although it is considered daring for a theatre to put on a show after blackout time I found the big supper restaurants, the so-called day clubs. and the night clubs or bottle parties crowded everywhere.

A few of the clubs have shady reputations, but most of them are well run and orderly. If they were not the Services would soon put them out of bounds.

Night life in London now is a considerable industry and a fairly profitable one. There are thousands of civilians and troops on leave who like to spend an evening or a night dancing, drinking and watching a cabaret show.

THE really big spenders of peacetime are not often seen in the West End these nights, except at the private gambling parties. But one man who has frequented the clubs during the war was as free with his money as the best of them.

He is Private Gordon Roll, the 27-year-old racehorse owner, who is now a prisoner of war. After inheriting part of the £460,000 estate of his father, Sir Cecil Roll, Gordon Roll was said to have lost £30,000 on the Turf in five months. In the West End he must have spent close to £10,000 within three months.

Young Roll has been known to order 30 bottles of champagne for his party at one sitting. When he invited a hostess to join his table he would give her a cheque for £50. The manager of a certain club has given me an example of his methods of tipping. When he was ready to leave Roll called the manager and said : " Do you think the waiters would be satisfied with £30?"

"I should think they would be highly delighted," said the manager.

Roll wrote a cheque for £30. Then as an afterthought. he took four £1 notes from his pocket and threw them down with the cheque.

One night Gordon Roll was introduced to a girl who qualifies as about the smartest dance hostess in London.

This girl, whom I will call Helen, was brought to Gordon Roll's table. They danced together and sat chatting over a bottle of champagne. When he said good-bye Roll handed her a cheque for £60. As soon as she cashed the cheque Helen went to Bond-street and chose a seven guinea silver cigarette case. She had a simple inscription engraved inside it.

Next Helen caught a train for the South Coast town where Private Roll

was then stationed and made the presentation in person.

Roll was so pleased with this gesture that he gave her a cheque for £250.

◆ ◆ ◆

IT is not often that a hostess receives tips on this scale. Nevertheless, these girls regularly earn about £12 a week. They are not paid a salary. On the contrary, they pay £1 or £2 a week for the privilege of being employed. The house collects this money by presenting a formal bill each week for coffee and sandwiches. These refreshments are actually supplied to the hostesses, and it would cost them that much if they ordered as ordinary guests.

A hostess expects at least £1 from each man with whom she drinks or dances. She also expects him to spend freely while she is at his table. In some clubs a hostess must produce £5 of business a night to keep her job.

A hostess of my acquaintance named Mary is typical of them all. She is reasonably pretty, wears attractive evening dresses, is normally intelligent, and, of course, a good dancer.

Mary never has to think twice when she is invited to have a drink. She would like champagne.

When you offer her your cigarettes it develops that Mary does not like Virginia tobacco ; she always smokes Turkish. The particular brand she favours cost 6s. for a box of 25.

Later the cigarette girl comes round again. This time she has a tray of dolls and chocolates, or fresh flowers. There is a velvet doll that Mary likes especially. She ought to like it, because the same doll is bought for her about three times a week. The value of this toy is 16s. The customer pays three guineas for it. And Mary sells it back to the cigarette girl for £1.

Of course, Mary enjoys chocolates. too. Flowers make her happy. She has never refused either of them.

Night club chocolates are made up artistically and with enormous economy. The chocolates and the boxes are bought separately, and the cost to the management is 5s. or 6s. The guest is charged from one to two guineas. Flowers are supplied usually on a sale-or-return basis. A spray of three carnations, worth 2s. 6d or 3s. is sold for 17s. 6d

By 3 o'clock in the morning Mary, like everyone else in the club, begins to feel hungry. She is quite content with a snack : bacon or scrambled egg. dried toast and coffee. This comes to 7s. 6d a head.

Take another look at Renee, the cigarette girl. She earns anywhere from £10 to £15 a week. Her wages are £1. She gets 5 per cent. commission on sales. She keeps all tips.

◆ ◆ ◆

IN the night club business the doorman is known by the old-fashioned name of linkman. His earnings are hard to compute. They are affected by

the weather. When it is raining everyone wants a taxi.

He does not get wages. He relies on tips. But they add up to a substantial sum. At a prosperous club, he may have to pay the house as much as £3 a week to employ him.

The dance band are all members of the Musicians' Union. They receive union rates of pay.

Restaurants, day clubs and bottle parties are assessed at different standards by the Musicians' Union. A high-class place is required to pay nine or ten guineas a week to each member of the band. The leader receives twice as much. His salary is usually arranged privately with the management. Each band also has one or more key men, who receive a little more than the others. The first saxophone may be paid 12 guineas, for example.

The cabaret artists' earnings are restricted only by their popularity. A man or woman with a big following can ask as much as £90 a week. His agent receives 10 per cent. of this sum. Often there is an accompanist to be paid, too.

At £4 a week, the girls who dance and show off their figures may seem underpaid. But their costumes are provided, whereas hostesses and cigarette girls have to spend freely on clothes and silk stockings.

◆ ◆ ◆

HOW much does a waiter earn? The amount varies so much that you cannot name a specific sum. In the day clubs, where drinking is allowed only until 11 p.m., or, if there is a supper licence, until midnight, and in the lower grade of bottle party, the waiter is not paid. But he is allowed to keep all his tips and he is given free meals.

In public restaurants, where drinking is permitted until midnight, and in the higher grade of bottle party, which is open from 11 p.m. to five, six or seven in the morning, the "tronc" system is used. "Tronc" is the French name for alms box.

All tips are put in the tronc. and the waiter writes on each bill his name or number and the amount of the tip. At the end of the week the tronc is divided in a rather complicated way.

The result. however, is that if the station waiters received £7 or £8 each, the captain would get £9 or £10 and the head waiter £15 to £20.

◆ ◆ ◆

THE cloak room is commonly run by a concessionaire. who pays the house from £2 to £5 a week, pays the wages of two men or girls and a lavatory attendant, and still makes a profit.

Day clubs and bottle parties are generally financed by syndicates. It would be hard to name a bigger gamble, but with luck there will be £300 a week profit. That is why new

clubs are always sprouting in the West End.

To open a brand new place requires an investment of anything from £850 to £5000, depending on the fixtures

and decorations. But that is not necessary. You can always find a bottle party which has been closed, give it a new name and a fresh coat of paint. and send out the invitations.

See what the boys in the back room will have And tell them we'll all have the same

MINISTRY OF AIRCRAFT PRODUCTION
MILK BAR
OUR MOTTO: "CIVIL SERVICE"

RESEARCH

LOW

with Lord Beaverbrook's apologies to Marlene Dietrich

BEAVERBROOK WILD WEST   (Copyright in All Countries.)

Continuing low cloud, rain, mist and drizzle kept the German bombers grounded at their bases in Continental Europe.

197. The 1941 dining room complete with a comfortable concrete and steel shelter.

198. Workers clearing damage and debris from Law Courts in the Strand.

Shelter

Artists in Uniform

To-day was sending-in day for this year's Royal Academy and the Services were well represented among the artists who arrived with their exhibits. Above: Miss P. C. Potts, of the Auxiliary Fire Service. Below: Lieut.-colonel Leon Jones.

The Average Woman

"The average woman is more conscious of her surroundings than the average man," Sir George Stapleton said to a conference of the Garden Cities and Town Planning Association at Oxford to-day.

"Since the home and food are so essentially the affairs of women, women should take a large and authoritative share in planning for the future.

"We must plan for a new age, and not for a new generation, and success will largely turn on holding a just balance between town and country."

Son-in-law Accused of Murder Attempt

A 30-year-old aircraftman, Owen Calog Davies, was remanded in custody at Watlington, Oxford, charged with the attempted murder of his father-in-law, Owen Figg Davies.

His wife, Kitty, was charged, jointly with Davies, with assaulting her father with intent to rob him of a wallet containing £39.

'Flu' Deaths Fall

Influenza deaths fell from 309 to 116 from February 22 to March 22.

In the 126 great towns of England and Wales were 5322 births and 6733 deaths during the week ended last Saturday. Greater London's figures were 1261 births and 2061 deaths.

Admiralty Death Fall

Arthur George Carter, 63, of Paddock-gardens, Upper Norwood, fell down a flight of stairs at the Admiralty, where he was employed as a messenger, and died from the effects of a fractured skull, it was stated at an inquest at Westminster to-day.

Concerts May Be Stopped

FEES CLAIM ON SONGS AND RECORDS OPPOSED

Evening Standard Reporter

Gramophone and informal concerts in public shelters may have to be abandoned if fees are not paid for the use of songs or records.

Various authorities have been reminded by two societies that a licence and royalties are due for these performances.

An official of the London Transport Board told me to-day that they had received letters from the Performing Right Society (which represents the composers) and the Phonographic Performance, Ltd. (acting on behalf of gramophone record manufacturers).

"We have sent the communications to the Ministry of Home Security, for whom we are acting as agents," he said.

At the Ministry of Health I was told that they had also received claims, "which are now being scrutinised."

I understand that the fee demanded by Phonographic Performance, Ltd., from the London Transport Board is two guineas a year for each tube shelter.

Eighty shelters are now used.

This fee is apart from the amount said to be due to the Performing Right Society.

Informal concerts have taken place in the tube shelters for some months.

Recently the American Red Cross presented radio-gramophones and loudspeakers to London Transport Board. Records are played when the shelter marshals ask for them.

Considerable opposition has been raised to the claims by local authorities and it is probable that the Ministries will resist the demands.

Westminster City Council have already stopped gramophone concerts in some of their public shelters.

When they applied to manufacturers for records they were informed that a licence would have to be obtained.

"No money is allocated for this purpose," a council official told me, "so we decided to abandon the scheme."

P.-c. Dies in Fire Rescue Attempt

Mrs. A. Campbell, 43, her son Patrick, 15, and daughter Annie 9, and P.-c. T. A. Benn, 25, lost their lives in a fire at a house in Liverpool during the night.

The Campbells were trapped in upper rooms. Constables Benn and Lacey, having supper in the police-station, rushed to the scene, broke into the house and tried to rescue the Campbells.

James Campbell, the father, who jumped from an upper window and broke his leg, and P.-c. Lacey are in hospital.

"Lower Than The Crocodile"

Eleven ambulances were to-day presented to the Free French Forces in London by Mrs. Somerville-Smith (President) on behalf of the British-American ambulance corps and individual donors.

Mrs. Somerville-Smith spoke of the grief with which those of French descent in the United States found their beautiful France under the heel of a people "to whom God had certainly given the appearance of men, but who have the instincts of something lower than the crocodile."

Hospital Carries On

The governors of St. Thomas's Hospital state that although they are to open a country hospital as an annexe, the normal services for out-patients will be maintained in London; also the existing facilities for air raid casualties and "acute sick."

Lofts Not Cleared

Twenty-three Croydon people who have not cleared the lofts of their houses have been reported to the police by Croydon Fire Brigade. The brigade have now inspected the lofts of 60,800 houses.

Missing

The name of Squadron-leader A. R. D. Macdonell is announced to-day as missing. He is the elder son of Macdonell, Chief of Glengarry. He married Miss Diana Keane last October.

Headwaiter's £4526

Mr Guiseppi (or Joseph) Benini, of Tottenham Court-road, W., former headwaiter at the Piccadilly Hotel, who died at sea in July, left £4526 (net personalty £1987)

Hospitality Abused

Told he had abused the hospitality of this country, Szyja Dynerman, a Pole, living at Hyde Park-mansions, London, was sentenced to six months' hard labour at Luton to-day for stealing £44 from the pocket of a Luton hat manufacturer.

He was said to have three convictions since he landed here in 1938 from Amsterdam and was also said to have been recommended for deportation.

£200 in Stolen Safe

A safe containing money and stamps to the value of £200 was stolen to-day from premises in York-road, Kennington.

She Got Her Medal 27 Years After

Miss Mabel Johnson looking at her medal.—Evening Standard picture.

Twenty-seven years after the historic Serbian retreat of the last war, Miss Mabel Johnson, Commandant of the British Red Cross Society, has been presented with the Serbian Retreat Medal commemorating that occasion.

The presentation has been made by the Jugoslav Minister in London, M Ivan Soubbotitch

Commandant Johnson is now working at a first-aid post in London

Eleven other people who have just received the medal are three doctors, four V.A.D. nurses and four orderlies.

"We should have received the medal in 1918," said Miss Johnson. "But all our records were lost."

'WILL SINGE HITLER'S MOUSTACHE'

"Our seamen in the Battle of the Atlantic will singe what there is of Hitler's moustache as surely as their forbears singed the king of Spain's beard."

Lieut.-commander R. Fletcher, M.P., Parliamentary Private Secretary to the First Lord of the Admiralty, said this at Weston-super-Mare, Somerset, to-day.

"We see the exploits of Drake and Hawkins and many another seaworthy through the golden haze of history," he went on. "But no braver men have ever left our harbours than the officers and men of the rusty, gale-battered tramps upon which our survival depends.

Though the sinkings of our ships were serious, they were not on a scale large enough to give Hitler his victory.

Lieut.-commander Fletcher said that Mr. Matsuoka's Berlin visit was likely to lead many people here to consider what was the position of the Japanese Ambassador in London.

An ambassador and his staff had many opportunities for reporting matters of interest to our enemies.

"I see no reason why we should wear kid gloves, or even three-ounce gloves, in this matter and tolerate what are presumably hostile observers in our midst when we are fighting the enemy with bare fists and knuckle-dusters," he added.

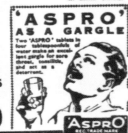

MARCH

28 Friday

No bombing again due to bad weather.

29 Saturday

A slight improvement in the weather around *Luftwaffe* bases in North West France enabled some missions to be flown but Bristol was chosen as an easier target to reach and London had a further night of calm.

30 Sunday
31 Monday

Weather conditions continued to hamper *Luftwaffe* operations and those aircraft that did fly did not attack London.

199. Damage to 'Jack Straw's Castle' the famous inn situated on Hampstead Heath – the highest point in London.

200. The Mayflower Church, Southwark, destroyed by bombs.

THEY SHELTERED IN A CHAMBER OF HORRORS

At Cut Rate Fee of 2s. 6d. a Night

A basement "chamber of horrors" in a former provincial place of entertainment which is now used as a raid shelter was described to-day by Lord Horder, the King's physician, in an address in London to the Royal Society of Arts.

He said that the owners or lessees of the building did a good trade letting out shelter accommodation at so much a night.

The only part which could reasonably be regarded as relatively secure was this basement.

Paintings on the wall included horrific subjects, such as the beheading of Charles I. and the hanging of Charlie Peace.

The shelter fee here was the "knockdown price" of 2s. 6d., but on the ground floor the price ranged from 5s. to 10s.

In one town a disused railway tunnel had been converted into an underground street—"and a mean street at that"—and the tendency for the population to become residential was increasing.

Raids or no raids, the children did not see the sun, or even the daylight for weeks on end, and the old and infirm came to the surface less often.

Chemin-de-Fer Fines

Alec Taylor (40), Reeves-mews, South Audley-street, W., was summoned at Marlborough-street to-day for being the keeper of a common gaming-house in Gloucester-place and for using premises for unlawful gaming. He was fined £5 with £15 costs.

David Falcke (49), Brompton-road, S.W., summoned for acting in the conduct of a common game-house, and assisting, was fined £2 with £2 costs.

It had been alleged that the police found a game of chemin-de-fer in progress, and that chips to the value of £3712 were in a box.

Aussies at Singapore: First Picture

First picture, received to-day, of Australian troops lined up on the deck of a transport before disembarking at Singapore. Thousands of them packed the rails of the ships, singing "Roll Out the Barrel."

In an address of welcome, Vice-admiral Sir G. Layton, C.-in-C., China Station, said: "The safe arrival of these strong reinforcements . . . is yet another demonstration of our command of the sea, which enables us to station forces . . . in the areas in which they are most needed."

New Air Mail Postcard Service For Middle East

A new air mail postcard service has, with the co-operation of the Service departments and the British Overseas Airways Corporation been introduced, announces the Postmaster-General to-day.

It will provide a means of communicating cheaply and quickly by air mail with men of the Army and R.A.F serving with Middle East Forces.

The air postcard rate for this new service to the destinations mentioned is threepence. The postcards will be forwarded by air all the way to their respective bases.

A blue air mail label (obtainable free of charge at any post office) must be affixed in the top left hand corner of the address part of the postcard, or alternatively the words " By air mail," may be written prominently in the same position

Many Girls Are Going Grey: No Hair Dyes

Evening Standard Reporter

There is a shortage of hair dyes and bleaches.

Many London hairdressers are unable to supply clients with dyes to use at home. Women have to go to the salons for treatment

Those who have been accustomed to " touching up " their hair themselves are in some cases going grey with surprising rapidity.

Synthetic blondes are resorting to peroxide of hydrogen and other homely bleaches because they cannot get their favourite proprietary brand.

"The difficulty is less acute in London than in the provinces, where some towns have thousands more women than usual," said a leading hair-dye manufacturer.

A hairdresser told me : " We have a good stock, but we are using it up rapidly "

"Sea of Danger" In Black-Out

Gardiners Corner, Aldgate, a busy traffic junction, was described to-day by the East London coroner, Mr W H R Heddy, as " very perilous for pedestrians in the day-time and in the black-out a veritable sea of danger "

---

8 KILLED BY BOMB: PROBLEM OF WILL

Bequests to Dead Wife and Servants

Mr. Arthur Fitzhardinge Berkeley Portman, editor of the Horse and Hound, for which he wrote under the name of Audax for 50 years, left £105,786 (net personalty £101,876).

With his wife and six of their seven servants he was killed in an air raid in September. He was 79.

He bequeathed:

The picture of Persimmon winning the Derby in 1896 to his wife for life, and then to the Jockey Club ;

All his shares in the Horse and Hound Publications, Ltd., and the " diaries of my life," scrapbooks and his Weatherby stud books, to his wife, with £500 and his effects, and the residue after certain other bequests had been made ;

Annuities of £300 each to his servants, Thomas and Sylvia Crisp and Ivy Cleverley, and on their death the capital sum to University College Hospital.

The deaths in the same raid of Mr. and Mrs. Portman and their servants raises a difficult legal problem which must be settled by the courts.

All three servants to whom Mr. Portman left annuities were killed.

"The point at issue is whether the capital sums of these annuities, which, of course, were never paid, will go to University College Hospital or not," said Mr. F. C. Maples, to whom probate of the will has been granted in conjunction with the Westminster Bank.

"As these annuities were to be tax-free, they involve a large sum of money—£40,000 to £50,000."

Mr Portman, who was older than his wife, was presumed to have died first. Mrs. Portman, in her will, left everything to him.

Fainted in Bath

Mrs. Golda Drakinsky, aged 65, of Chicksand-street, Stepney, was found dead in a public bath at Whitechapel.

At the Hackney inquest to-day it was stated that she probably fainted while in the bath.

Verdict, death from misadventure.

Jersey Fabrics

By CORISANDE

Jersey fabrics play a leading part in spring and summer fashions. In many cases these knitted materials look so much like woven ones that it is difficult to tell the difference.

The jacket sketched to-day looks like brown tweed, but comes from the knitwear department at Debenham and Freebody Ltd., Wigmore-street.

Another Jersey fabric looks like herringbone tweed. It is used for a tailored dress with three stitched box pleats down the front of the skirt. Yet another looks like grey flannel.

For the afternoon and evening there are fine Jersey fabrics run with a tinsel thread.

Sketch by DOROTHY THATCHER

☆

Soldier of 21 Cited by Colonel Dismissed from Suit

Mr. Justice Henn Collins to-day dismissed the petition of Lieut.-colonel William Anderson Swales, of Framlington place. Newcastle, who charged his wife Dorothy, with adultery.

He cited Robert R Walker, lance-corporal in the London Scottish, 21-year-old son of his former honorary colonel, as co-respondent The allegations were denied, and Walker was dismissed from the suit.

Mr. Justice Henn Collins said the substance of the charge rested upon the allegation that Mrs. Swales and Walker, who was 20 years her junior, spent much time in a bathroom

The evidence against the wife was that of servants.

If there were a guilty intrigue, one would expect some sort of familiarity at other times.

Two people in love with each other would find it difficult, while living in the midst of a crowded household, to disguise the real state of affairs There was no such evidence

Fewer Use Shelters

Although many councils in North London are still building public shelters, the number of shelter users is declining

A census at Hendon during an alert has revealed that of a total shelter capacity of 29,950 people only 1502 people were using them

Disciplinary Code

Finchley Borough Council are supporting the plea of Edmonton Borough Council to the Regional Commissioners for Civil Defence asking for the introduction of a disciplinary code for civil defence workers to prevent absences from duty and other breaches of conduct

Stole Newspapers

Three boys aged about 15 admitted at Southwark Juvenile Court to-day, having stolen newspapers and periodicals worth £5 17s. 3d. The case was adjourned for a week.

It was stated that they took the papers from outside a newsagent's shop at 4.45 a.m. and sold £1 worth.

APR

1 Tuesday

2 Wednesday

Again, *Luftwaffe* night bombing operations were grounded by bad weather.

3 Thursday

4 Friday

In a window of slightly improved weather the *Luftwaffe* targeted Bristol for two consecutive nightly attacks. London was again quiet.

5 Saturday

As the bad weather returned all *Luftwaffe* bomber operations by night were cancelled. Even in good weather there had been no daylight attacks on the capital for several weeks and the Germans restricted their daytime activities mainly to attacks on coastal shipping which meant their planes did not trip the coastal radar warning station alerts and could operate with greater success and minimal losses.

Radar was still top secret. The British public were not informed of its existence until later in 1941 when it was called Radio Location or Radio Direction Finding. At this period of the war the myth of fighter pilots being fed carrots to aid night vision was born in an attempt to cover up the existence of radar on board aircraft.

201. London's largest crater again at Bank in the City. This picture, taken on 1st April, shows that the temporary bridge had been removed in preparation for proper repairs.

"Don't Bring Children Home at Easter"

PARENTS WARNED

MR. ERNEST BROWN, THE MINISTER OF HEALTH, IN AN APPEAL TO-DAY TO PARENTS NOT TO BRING THEIR EVACUATED CHILDREN HOME FOR THE HOLIDAYS, STATES:

"The children would be running great risks in the danger area. Leave them where they are until the Government says it is safe to return."

School premises and play-grounds are to be kept open.

WEST END GAS TEST TO-NIGHT

Evening Standard Reporter

Three West End streets will be "danger zones" to-night, in the first black-out gas test to be carried out by A.R.P. officials.

The "raid" will probably catch many people without their gas-masks because the streets in which the exercise is to be carried out have not yet been named.

Blue lights, blue flags and the gas protection clothing of the A.R.P. workers will indicate that the attack is on.

All the services of Westminster City Council will take part.

It will be a full-scale rehearsal with casualties to attend, and food, furniture, buildings and streets to decontaminate.

It depends on the weather whether tear-gas or an aniseed preparation will be used, but those caught without their gas-masks will find both gases unpleasant.

Dogs are Safe from Tear Gas

Tests have shown that dogs are immune from the effects of tear gas, state the National Canine Defence League, who have prepared a leaflet giving directions to dog owners for the construction of a simple home made gas-resisting box.

Good Friday Shopping

It was stated to-day by the Drapers' Chamber of Trade that the following West End shops will open on Good Friday and Saturday during their usual hours and close on Easter Monday:

Harrods, Selfridges, John Barkers, D. H. Evans, Bourne and Hollingsworth, Swan and Edgar, Stagg and Russell, Ponting.

These firms have decided to close on Good Friday and Monday:

Debenham and Freebody, Marshall and Snelgrove, Harvey Nichols, Peter Robinson, Peter Jones (Sloane-square), Jays (Oxford-circus). Half-day on Saturday.

Most drapers' shops in the suburbs are expecting to close on Good Friday.

Mr. Jordan Kicks Off

Mr. W. J. Jordan, the New Zealand High Commissioner, kicked-off in the Rugby match between H.M.S. Ganges and H.M.S. Ganges New Zealanders.

open all day on Saturday and close on Monday.

In provincial centres this will, as a rule, also be the practice.

Butchers will, in the main, close on Easter Monday. On Good Friday, it was stated by a trade official, they will use their discretion, according to local conditions.

Provision dealers will probably close both Friday and Monday in most districts.

Where there are large numbers of war factory workers who need them, shops will open on one or both days. It is being left to local arrangement.

Many tobacconist shops will be closed on two half days during Easter.

The National Union of Retail Tobacconists have recommended to their members that they should close at 1.30 p.m. on Good Friday and at the same time on Easter Monday.

This has been suggested for the benefit of shop assistants.

Many Government employees who have been evacuated will work on Good Friday and take Easter Tuesday off. They have already been given Easter Monday free, so that they will have from Saturday midday until Wednesday morning to visit their families.

Home Guard Officer Pose: "No Evidence"

Mr. Law, Financial Secretary, War Office, said in the House of Commons to-day that he had been unable to discover any evidence for the report that men posing as officers of the Home Guard, and dressed in uniforms similar to that body, recently visited the homes of various Home Guard members in their absence and persuaded the womenfolk to hand over rifles and ammunition.

LADY LOUIS AND GUEST

Mr. Quo-Tai-Chi, the Chinese Ambassador, who was guest of honour at an Anglo-Chinese luncheon in London to-day, had Lady Louis Mountbatten as his right-hand neighbour.

75 D.S.O.s and M.C.s Get Home Guard Commissions

A hundred and seventy-two more Home Guard commissions announced to-day by the War Office include, one second in command to area commander—Brigadier-general Adolphe Symons, late commanding the 13th Hussars—26 zone commanders, 36 group commanders and three assistants to area commanders.

There are 40 D.S.O's in the list, 28 M.C's. and 7 who hold both the D.S.O. and M.C.

Among the 106 battalion commanders is Lord Wigram, who, as Sir Clive Wigram, was King George V.'s private secretary from 1931 to 1935. He is now Permanent Lord-in-Waiting to King George VI.

An Englishman's Word

Collector at Tottenham Police Court.—We always live in hopes of getting paid. In this case the debtor is an Englishman, and our hopes are sure to be realised.

Stored Furniture Profiteering

Captain Waterhouse, Parliamentary Secretary to the Board of Trade, asked in the Commons to-day about large increases in charges originally agreed upon for the storage of furniture, said that it was proposed to introduce legislation to give the Board of Trade power to deal, among other things, with the charges for certain services including furniture storage.

Sir William Davison (Cons., Kensington S.), said that some of these charges were regarded as being in the nature of profiteering. He asked if any additional expenditure was falling on owners of repositories to justify the increases.

Capt. Waterhouse replied that some increased expenditure was falling on these people but there were other cases as well.

Petrol Case Witness Loses His Job

Questioned about a statement made by the leading counsel against the chief witness for the prosecution in the petrol case at Newton-le-Willows, Lancs., Mr. Geoffrey Lloyd, Petroleum Secretary, said in the Commons this afternoon that the employment of the officer in question had now been terminated.

The officer was recruited through the usual channels of the Ministry of Labour for temporary Government employment. All his references appeared to be satisfactory. Every possible precaution was taken to secure fit and proper people for Government employment.

Accused Widow And Mr. "B"

Norah Bane, aged 45, a widow, of Northampton Buildings, Rosoman-street, E.C., was remanded in custody at Clerkenwell Police Court to-day, when accused of demanding with menaces a sum of £100.

The name and address of the prosecutor were withheld at the request of the police. He was referred to as "Mr. B."

Detective-inspector Knapp said he concealed himself in a room yesterday afternoon with another officer and overheard a conversation between the woman and "Mr. B."

When he told her she would be arrested for demanding money with menaces, he said she remarked, "What do you mean by menaces?" He replied: "It is commonly called blackmail."

Grandson for M.P.

The birth of a son at Clifton Hampden, Oxfordshire, to the wife of Mr Eric Leigh, son of Sir John Leigh, Conservative M.P. for Clapham, is announced to-day.

He Lacked Knowledge Of Bombs

BUT "DEALT WITH THEM"

The King has awarded the George Medal to Acting Flight-lieutenant J. W. Sim, and Acting-Sergeant Sidney Boys.

Acting Flight-lieutenant Sim dealt with unexploded bombs although he lacked special training and experience. His home is at Northaw, Herts.

Acting-sergeant Boys was in charge of a station fire tender. One night last September he drove his fire tender up to a crashed airplane loaded with bombs manned the hose himself and extinguished the fire He acted similarly on two other occasions and saved three airmen.

The British Empire Medal has been awarded to Corporal G W Gazeley, who, on a night in October, dealt with three unexploded bombs.

Aircraftman First-Class A. L. Watkins is awarded a similar medal for bravery when an aircraft crashed on an airdrome and burst into flames in December Aircraftman Watkins jumped on to the blazing aircraft to assist the pilot to get clear Aircraftman Watkins's home is at Clapham.

Mr. Attlee Defends Sir R. Vansittart

When Mr. Stokes (Soc., Ipswich) asked in the House of Commons to-day whether "in view of the damage done to our cause by the broadcasts of Sir Robert Vansittart," the Prime Minister would dispense with Sir Robert's services and appoint another diplomatic adviser, Mr. Attlee, Lord Privy Seal, replied: "No, sir."

Sir Waldron Smithers (Con., Chislehurst) suggested that the question was an unjust and unfair attack upon a public servant."

Asked if any evidence had come to the notice of the Government bearing out the statement that damage had been done, Mr. Attlee replied, "No, I do not accept the allegations made in the question."

APRIL

6 Sunday

In poor weather only a few *Luftwaffe* missions were flown but none touched London and the capital had its seventeenth consecutive night of relative peace on the home front.

7 Monday

Clydeside and Glasgow received another major attack but bombs were dropped the length and breadth of the country including London.

8 Tuesday

9 Wednesday

Two quiet nights in London as the Midlands towns of Coventry on Tuesday and Birmingham on Wednesday were targeted for major raids by the *Luftwaffe*.

10 Thursday

Birmingham again received a major attack but some bombs fells in London.

11 Friday

Good Friday and Bristol suffered another major attack just as Winston Churchill arrived there for a visit.

202. *German bombs find their targets again. This* Daily Mail *picture shows a nurse salvaging in the wreckage of a London hospital for the aged and infirm, which was bombed on Monday night.* Daily Mail, *9th April 1941.*

203

204

APRIL

12 Saturday

13 Easter Sunday

14 Monday

15 Tuesday

No bombs were reported in the London area but Belfast suffered a major attack on the Tuesday. The death toll in the Belfast raid was around 700 and reflects the fact that the city was poorly provided with shelters and defences in the belief that it was too dangerous a mission for *Luftwaffe* long-range bombers to fly the 1000 miles from their bases.

16 Wednesday

The capital's weeks of relative peace were shattered by the heaviest air attack on Britain to date. Some 890 tons of HE and more than 100,000 incendiary bombs were dropped in a raid on the capital that lasted for about nine and a half hours.

Damage was severe over a wide area of London. Many fires – 8 major, 41 serious and 2200 smaller – were started. There were the inevitable interruptions to road, rail and utilities. Many landmark buildings such as St Paul's Cathedral, the Houses of Parliament, the Law Courts and many churches were damaged to varying degrees.

Casualty figures of 1180 dead and 2230 badly injured were the highest for any single night's bombing and reflected the severity of the attack.

203. Nurses salvaging in a wrecked hospital.

204. In the major raid of 16th April St. Paul's was hit again – here is a close-up of the huge hole the bomb tore in the North Transept floor.

205. This picture of damage at Blackfriars caused by a bomb in September 1940 was not released for publication until April 1941.

APRIL

17 Thursday
18 Friday

Two days and nights free from the bombers as the clearing up from Wednesday's raid got under way.

19 Saturday

Another massive blow against London – this time a 1000-ton raid in 'celebration' of Hitler's fifty-second birthday. Damage and casualties (1200 deaths) were severe but the impact of this heavy attack was limited a little by poor visibility. This meant that a concentrated attack on a specified target or concentration point – in this case eastward along the river from Tower Bridge to Woolwich – was not easy to achieve and bombing was scattered over a wide area.

20 Sunday

At the end of a week which had seen two of the heaviest attacks anywhere in Britain launched against London, the capital had a quiet night.

206. This picture of clearing up in Piccadilly after the raid of 16th April was embargoed under the '28-day rule' – 'not for publication before the daily paper on Friday May 16th'.

207. Fire-fighters at work on a blaze in Pimlico on the night of 16th April.

208. *'Leaping flame and billowing smoke rise over the London roof-tops'. This was the height of Wednesday night's raid recorded by staff cameraman W.R. Turner from a rooftop while high explosive bombs crashed into the flames. Daily Mail, 16th April 1941.*

IAN COSTER'S LIGHTER LONDON

Day in the life of a wartime Londoner

THOUGH he didn't want to be an actor again Harold Huth accepted part in "You Can't Escape Forever" at Teddington. But he plans to produce, direct and act in film called "Greater London" about 24 hours in lives of ordinary Londoners at this time. "It won't be about luxury hotel people." he says.

Story is based on tale by Roland Pertwee. Huth, who directed films for Mycroft, and produced "Busman's Honeymoon" has just finished job as associate producer on Leslie Howard's "Pimpernel Smith."

HANDSOMEST male trio in British pictures, John Clements, Michael Wilding and Michael Rennie stood on smoky deck of aircraft carrier at Ealing studios when I looked in. They are the three Rover boys of the Fleet Air Arm in Balcon's "Ships With Wings."

Commander "Shorty," R.N. (retired), *was there to see that naval tradition was upheld. "Shorty" had already held up the film because of a soft collar which one officer was wearing. "No man would face his captain in a collar like that," said the naval adviser. So the collar had to be changed.*

Surprise is that ballet dancer Beatrice Appleyard does a *danse de ventre* in "The Camp of Ratilla." murders a young merchant (George Carden) and eats a grape with the nonchalance of a Borgia.

OLD woman's comment, overheard by Rodney Ackland on a bus: "There's an awful lot of fate about these days."

REVIVAL of "Kismet," with Harry Welchman in Oscar Asche part, is being considered by Tom Arnold.

BACK at the May Fair Inga Andersen gives two new numbers first airing. "He may be your man Friday but he's my man all the week" and "I'm Zara the vamp of the Sahara."

COTTAGE To Let," which should have reopened at Wyndham's to-day has been postponed for fortnight

MINOR casualty in raid was Judy Campbell "I got a cut and a bang on the head though I'd dined under the bedclothes," she said She rescued a bottle of brandy and went to the Savoy, where she interested Carroll Gibbons in a new lyric she's written and celebrated escape She didn't miss performance of "New Faces."

Funniest turn in new show is

Summit Shirts
are a good thing to put on

True to form in cut, fit and good workmanship. Colours as faithful and materials as well chosen as ever. And, of course, still three lengths of sleeve. In fact, the good job which you expect from

AUSTIN REED

Bath, Belfast, Birmingham, Bournemouth, Bristol, Edinburgh, Glasgow, Hull, Leeds, Liverpool, Manchester, Norwich, Nottingham, Oxford, Sheffield, Southampton.

Rescued 18 in a Hurricane

The Royal National Life-boat Institution has awarded its gold medal, given only for conspicuous gallantry, to Coxswain John Boyle, of Arranmore, on the West Coast of Ireland; its silver medal to Teague Wards, the motor mechanic; its bronze medal to each of the other six members of the crew, and money awards of £8 15s. 6d. to each man, for the rescue of eighteen lives from a steamer which had struck on a reef.

The rescue was carried out in a hurricane with fierce gusts of snow and sleet. Both life-boat and wreck were exposed to the full force of mountainous Atlantic seas.

The rescue took four hours, and each of the eighteen men was over five minutes in the breeches buoy being hauled through the breaking seas from the wreck to the life-boat.

The life-boat was out altogether for sixteen hours.

R.A.F. Triumphs in Middle East

Fighter aircraft of the R.A.F. are proving their superiority over German aircraft of all types as completely in the Middle East as they have done in Europe, states the Air Ministry news service.

Since the beginning of the year 122 enemy aircraft have been shot down. These include Ju. 88's used for dive-bombing and carrying highly-trained crews.

German fighters have been shot down with the same regularity as those of the Italians. More than 50 Messerschmitt 109's and 110's have been destroyed since they made their appearance on the Middle East fronts.

The figures are all the more remarkable in view of the fact that the Royal Air Force losses in the first three months of the year were only 62.

In a great number of cases the pilots were saved.

Till for Treasury

The proprietors of a Brighton store have sent their takings during Brighton and Hove's war weapons week—£1659—to the Treasury as a free of interest loan

Standard quiz

1. What is the highest decoration bestowed by Hitler on his submarine aces? 2. Deanna Durbin is now ——? 3. What coin measures exactly an inch across? 4. What insignia does a general wear on his shoulder? 5. How many sides has a bee's cell?—Key on PAGE SEVEN

War Loan Leads Rise in Markets

City Editor—S. W. ALEXANDER

News of the naval action at Tripoli had a stimulating influence on Stock Markets to-day, where prices generally improved under the lead of British Government securities.

Heavy buying of War Loan took place in anticipation of the stock going ex dividend on Friday. The 3½ per Cents put on ⅝d. at £104 1s. 3d., other Gilt-edged issues being about 2s. 6d. higher.

Losses Regained

Home Rails regained early losses, and in the Industrial section several issues were actually better on the day, after being dull. United Steel, Chemicals, Dunlops, Pinchin Johnson and Courtaulds were among the firmest features.

Oil shares were generally harder, and Mines, as a result of the midday recovery, finished higher on the day.

Diamond Exports Jump

South Africa's diamond exports showed a considerable increase last month.

The total, according to cabled advice received by Barclays Bank (Overseas) was £486,000, against £236,000 in March 1940.

Sales of uncut gem and industrial diamonds are expected to show a further improvement this month The revival of this industry since the German occupation of Holland has been one of the features of the war.

Dividends Resumed

Two companies announce a resumption of Ordinary dividends.

Carpet Trades is paying 5 per cent., the first since 1937, and E. Pollard a dividend at the same rate. The last payment by the latter was 7 per cent. in 1938. Carpet Trades' profits have risen from £32,000 to £39,000 and those of E. Pollard from £29,800 to £51,400.

Romac Motor Accessories.—Dividend 7½ p.c. (against 5 p.c.).
Broken Hill Proprietary.—Halfyearly dividend 9d
Madras and S. Mahratta Railway.—Int. on Cap. stock 2½ p.c. (same).
General Mining and Finance.—Final 15 p.c. (same).
Kitchen and Wade.—Second int. 12½ p.c.
Monte Video Gas and Dry Dock.—Final 5 p.c. (pay 2 p.c. in May, and 1 p.c. in Dec.).

Rubber Prices Lower

Spot rubber to-day declined 1-16d. a lb. to 1s. 2 15-32d. May to September quoted 1s. 2 13-16d., Oct.-Dec. 1s. 2¾d.

Tin.—Cash £271 5s. a ton (unchanged), three months £267 2s. 6d. (decrease 7s. 6d.). Turnover 100 tons.

"Made-up" Pay Appeal

A "test" case of import to many local councils, involving hundreds of thousands of pounds of ratepayers' money, is to be reviewed in the Court of Appeal during the present sittings.

Bolton Corporation are appealing against a majority decision in the King's Bench refusing an order prohibiting the National Arbitration Tribunal from adjudicating in a dispute.

The dispute concerned payment of employees serving with the Forces or on civil defence.

Corporation officials assert that they should have their pay made up if they joined the Forces or undertook civil defence work, and the corporation refused.

APRIL

21 Monday
22 Tuesday
23 Wednesday

Three further quiet nights in London while
Plymouth–Devonport was in receipt of three
major attacks on three consecutive nights.

24 Thursday
25 Friday

The *Luftwaffe* turned their attentions to raids
on Portsmouth on the Thursday and
Sunderland on the Friday. London had two
further nights of calm.

As Hitler's planned invasion of Russia –
codenamed 'Barbarossa' – drew nearer, some
Luftwaffe units were beginning to be moved
east from their bases in Western Europe to aid
a *Blitzkrieg* on the Russian border in June.

209. Inspecting damage to St George's Roman
Catholic Cathedral, Southwark, on St George's
Day.

APRIL

26 Saturday
27 Sunday

Two more quiet nights in the capital as Winston Churchill returned to London after a week's tour of the bombed provincial cities on Sunday the 27th. That night he broadcast to the nation. He praised the spirit of every man, woman and child in Britain and gave his impressions of this trip: 'What a triumph the life of these battered cities is over the worst which fire and bombs can do. What a vindication of the civilised and decent way of living we have been trying to work for and work towards in our island.'

28 Monday
29 Tuesday
30 Wednesday

Plymouth–Devonport suffered two major raids on consecutive nights on Monday and Tuesday. The city was an easy target for the *Luftwaffe* as it was so near bomber bases on the French coast. This attack, coming on top of the three earlier in the month, left the city almost in ruins. Morale too, despite Churchill's speech on Sunday the 27th, was shaky as Plymouth had been exposed to perhaps the most devastating form of aerial bombardment – namely, concentrated heavy raids for several nights followed by a lull before more nights of heavy raids. The fear and uncertainty such a pattern engendered was guaranteed to hit morale.

210. Leicester Square after the raid on 16th April.

211. St George's Day service held amid the ruins of the Church of St Andrew-by-the-Wardrobe, Queen Victoria Street.

212. The damage in the City Temple – the only Free Church in the City.

213. This is the porch of a London church where a vicar was killed while on duty fire-spotting during the raid on 16th April.

214

215

MAY

The first seven days in May saw Merseyside in receipt of similar treatment to Plymouth in March and April – namely several, in this case seven, nights of concentrated heavy attack. It became known by the somewhat festive sounding title of 'Merseyside's May Week'. Damage was severe, casualties amounted to around 3500 deaths and serious injuries, and as many as 70,000 people made homeless. The worst feature of Merseyside's experience was the way in which local organisations almost broke under the strain of the bombing, as much because of their own ineptitude as the *Luftwaffe* attacks. Morale was seriously undermined by rumours of tens of thousands of deaths, homeless people with nowhere to go and a lack of food for all the population.

During 'Merseyside's May Week' other targets in the North of England and Clydeside and Belfast were also attacked, but London escaped the bombers until the night of Saturday 10th May.

214. A messenger puzzling out the new addresses of blitzed firms.

215. The scene near the Old Bailey after the raid on 10th May.

216. St Stephen's Church, Walbrook, burnt out during the raid of 10th May.

The attack on London on 10th May came at a full or bombers' moon when the River Thames was at its lowest level. Perfect conditions for the bombers enabled concentrated bombing on the target area around the docks and the East End. During an eight-hour raid, more than 700 tons of HE and 100,000 incendiaries were dropped into that concentration point by around 550 *Luftwaffe* aircraft, many of which had to fly two sorties to maintain the numbers required for this attack. *Luftwaffe* numbers were depleted as many units had been moved east in preparation for the assault on Russia.

217. Fetter Lane after the raid. The object in the left-hand foreground is a fire-fighter's hose.

218. Office workers who have been bombed out of their workplaces waiting for instructions.

219. *City clerks and typists turned up as usual on Monday morning. Many of them found that for the time being they had been blitzed out of their offices, but they took the news with the same good humour that they have shown on former occasions. Daily Mail, 13th May 1941.*

Fire-fighters had an awesome task. There were 9 conflagrations together with 20 major and about 2200 other fires in an area covering around 700 acres. In some cases water supplies with which to fight the fires ran out and all the fire-fighter could do was watch the flames consume the building.

220. Pump Court in the Temple. Note the fire hose attached to the hydrant.

221. The bronze bust of Sir William Owen, a conservator of the Museum in the nineteenth century, lies amid the twentieth-century rubble of the Royal College of Surgeons.

222. More damage at the Royal College of Surgeons – in this case the 'Skullery pantry' holding skulls of all ages, shapes and sizes was damaged by fire in the raid.

Casualties from the raid on Saturday 10th May were the largest for any night of the Blitz. 1436 people died, 1792 were seriously injured. Damage was severe, mostly from fire although high explosive bombs also made their mark. More than 5000 houses were destroyed making around 12,000 people homeless. Many public buildings suffered damage by fire or HE or both, including the Houses of Parliament, the Law Courts, the Guildhall, Westminster Abbey, Mansion House, the Royal College of Surgeons and the British Museum (where a quarter of a million books were destroyed).

On the morning of the 11th smoke clouded the sun and in the streets of London the fire-fighters continued their relentless task. It was not until 21st May that some of the most serious fires were under control and could cease to be hosed down. Transport and utilities suffered severe dislocation. Most railway stations were blocked for weeks. A third of London's roads were impassable on 11th May and 155,000 families were without gas, water or electricity.

223. Jermyn Street in SW1 after the raid.

224. *The King and Queen paid a visit yesterday to Westminster Abbey, where they were crowned four years ago. It was a sad pilgrimage for the Abbey suffered badly in Saturday night's savage raid. In this picture they are seen standing on the exact spot in front of the High Altar where they received their crowns.* Daily Mail, 15th May 1941.

For several days Londoners waited with fear for the follow-up attack. Middlesborough was attacked on the following night, 11th May, and then for four nights *Luftwaffe* operations over Britain were only minimal.

On Friday 16th May Birmingham suffered a major attack which was the last air attack of the Blitz before Hitler turned his attention east towards Russia and his invasion on 22nd June.

225. The verger on the right inspects the damage to Westminster Abbey, while workmen begin to clear up.

226. A picture taken in late May of Queen Victoria Street to show that despite the scars of many bombings life in the street was carrying on as usual.

227. The burnt out remains of the Salvation Army headquarters. The fires on 10th May were so severe and overwhelming that in some cases there were not enough fire-fighters free to attend to a fire and in others, like the situation at the Salvation Army building, there was no water available with which to attack it.

228. Damage to St. James's Palace.

229

230

By the end of the Blitz 43,000 British civilians had lost their lives, more than half of them in London, and hundreds of thousands had been injured to greater or lesser degrees.

Despite the death and destruction caused by the *Luftwaffe*'s onslaught in the last four months of 1940 and the first five of 1941, the bombing singularly failed to achieve its stated aims of stopping war production and terrorising the civilian population into surrender. If anything, it strengthened civilian resolve. For apart from a few cracks at times of the severest bombing, morale remained good with people working on production lines in the open air if it were necessary to maintain production; forgoing luxuries with relatively good cheer and contributing with their time, money and energies to aid the war effort in every conceivable capacity.

229. *The road to business was not easy. But the girls picked their way through the debris with a laugh and a smile. These* Daily Mail *pictures show the spirit of the City after 'reprisals'.* Daily Mail, 13th May 1941.

230. . . . *a London Street scene after a Blitz: battered motor cars, shattered masonry litter the street. It was the most savage raid London has endured. Firemen fought the flames: Home Guards, demolition workers, rescue squads played their part. The Germans called it a 'reprisals' raid. They can call it what they will. London, still slow to organise her defences, will go on fighting the night horror. For London, though it can burn, can never yield.* Daily Mail, 12th May 1941.

231. *Old Bailey, scene of many famous trials, had its north-west wing torn away. No. 2 Court was demolished.* Daily Mail, 16th May 1941.

MAY 1941 – MAY 1945

Throughout the summer of 1941 much work had to be done to repair, if only temporarily, the damage to London and the other cities, towns and even villages that had suffered in the Blitz. By August of 1941, 1,100,000 houses had been made weatherproof ready for some of the homeless to move into. The ending of the Blitz did not mark the end of air attacks on Britain or London. Hull was attacked in the summer of 1941 and in April and June 1942 there were the Baedeker raids on towns like York, Exeter, Bath and Canterbury. In these raids towns of outstanding beauty, listed in the Baedeker Guide to Britain, were chosen for attack.

London was not attacked by air again until January 1943 when during the 'Little Blitz' that lasted until the end of March it was hit thirteen times. After that, *Luftwaffe* planes never attacked Britain again but London was not safe from aerial attack. In the summer of 1944 the V1 rockets, followed by V2s, began to fall in London. The V1 'doodle-bugs' or 'buzz bombs' as they were called were pilotless rocket-propelled bombs launched from Europe, but the Allied successes in the war eventually stopped the V rocket menace.

232. A service in the wrecked Roman Catholic Cathedral of St George's, Southwark. Throughout the summer of 1941 many open-air services were held in ruined churches throughout London.

233. In the autumn of 1941 the *Daily Mail* took a series of photographs under the title 'The Miracle of St Paul's' showing the devastation to all the surrounding areas. This picture could not have been taken in early 1940 as Cannon Street's many high buildings shielded St Paul's from view.

234. The Queen came to inspect the damage to St Paul's in the summer of 1941.

Maureen Hill is the author of two books for younger readers; *Growing up at War*, a detailed account of life during the Second World War, and *The Green Guide* which deals with all today's ecological issues. Both are published by Collins Armada.
A former teacher, Maureen Hill is married with four young children and lives in Croxley Green, Hertfordshire.

Acknowledgements

Our thanks are due to all those at Associated Newspapers archive, picture library and photo services without whose help this book would not have been possible. In particular:

Bob Dignum
John Emery
Paul Rossiter
David Sheppard
Steve Torrington

We would also like to thank

John Dunne and Roger Lightfoot for their help in producing the book.